MEDITERRANEAN BY CRUISE SHIP

DOCUMENTATION

Passenger Name_____

Ship Name _____

Date of Voyage_____

Stateroom_____

D1016564

MEDITERRANEAN
By Cruise Ship

ANNE VIPOND

FIFTH EDITION

*YOUR PORTHOLE
COMPANION*

TM

**OCEAN
CRUISE
GUIDES**

Vancouver, Canada   Pt. Roberts, USA

Published by: Ocean Cruise Guides Ltd.

Canada
325 English Bluff Road
Delta, BC V4M 2M9

USA
PO Box 2041
Pt. Roberts, WA 98281-2041

Phone: (604) 948-0594   Email: info@oceancruiseguides.com

Fifth Edition

Visit our web site: www.oceancruiseguides.com

Editors: Mel-Lynda Andersen, Debbie Parker (UK), Karen Stevens, Stephen York (UK), Michael DeFreitas, William Kelly
Cover Artwork by Alan H. Nakano.
Cover Design by Ocean Cruise Guides.
Cartography: Reid Jopson, Doug Quiring, Cartesia – USA, OCG.
Design: Ocean Cruise Guides Ltd
Publisher: William Kelly

Printed in China.

Library and Archives Canada Cataloguing in Publication

Vipond, Anne
Mediterranean by Cruise Ship : the complete guide to Mediterranean cruising / Anne Vipond. -- 5th ed.

Includes index.

ISBN: 978-0-9809573-4-1   ISSN 1921-8028
1. Cruise ships--Mediterranean Region--Guidebooks.
2. Mediterranean Region--Guidebooks. I. Title.

D973.V56 2010   910'.91822   C98910623-3

(Opposite) Villefranche

Contents

Part One

General Information

Santorini

PART TWO

THE VOYAGE & THE PORTS

Villefranche

Back in the mists of antiquity, the Mediterranean was the center of the known world. Even after the seafaring Phoenicians ventured beyond the Pillars of Hercules, the Mediterranean remained the cradle of Western civilization. Empires rose and fell along its shores, and over the millennia much blood was spilled into Homer's wine-dark sea as various nations battled one another for world supremacy. Great armies marched up and down its coastal plains, and fleets of war ships sailed across its waters.

Today, as the birthplace of Western civilization, the Mediterranean offers cruise passengers a rich variety of destinations spanning 5,000 years of human history. Nowhere else in the world is there such a concentration of architectural wonders and artistic masterpieces. Cities of past glory now disarm visitors not only with their ancient ruins and Renaissance palaces, but with their waterfront promenades, outdoor cafes and chic boutiques. Baroque churches face fountain-filled squares, medieval castles overlook golden beaches, and subtropical flowers flourish in a mild climate and sensuous setting that has long appealed to poets, painters and romantics. The Mediterranean is a storied sea, and its layers of history and human drama inspire a passion for living. This intensity extends to affairs of the heart, with many a star-crossed romance unfolding beneath the Med's sunny skies.

Mark Twain described his Mediterranean cruise, which he took on board a steamer from New York in 1867, as "a picnic on a gigantic scale." By then the fashionable 'grand tour' of Europe was so popular with British and American travellers that members of the wealthy class began seeking ever more exclusive modes of travel in the form of Pullman rail cars, stately hotels and lavish ocean liners. Today we can all embark on a grand tour of the Mediterranean, where an expanding fleet of modern cruise ships now carries passengers from port to port in unsurpassed luxury and comfort.

A Mediterranean cruise is a heady mix of high culture and hedonism, an opportunity to indulge in sybaritic pleasures while enriching the mind with art and learning. As the world embarks upon a new millennium, the need to look back and understand our beginnings is more compelling than ever. And cruising the Mediterranean Sea is an ideal way to revisit the past while thoroughly enjoying the here and now.

A cruise ship lies at anchor off Sorrento on Italy's south coast.

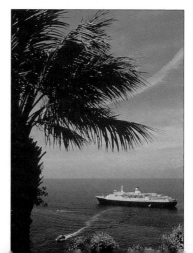

PART I

GENERAL INFORMATION

Choosing Your Cruise

The Mediterranean Sea, bordered by three continents and over a dozen countries, offers an extraordinary diversity of cruise destinations, with ports of call ranging from grand cities to idyllic islands. Ships plying the Mediterranean are as diverse as their destinations, and some of the newest and largest premium ships offer Mediterranean cruises, along with a host of small luxury ships. (For more detail, please refer to the Cruise Lines Glossary at the back of this book.) The length of a Mediterranean cruise can vary, usually ranging from one to two weeks, and both round-trip cruises and one-way cruises (which depart one port and terminate at another) are available. The ships dock at the large ports, but often anchor and

tender passengers ashore at smaller ports, such as those along the Riviera or among the Greek islands.

Each spring, following a winter in the Caribbean, cruise ships begin arriving in the Mediterranean. Their transatlantic crossings often include stops at the Madeira and Canary Islands, as well as Morocco and Lisbon, before entering the Mediterranean Sea. Some ships head to Southampton, England, which has become an important base port for cruises to the Med.

Western Mediterranean ports of call include Gibraltar, Malaga and the Balearic Islands of Majorca and Minorca, with Barcelona a popular base port. The French ports of Marseille, Nice and others along the Côte d'Azur are also featured in western itineraries, as are the Italian islands of Sardinia and Sicily. The 'boot' of Italy lies in the middle of the Mediterranean and its famous ports and nearby cities are included in both western and eastern cruises. The Italian Riviera, Florence, Rome and Naples are all popular stops, as of course is Venice, where most ships dock overnight so their passengers can fully enjoy this enchanting city.

Greece's mainland ports and far-flung islands are highlighted in eastern cruises, as are the intriguing Turkish destinations of Istanbul and ancient Ephesus. An eastern cruise might also include the Black Sea and Egypt's seaports of Alexandria and Port Said,

Santorini is one of the Greek islands visited by cruise ships.

both providing access to Cairo and the Great Pyramids.

When choosing a cruise, you're well advised to visit a travel agent who specializes in cruises. Look for an agency displaying the CLIA logo, indicating its agents have received training from the Cruise Lines International Association. The cruise lines strongly encourage their clients to book through a travel agent with CLIA accreditation, and these qualified agents are a good source of information, with personal knowledge of many ships. They are able to provide pertinent detail regarding on-board atmosphere, cabin selection and pricing. Supplied with the relevant information, i.e. which countries or specific destinations you would like to visit, the length of cruise you wish to take, and the type of onboard atmosphere you are seeking, a travel agent can recommend suitable itineraries and ships.

The cruise lines' websites and brochures are another good source of information regarding itineraries and the onboard atmosphere offered on their ships.

Arriving in Venice by ship is one of life's most memorable travel experiences.

Flights can be booked through the cruise company, and it is worth paying the optional variation fee (about $50), which lets you pick your dates of travel, airline, routing and advance seat assignment. Basic air/sea arrangements include ground transportation between airport and pier, along with baggage handling. Hotel packages are also available through the cruise lines, enabling passengers to spend an extra day or two in port before boarding their ship or after disembarking at the end of a cruise, and these packages include transfers between airport, hotel and pier.

Spring and fall are considered the best months for cruising the Med, although ships remain there throughout the summer. Mid-summer temperatures in southern Italy and parts of Greece can climb into the 90s, while the weather in fall is pleasantly warm and sunny. August is the month in which many Europeans like to take their vacations, temporarily closing their businesses in the city and heading to the coastal resorts.

Shore Excursions

The cruise lines offer **organized shore excursions** for the convenience of their passengers, and these are described in a booklet that is enclosed with your cruise tickets, as well as at on-board presentations given by the ship's shore excursion manager. Most cruise lines provide shore excursion information on their websites, with the option of pre-booking your shore excursions on-line. Regardless of whether you book an excursion before or during your cruise, the charge for such excursions varies, depending on

its length (half day / full day) and the activities involved. Most shore excursions are fairly priced and the local tour operators used are reliable and monitored by the cruise companies, with the added advantage that the ship will wait for any of its overdue excursions.

Full-day shore excursions organized by the cruise lines are usually a combination of driving tour, guided walking tour and lunch at a local restaurant, with an interlude for shopping. The tour guides are local people providing narration of the sights and answering any questions you might have. When joining a ship-organized excursion, the decision to tip your guide or driver is personal. If you like the service, a tip of US$1 per person for a half-day tour and $2 per person for a full-day tour is standard.

Independent-minded passengers need not feel that pre-booked shore excursions are their only option when exploring various ports of call. If the ship docks right beside a town or city center, a person can simply set off on foot to do some sightseeing and shopping. If the town center is a few miles from the port, the cruise lines often offer a **shuttle service**. In some instances, such as Rome and Florence, where the city is an hour or more away from its seaport, your options include taking a train or hiring a taxi. Passengers who like the idea of exploring these cities on their

Local attractions can often be reached on foot, such as those on the Greek island of Patmos.

own but wish to avoid any anxiety about getting back to the ship on time, may want to consider a ship-organized excursion that provides transportation to and from the city center but leaves you to see the sights on your own before reboarding the coach at a pre-appointed time for the ride back to the ship.

Train travel in Europe is very efficient and is a convenient way to see a port's nearby attractions. The ship's shore excursion manager will likely have a current schedule, which is also posted at the local train station. Double-check the schedule at the other end before leaving the station to take in the local sights. Although the trains generally run on schedule, it's best not to plan your return train ride too close to the ship's time of departure, just in case there's an unforeseen delay. Local currency is needed to purchase a ticket. There are two classes of tickets, with first class being more expensive but allowing you to ride in slightly better cars. (A rail pass is another option for passengers planning an extended stay in Europe before or after their cruise; for details, see page 17). The local buses are often a good way to cover short distances, but are not recommended for longer trips, as they make frequent stops and are not always as reliable as trains for keeping to their schedules. Bus tickets are usually sold at local newsstands.

Taxis may seem expensive, but if you're splitting the fare with a few other people it can often be more economical than a ship-

Rented scooters are one way to get around small ports of call.

organized excursion. Keep in mind that some taxi drivers make better 'guides' than others, and be sure to agree on the fare before getting into the taxi. To avoid possible miscommunication due to a language barrier, it's a good idea to write on a piece of paper the exact amount both parties have agreed upon and show it to the driver to be certain he understands what you are willing to pay at the end of the trip. Don't hesitate to bargain with a few drivers before making your decision, and remember that a tip is certainly warranted if the driver proves to be pleasant and helpful. If you hail a taxi in a large city, the driver will simply charge you the metered fare.

Renting a car or motor scooter is often a good way to explore an island destination, but it's not recommended when visiting large cities where traffic can be extremely congested and fast-

Sightseeing in car-free Venice is done by boat and on foot.

paced. Boat travel is another option in some ports such as Venice, where large boats serve as local buses, and taxis come in the form of motor boats. At Naples, ferries and hydrofoils transport visitors to the nearby isle of Capri, and at some small ports, boat transport is often the best way to tour the area.

The local sights to be seen on Mediterranean shore excursions include ancient ruins, medieval fortresses and Renaissance palaces. There is often a fair amount of **walking** involved, especially at the ruins where stone steps and uneven grades are common. In medieval towns and city quarters, where the roads are too narrow for vehicles, on foot is often the only way to explore the winding cobblestone streets.

Pre- and Post-Cruise Stays

If time allows, fly to your port of embarkation at least a day before the cruise begins, thus avoiding the stress of making same-day travel connections. Better yet, stay two or three nights at your embarkation port to recover from jet lag, relax and have time to enjoy the local sights. Southampton, Lisbon, Barcelona, Nice, Savona, Genoa, Rome (Civitavecchia), Venice, Athens (Piraeus) and Istanbul are all used as base ports for Mediterranean cruises. Thus, you could, for example, fly to Athens and spend a few days visiting the Acropolis and other famous sites before embarking on an eastern Mediterranean cruise that terminates in, for instance, Rome – where you could spend a few days exploring and enjoying the city before flying home.

Be sure to book your accommodations ahead of time, either

through your travel agent or as part of a pre- or post-cruise package offered by the cruise line. The hotel packages offered by the cruise lines usually utilize 4- and 5-star hotels, thus ensuring their clients a consistent level of comfort and service, and transfers between hotel and pier are included. If you're booking a hotel independently, reservations are advisable in the major cities.

Once you have checked into your hotel, remember that the concierge and front desk staff offer a wealth of information for foreign visitors. They can direct you to the best shops and restaurants, and will usually provide miscellaneous services upon request, such as obtaining information on local tours or calling a taxi and confirming the destination and fare with your driver. If you're part of an organized cruisetour, an experienced guide employed by the cruise line will be available to answer questions (see next section on Land Tours).

Land Tours

A cruise is a perfect opportunity to combine a vacation at sea with a land-based holiday, and a fully escorted cruisetour is an ideal way to see more of a European country. The tours offered by the cruise lines are a seamless form of travel, for the cruise companies maintain the same level of service on land as at sea, with well-planned itineraries, first-class hotel accommodations and professional tour direction. Hotels are centrally located, within walking distance of major attractions and shopping streets, and several hosted meals are often part of the package, while plenty of free time allows clients to do a bit of independent sightseeing, leisurely shopping or lingering in a sidewalk cafe. The group trav-

A water taxi pulls up to the entrance of the four-star Luna Baglioni Hotel in Venice.

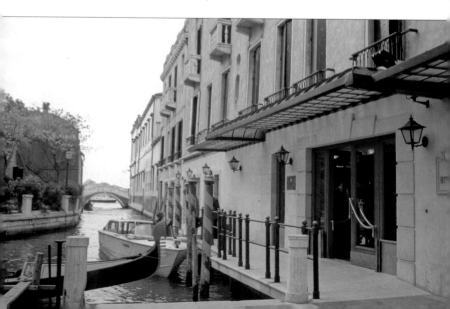

els by comfortable motor coach or high-speed train, and the tour guides employed by the cruise companies are well-educated and highly qualified to introduce visitors to the history, culture and cuisine of the country they are visiting. All tours must be booked at the same time as the cruise, as part of a cruisetour package. Land tour itineraries vary with each cruise line.

Italy is well covered by land tours, including a variety of three- and five-day trips that feature Venice, Rome and Florence. Milan and Lake Como are also featured in some land tours, as are the hilltop towns of Tuscany. Spain's interior is covered by land tours combined with cruises out of Barcelona, with Seville and Madrid included in five-night itineraries.

Touring On Your Own

If you plan to embark on an independent tour outside the major cities, your options include renting a car or purchasing a rail pass. If you cherish total independence and the freedom to hop from village to village, stopping on a whim to admire a valley view or coastal lookout, then **renting a car** is probably for you. Obtain an International Driver's Permit before leaving home, especially if you'll be travelling in areas where you are not fluent in the language. When reserving a car, confirm a number of details, such as whether the 'all-inclusive' rate includes taxes, drop-off charges and unlimited kilometers. European cars are generally smaller than North American models, with a 'compact' comfortably holding two people and two pieces of luggage; the next size up is usually worth the extra cost. Standard-shift transmissions are popular in Europe, but automatics are available in larger cars

An independent tour of Spain could include staying in a monastery overlooking Toledo.

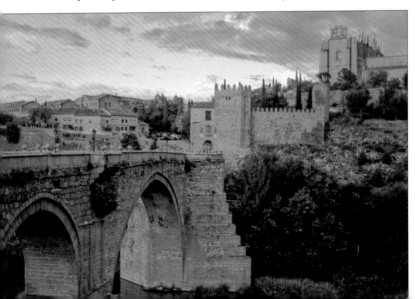

at higher rates. If you plan to use a credit card for insurance, ask for a copy of the policy's coverage; theft protection insurance is also required in some countries. One tip for deterring thieves is to leave a local newspaper lying on the dashboard or passenger seat whenever you're parking the car.

Rail travel is another option for independent travel in Europe. It is efficient and comfortable, and is a relaxing way to see the countryside as you settle into your window seat and watch the scenery slide by. An extensive rail system connects countries, cities, towns and villages, and most train stations are centrally located – whether in a resort town or a large city – so your hotel will likely be just a short taxi ride away.

In 1958, Western Europe's railroads developed the idea of an easy-to-use, multi-country, pre-paid ticket for unlimited mileage use, and that concept evolved into the popular Eurailpass, which now comes in a variety of forms. The range of passes offered by Rail Europe is exhaustive, including the EurailDrive Pass with which a person can combine four days of unlimited train travel with two days of car rental through Avis or Hertz. The flexible Eurorail Select pass has replaced the Europass and provides unlimited first-class train travel within a two-month period for lengths of five, six, eight, 10 or 15 days, and is valid in three, four or five bordering countries, depending on the specific pass purchased. To obtain more information about Rail Europe's selection of passes, visit the company's website at *www.raileurope.com.* All passes must be purchased before you leave for Europe, and reservations are required for some trains. Porters and luggage carts are not always available, so you must be

High speed trains pull into the Atocha Station in Madrid.

Train travel in Europe is an efficient and relaxing way to get around. (Above and left) Nice's train station.

prepared to handle your own baggage if travelling by train.

Accommodations should be reserved in advance when travelling by train, while car travel affords more flexibility. Each country offers unique and varied accommodations, and it's best to do some research ahead of time. Places to stay in Portugal include *pousadas* (stately castles), which are palaces and private manor houses that have been converted into hotels. In Spain, many of the *paradores* (state-operated tourist hotels) are housed in castles, palaces, monasteries and convents that have been refurbished into three- and four-star hotels. France offers everything from grand hotels to family-run country inns serving regional cuisine. And in Italy, an umbrella organization called Agriturismo ('farm stays') provides information on an extensive network of rural bed-and-breakfast inns. Located on quiet country roads, with views of valley fields and vineyards, these Italian B&B's are housed in country estates and quaint farmhouses.

There are hundreds of monasteries and convents throughout Europe, many of which welcome overnight visitors who enjoy the spartan but clean accommodations and the warm hospitality. For example, Villa del Foro, a 16th-century monastery in Rome, rents room starting at US$110 (double) per night.

Villa rentals are also popular with people travelling as a small group, and properties are available in Greece, France, Spain and Portugal, as well as Italy. It's possible to rent a *palazzetto* in Venice that accommodates eight people and is within walking distance of St. Mark's Square for about US$3,000 per week. There are numerous websites providing information on villa rentals. Those that include details and photos of each property, and that allow travellers to book directly with a villa owner, are your best bet. Each country's official tourism department is another source of helpful information regarding local accommodations, as is your travel agent.

Accommodations include famous grand hotels such as the Ritz in Madrid (above) and converted monasteries, such as the Hotel Loggiato dei Serviti in Florence (below) – an elegant three-star hotel overlooking Piazza SS. Annunziata.

Documentation

Several weeks prior to your cruise's departure date you will receive (or be able to print out) all pertinent documentation for your trip, including your cruise ticket, airline ticket and a mandatory pre-registration form that can be completed online, or faxed or mailed to the cruise line. Before your departure, leave a detailed travel itinerary with a family member or friend, in case someone needs to contact you while you're away. Include the name of your ship, its phone number and the applicable ocean code, as well as your stateroom number – all of which will be included in your cruise documents. With this information, a person can call the international telephone operator and place a satellite call to your ship in an emergency.

A valid passport is required for travel to all countries bordering the Mediterranean. A few countries in the Mediterranean region also require an entry visa, and your travel agent or the cruise line can advise you beforehand of any visa requirements your cruise might entail. As a precaution, you should photocopy the identification page of your passport, along with your driver's licence and any credit cards you will be taking on your trip. Keep one copy of this photocopied information with you, separate from your passport and wallet, and leave another copy at home.

Travel insurance is recommended. A comprehensive policy will cover trip cancellation, delayed departure, medical expenses, personal accident and liability, lost baggage and money, and legal expenses. You may already have supplementary health insurance through a credit card, automobile club policy or employment health plan, but you should check these carefully. Carry details of your policy with you and documentation showing that you are covered by a plan.

Currency

When travelling abroad, it's best to take various forms of currency – cash, credit cards and bank cards. If you're staying in a foreign city for a few days before or after your cruise, obtain some petty cash in that country's currency to cover taxi fares and other incidentals. Major credit cards are accepted by most hotels and restaurants, and ATM machines are widespread in larger cities.

Once you're aboard your ship, travellers checks can be cashed at the Front Desk and many of the ships have an ATM on board, usually located near the Front Desk.

Most ships also have a currency exchange facility on board, offering a competitive rate on foreign currencies, so that passengers needn't spend time at each port of call exchanging funds into local currency. The rates offered by local currency exchange offices can vary and some will charge a higher commission on Sundays. The euro is the official currency in the majority of member nations of the European Union, making money transactions much simpler for cruise passengers visiting Greece, Italy, France, Spain, Portugal, Malta and Cyprus. One euro is divided into 100 centimes and there are eight coins, worth 1, 2, 5, 10 ,20 and 50 centimes, and 1 and 2 euros. There are seven banknotes in denominations of 5, 10, 20, 50, 100, 200 and 500 euros. The approximate rate of exchange is one euro costing $1.25 US and $1.35 CAN.

For major purchases or expenses, a credit card is recommended (rather than carrying large amounts of cash) and although a currency conversion fee is charged (usually 2 or 3%), the difference in service charges between using a credit card or withdrawing cash in the local currency from an ATM is not substantial. It's best to carry several credit cards, and married couples should arrange for at least one set of separate cards (without joint signing privileges) in case one spouse loses his or her wallet and all of the couple's joint cards have to be cancelled. It's also wise to take along a handful of small US bills and euros to cover possible tips for guides and other sundries when ashore.

What to Pack

Pack casual attire for daytime wear – both aboard the ship and in port. The weather will be generally dry and sunny, but spring and fall temperatures in the Mediterranean can vary from cool to hot, so pack clothes that can be layered. Cool, loose cotton clothes are recommended for the summertime heat, as are sunglasses and a wide-brimmed hat. A comfortable pair of rubber-soled shoes is essential for walking along cobblestone streets, and a light sweater or jacket will fend off the air-conditioning in restaurants, museums and aboard motorcoaches. Some European ports, such as Venice, can be chilly in late October, so pack one warm sweater or jacket if you're travelling at this time of year.

The dress code for churches and monasteries dictates that legs and shoulders be covered, so keep this in mind when heading ashore – either wear slacks or carry a wrap that can be tied around your waist as an ankle-length cover-up before entering religious sites. In Muslim countries, conservative attire is recommended, and removal of shoes is mandatory before entering mosques.

Your evening wear should include something suitable for the two or three formal nights held on board most ships. Women wear gowns or cocktail dresses, and men favor suits. For informal evenings, the women wear dresses, skirts or slacks, and

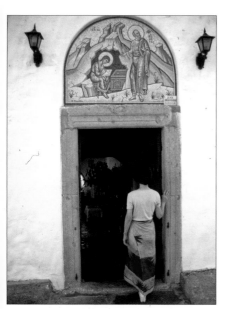

Visitors to monasteries must cover their shoulders and legs.

the men wear jackets with either a shirt and tie or an open-necked sports shirt.

Check with your travel agent regarding on-board facilities; for instance, most cabins will have a built-in hair dryer. Many ships have coin-operated launderettes with ironing boards; those that don't usually provide laundry service at an extra charge. Steam pressing and dry cleaning are standard services on most ships, and it's easy to do hand washing in your cabin. Poolside towels are provided by the ship, as are beach towels – upon request – for taking ashore.

To save room in your suitcase, pack sample sizes of toothpaste and other toiletries, which can also be purchased on board the ship. If you wear prescription

eyeglasses, consider packing a spare pair. Keep prescribed medication in original, labelled containers and carry a doctor's prescription for any controlled drug. Other items you may want to bring along are a small pair of binoculars and a pocket calculator for tabulating exchange rates. And be sure to keep all valuables, such as travellers checks, camera and expensive jewelry, in your carry-on luggage, as well as all prescription medicine and documentation, such as your passport, tickets and a copy of your insurance policy. Last but not least, be sure to leave room in one of your suitcases for souvenirs.

Health Precautions

Vaccinations are not compulsory for a Mediterranean cruise, but you may want to consult your doctor in this regard. All ships have a fully equipped medical centre with a doctor and nurses. Passengers needing medical attention are billed at private rates which are added to their shipboard account. This invoice can be submitted to your insurance company upon your return home. You may already have supplementary health insurance through a credit card, automobile club policy or employment health plan, but you should check these carefully. Whatever policy you choose for your trip, carry details of it with you and documents showing that you are covered by a plan.

The overall standards of cleanliness on board cruise ships are extremely high, yet contagious viruses that are spread by person-to-person contact (such as the Norovirus, which is a brief but severe gastrointestinal illness) do occasionally plague a small percentage of passengers. To avoid contracting such a virus, practice frequent, thorough handwashing with warm, soapy water.

Motion sickness is not a widespread or prolonged problem for most passengers, but for those who are susceptible, a number of remedies are available. One is a special wrist band, the balls of which rest on an acupressure point. These 'sea bands' are available at most drug stores. Another option is to chew meclizine tablets (usually available at the ship's infirmary) or take Dramamine, an over-the-counter antihistamine. It's best to take these pills ahead of time, before you feel too nauseous, and they may make you drowsy. Fresh air is one of the best antidotes, so stepping out on deck is often all that's needed to counter any queasiness. Other simple remedies include sipping ginger ale, nibbling dry crackers and an apple, or lying down.

To avoid traveller's diarrhea, it's best to drink bottled water when ashore, but don't worry about drinking the wine. Recent studies have shown that a glass of wine – either red or white – is a good way to fend off traveller's diarrhea. Wine contains a mild disinfectant that quickly destroys a variety of bacteria that can cause stomach problems. Wine loses its antidiarrheal advantage over time, so don't rely on vintages over 10 years old to be effective.

Connecting with Home

Text messaging and e-mail are replacing phone calls as the most convenient way to reach someone while you're away. Many of the ships provide satellite-based broadband services that allow you to use your wireless devices while at sea. Mobile phones are the easiest way to call home and, if you currently have the service through your home provider, you can also send and receive text messages. Be careful about using your mobile phone to call fellow travellers on the ship, because the roaming charges can add up.

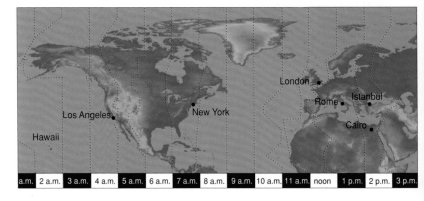

International roaming rates start at $1.50 per minute. Calls can also be placed through the ship's radio office or by placing a direct satellite telephone call. This is expensive, however, and unless the call is urgent you may want to wait and place your call from a land-based phone. Refer to the map (previous page) to determine the time difference before placing a call.

E-mail is another way to keep in touch and most ships now have internet cafes where passengers have access to on-line computers and are charged for their use on a per-minute basis. If you plan to send frequent e-mails while on your cruise, you may want to open a hotmail account upon embarkation. On some ships, passengers can use their own laptop computer to plug into the ship's connection.

Vacation Photos

Digital images have largely replaced photographs, but the goal of capturing your holiday's highlights remains the same. If you're using a digital camera, be sure to have a total of at least 128 mb of flash card memory storage and pack an extra battery pack, which can be recharged in your stateroom. Shoot at a fine setting for print-quality reproduction. A laptop computer will of course provide lots of storage, and most on-board photo departments can develop digital images into prints.

The ship's photo gallery is a good place to purchase shots of yourself, friends and family members as you disembark at each port of call. These make nice mementos of your cruise. On formal nights, when everyone is looking their best, the ship's photographers are set up to take formal portraits that are displayed the next day in the photo gallery. There is no obligation to purchase these framable prints but people often do because it's a convenient way to obtain a professional portrait.

Security

While security is not a major concern when on board the ship, you should take some precautions when venturing ashore. Property crime can occur anywhere, but tourists are especially vulnerable because they carry large amounts of money, as well as cameras another valuables. Keep all credit cards and most of your cash securely stowed in an inside pocket of your clothes or shoulder bag, and keep a few small bills in a readily accessible pocket so you're not pulling out your wallet to pay for small impromptu purchases from street vendors.

Be aware of potential thieves. Many operate in pairs, with one creating a distraction, such as dropping a handful of coins, while the other lifts their victim's wallet. Don't wear expensive jewelry and don't wear a fanny pack because a professional pickpocket with surgical scissors can quickly snip the strap and lift your pack without you even noticing. An inside jacket pocket with a zipper or a money belt concealed beneath your clothes are more secure ways to carry money.

Situations requiring caution include any place where there are crowds of people, and at airports and train stations, where you should never turn your back on your luggage. When hiring a taxi, watch to make sure every piece of luggage is loaded into the trunk, and never leave valuables in a rented car.

Shopping

Most stores and upscale shops accept all major credit cards, but it's best to have local currency (in most cases the euro) for small and impromptu purchases. Value Added Tax is attached to most purchases in Europe, and North American visitors can obtain a refund by first requesting a refund form in the store where they make their purchase, then having it stamped by customs staff in the airport prior to departure. Refunds can be obtained on the spot or after you are home, by sending the form to the appropriate office. Check with your travel agent or local customs office before leaving home to determine your duty-free allowances.

The Mediterranean is rich in centuries-old craftsmanship, and memorable souvenirs include hand-painted ceramics, lusterware, terracotta pottery and decorative tiles. Hand-woven carpets, embroidered linens and delicate laceware are other traditional crafts, as is gold filigree jewelry. In the major cities and tourist resorts you will find boutiques selling high-fashion clothing, leather goods and jewelry.

Italian craftsmanship on display in a Sicilian shop window.

Western civilization began along the shores of the Mediterranean, and its well-travelled waters have transported heroes and emperors, poets and prophets, to their appointments with destiny. Over the centuries this inland sea has inspired hope and instilled fear in mariners, living up to Homer's description of it being capricious and powerful, peaceful and calming. For the officers of modern ships, the Mediterranean no longer presents the same challenges it did to such legendary seafarers as Odysseus, and passengers cruising the Med can simply sit back and ponder the complex workings of a modern cruise ship.

Navigational Challenges of the Mediterranean

Although the Mediterranean is the world's largest inland sea at just under one million square miles, it doesn't possess the characteristics of an open ocean, such as swell, and ship captains generally regard the Mediterranean as one of the safest and easiest cruise areas to navigate.

Thoroughly charted, the Mediterranean is surprisingly deep in places. Thirty miles west of Greece's Peloponnese Peninsula, along a major subduction zone, the depths plunge to over 15,000 feet. Conversely, sea depths become shallow at river mouths, where silt carried downstream and deposited on the river's delta can alter the course of tributaries and reduce water depths at harbor entrances.

Although strong currents are not a prevalent hazard in the Mediterranean, two passes of concern are the Strait of Messina (lying between Sicily and the 'toe' of Italy) and the Dardanelles (leading to the Sea of Marmara and Istanbul). In both cases, however, currents rarely exceed five knots, which modern ships can handle without difficulty. (For a map of the prevailing currents in the Mediterranean, see page 41, Natural Phenomena.)

The upper decks of modern cruise ships provide excellent viewing for passengers. Shown here, a ship off the Sicily coast.

PORT SIDE OF SHIP

Telecommunication Domes · Funnel · Navigation Bridge · Anchoring Gear · Stern · Rudder · Propeller · Engine Room · Stabilizer · Thrusters · Bow Bulb · Bow

STARBOARD SIDE OF SHIP

The enclosed Mediterranean produces smaller waves than an open ocean, but there can occasionally be steep seas if the winds are strong. Although this normally doesn't present a problem for modern ships, the ship's motion can be uncomfortable for passengers if the ship is sailing broadside to the direction of the waves. Strong winds and choppy waves can occur in the Sea of Crete, the Tyrrhenian Sea (between the Straits of Messina and Naples), and the area between Barcelona and Marseille where ships cross the Gulf of Lions. At such times, the center of the ship in an inside cabin can be the most comfortable spot.

Many harbors of the Mediterranean are man-made, and some are quite old with narrow entrances. For example, the entrances to Marseille, Livorno and Civitavecchia are very tight and require close attention from the crew. The entrance to the ship dock at Venice is also very narrow, and the west side of the docking area is shallow, making maneuvering for large ships very challenging.

How Ships Move

Ships are pushed through the water by the turning of propellers, two of which are mounted at the stern. A propeller is like a screw threading its way through the sea, pushing water away from its pitched blades. Props are 15 to 20 feet in diameter on large cruise ships and normally turn at 100 to 150 revolutions per minute. It takes a lot of horsepower – about 60,000 on a large ship – to make these propellers push a ship along at 20 knots. The bridge crew can tap into any amount of engine power by moving small levers that adjust the propeller blades to determine the speed of the ship. Most modern ships use diesel engines to deliver large amounts of electricity to motors that smoothly turn the propeller shafts. The use of electric motors to turn prop shafts greatly reduces ship vibration and passengers rarely detect the workings of the ship. Some ships use electric motors mounted on pods hung from the stern of the ship, like huge outboard engines. These pods can swivel 360 degrees.

Ships normally cruise between 15 and 20 knots in the Med, although in the Greek islands – where distances are not great – ships go slower. Distances at sea are measured in nautical miles (1 nautical mile = 1.15 statute miles = 1.85 kilometers).

Most of the cruise ships currently sailing the Mediterranean were built in the last decade or two – a testament to the booming cruise industry. These new ships have been dubbed 'floating resorts' for their extensive onboard facilities, from swimming pools and health spas to show lounges and movie theaters. Cabins, formerly equipped with portholes, now are fitted with picture windows or sliding glass doors that open onto private verandas. Modern cruise ships are quite different from those of the Golden Age of ocean liners, which were designed for the rigors of winter storms in the North Atlantic. Ships built today are generally taller, shallower, lighter and powered by smaller, more compact engines. Although their steel hulls are thinner and welded together in numerous sections, modern ships are as strong as the older ocean liners because of advances in construction technology and metallurgy.

A ship's size is determined by measurements that result in a figure called tonnage. There are approximately 100 cubic feet to a measured ton. Cruise ships used to be considered large if they exceeded 30,000 tons. Most new ships being built today are over 80,000 tons and carry about 2,000 passengers.

At the stern of every ship, below its name, is the ship's country of registry, which is not necessarily where the cruise company's head office is located. Certain countries grant registry to ships for a flat fee, with few restrictions or onerous charges, and ships often fly these 'flags of convenience' for tax reasons.

A ship's bow bulb reduces the vessel's fuel consumption.

The Engine Room

Located many decks below the passenger cabins is the engine room, a labyrinth of tunnels, catwalks and bulkheads connecting and supporting the machinery that generates the vast amount of power needed to operate a ship. A large, proficient crew keeps everything running smoothly, but this is a far cry from the hundreds of workers once needed to operate coal-burning steam engines before the advent of diesel fuel.

Technical advancements in the last 40 to 50 years have helped to reduce fuel consumption and to improve control of the ship. These advancements include the bow bulb, stabilizers and thrusters. The bow bulb, just below the waterline, displaces the same amount of water that would be pushed out of the way by the ship's bow. This virtually eliminates a bow wave, resulting in fuel savings as less energy is needed to push the ship forward. Stabilizers are small, wing-like appendages that protrude amid-ships below the waterline and act to dampen the ship's roll in beam seas. Thrusters are port-like openings with small propellers that are located at the bow (and sometimes at the stern) which push the bow (or stern) of the ship as it is approaches or leaves a dock. Thrusters have greatly reduced the need for tugs when docking.

The Bridge

The bridge (located at the bow of the ship) is an elevated, enclosed platform that bridges (or crosses) the width of the ship, providing an unobstructed view ahead and to either side. It is from the ship's bridge that the highest-ranking officer – the Captain – oversees the operation of the ship. The bridge is manned 24 hours a day by two officers working four hours on, eight hours off, in a three-watch system. They all report to the captain, and their various duties include recording all course changes, keeping look-

A modern cruise ship bridge has banks of navigational aids.

out and making sure the junior officer keeps a fresh pot of coffee going. The captain does not usually have a set watch but will be on the bridge when the ship is entering or leaving port, and transiting a channel. Other conditions that would bring the captain to the bridge would be poor weather or when there are numerous vessels in the area, such as commercial fishboats.

An array of instrumentation provides the ship's officers with pertinent information. Radar is used most intensely in foggy conditions or at night. Radar's elec-

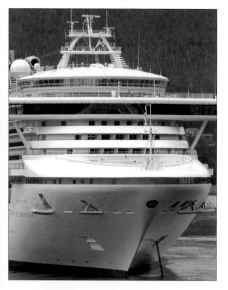

tronic signals can survey the ocean for many miles, and anything solid – such as land or other boats – appears on its screen. Radar is also used for plotting the course of other ships and for alerting the crew of a potential collision situation. Depth sounders track the bottom of the seabed to ensure the ship's course agrees with the depth of water shown on the official chart.

The helm on modern ships is a surprisingly small wheel. An automatic telemotor transmission connects the wheel to the steering mechanism at the stern of the ship. Ships also use an 'autopilot' which works through an electronic compass to steer a set course. The autopilot is used when the ship is in open water.

Other instruments monitor engine speed, power, angle of list, speed through water, speed over ground and time arrival estimations. When entering a harbor, large ships must have a pilot on board to provide navigational advice to the ship's officers. When a ship is in open waters, a pilot is not required.

Tendering

At some ports, the ship will anchor off a distance from the town and passengers are tendered ashore with the ship's launches. People on organized shore excursions will be taken ashore first, so if you have booked an excursion

Ships at anchor transport their passengers ashore in tenders.

you will assemble with your group in one of the ship's public areas. Otherwise, wait an hour or so to board a tender, when the line-ups will be shorter.

Ship Safety

Cruise ships are one of the safest modes of travel, and the cruise lines treat passenger safety as a top priority. The International Maritime Organization maintains high standards for safety at sea, including regular fire and lifeboat drills, as well as frequent ship inspections for cleanliness and seaworthiness.

Cruise ships must adhere to a law requiring that a lifeboat drill take place within 24 hours of embarkation, and many ships schedule this drill just before leaving port. You will be asked to don one of the life jackets kept in your cabin and proceed to your lifeboat station. Directions are displayed in your cabin, and staff are on hand to guide passengers through the safety drill.

Hotel Staff

The Front Desk (or Purser's Office) is the pleasure center of the ship. And, in view of the fact that a cruise is meant to be an extremely enjoyable experience, it is fitting that the Hotel Manager's rank is second only to that of the Captain. In terms of staff, the Hotel Manager (or Passenger Services Director) has by far the largest. It is his responsibility to make sure beds are made, meals are served, wines are poured, entertainment is provided and tour buses arrive on time – all while keeping a smile on his face. Hotel managers typically have many years' experience on ships, working in various departments before rising to this position. Most have graduated from a university or college program in management, and have trained in the hotel or food industries,

The front desk handles all passenger queries and accounts.

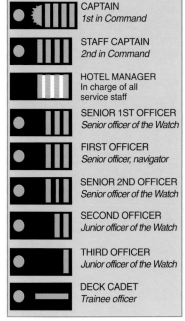

CAPTAIN
1st in Command

STAFF CAPTAIN
2nd in Command

HOTEL MANAGER
In charge of all
service staff

SENIOR 1ST OFFICER
Senior officer of the Watch

FIRST OFFICER
Senior officer, navigator

SENIOR 2ND OFFICER
Senior officer of the Watch

SECOND OFFICER
Junior officer of the Watch

THIRD OFFICER
Junior officer of the Watch

DECK CADET
Trainee officer

The ship's hotel manager oversees all of the service staff.

Excursion Manager. All ship's staff wear a uniform and even if a hotel officer doesn't recognize a staff member, he will know at a glance that person's duties by their uniform's color and the distinguishing bars on its sleeves. The hotel staff on cruise ships come from countries around the world.

Checking In

Upon arrival at your cruise ship pier, you will be directed to a check-in counter and asked to offer up a credit card to be swiped for any onboard expenses. In exchange, you will receive a personalized plastic card with a magnetic strip. This card acts both as your onboard credit card and the door key to your stateroom. It is also your security pass for getting off and on the ship at each port of call. Carry this card with you at all times.

where they learn the logistics of feeding hundreds of people.

A Hotel Manager's management staff includes a Purser, Food Service Manager, Beverage Manager, Chief Housekeeper, Cruise Director and Shore

*A standard outside stateroom
with balcony.*

Life Aboard

Cruise ship cabins – also called staterooms – vary in size, from standard inside cabins to outside suites complete with a verandah. Whatever the size of your accommodation, it will be clean and comfortable. A telephone and television are standard features, and storage space includes closets and drawers ample enough to hold clothes and miscellaneous items. Valuables can be left in your stateroom safe or in a safety deposit box at the front office, also called the purser's office.

If your budget permits, an outside cabin – especially one with a verandah – is preferable for enjoying the coastal scenery and orienting yourself at a new port. When selecting a cabin, keep in mind its location in relation to the decks above and below. Being above or below the disco is fine if

that is where you plan to be in the wee hours, but if you are below the dining room, you'll likely hear the scraping of chairs as a wake-up call. For those prone to seasickness, cabins located on lower decks near the middle of the ship will have less motion than a top outside cabin near the bow or stern. If you have preferences for cabin location, be sure to discuss these with your cruise agent when booking. Cruise lines often reward passengers who book early with free upgrades to a more expensive stateroom.

Both casual and formal dining are offered on the large ships, with breakfast and lunch served in the buffet-style lido restaurant or at an open seating in the main dining room. Dinner traditionally was served at two sittings in the main dining room, with passengers asked to indicate their preference for first or second sitting. While this traditional two-sitting format is still offered on the large ships, flexible dining times are

Specialty restaurants (one shown above) are an alternative to the ship's main dining rooms (left and bottom).

now also offered for passengers preferring to dine each evening at a time of their choosing. Luxury cruise lines usually offer a choice of open-seating restaurants.

Most ships also offer alternative dining – small specialty restaurants that require a reservation and for which there is usually a surcharge (about US$25 per person). Room service is also available, free of charge, for all meals and in-between snacks.

Things to Do

There are so many things to do on a modern cruise ship, you would have to spend a few months onboard to participate in every activity and enjoy all of the ship's facilities. A daily newsletter, delivered to your stateroom, will

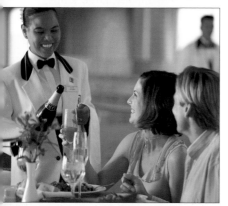

keep you informed of all the ship's happenings. If exercise is a priority, you can swim in the pool, work out in the gym, jog around the promenade deck, join the aerobics and dance classes or join in the table tennis and volley-ball tournaments. Perhaps you just want to soak in the jacuzzi, relax in the sauna or treat yourself to a massage and facial at the spa.

Stop by the library if you're looking for a good book, a board game or an informal hand of bridge with your fellow passengers. Check your newsletter to see which films are scheduled for the movie theater or just settle into a deck chair, breathing the fresh sea air. Your days on the ship can be as busy or as relaxed as you want. You can stay up late every night, enjoying the varied entertainment in the ship's lounges, or you can retire early and rise at dawn to watch the ship pull into port. When the ship is in port, you can remain onboard if you wish or you can head ashore, returning to the ship as many times as you like before it leaves for the next port. Ships are punctual about departing, so be sure to get back to the ship at least a half hour before it is scheduled to leave.

Although bridge tours (of the navigation area of the ship) have been largely discontinued due to security concerns, tours of the kitchen and of backstage entertainment areas are available on most ships. If you have an interest in these areas, check with the front desk for tour opportunities.

Children and teenagers are welcome on most cruise ships, which offer an ideal environment for a

(Top) The central atrium on a large ship. (Above and below) Games room and internet cafe.

(Top to bottom) Pool decks on moderns ships are expansive and often include dedicated areas for children. Outside teak decks are excellent venues for excercising.

family vacation. Youth facilities on the large ships usually include a playroom for children and a disco-type club for teenagers. Supervised activities are offered on a daily basis, and security measures include parents checking their children in and out of the playroom. Kids have a great time participating in activities ranging from ball games to arts and crafts, all overseen by staff with degrees in education, recreation or a related field. Each cruise line has a minimum age for participation (usually three years old), and some also offer private babysitting. Youth facilities and programs vary from line to line, and from ship to ship.

Extra Expenses

There are few additional expenses once you board a cruise ship. Your stateroom and all meals (including 24-hour room service) are paid for, as are any stage shows, lectures, movies, lounge acts, exercise classes and other activities held in the ship's public areas. If you make use of the personal services offered on board – such as dry cleaning or a spa treatment – these are not covered in the basic price of a cruise. Neither are any drinks you might order in a lounge. You will also be charged for any wine or alcoholic beverages you order with your meals. Some cruise lines offer beverage programs for teens and children, in which their parents pre-pay for a booklet of soft-drink tickets or for unlimited soda fountain fill-ups.

Gratuities for staff are an extra expense, with each cruise line providing their own guidelines on how much each crewmember should be tipped – provided you are happy with the service. On some cruise lines tipping is a personal choice while on others it is expected. A general amount for gratuities is US$3.50 per day per passenger for both your cabin steward and dining room steward, $2 per day for your assistant waiter, and $1 per day for the dining room management. Tips were traditionally given the last night at sea, in American cash, but most cruise lines now offer a service that automatically bills a daily amount for gratuities to your shipboard account – which can be adjusted at your discretion. Most ships are cashless societies in which passengers sign for incidental expenses. These are itemized on a final statement that is slipped under your cabin door during the last night of your cruise and settled at the front office by credit card or cash.

(Above) A poolside bar is an ideal spot for relaxing. (Below) A couple enjoys a romantic moment at the ship's rail.

Cataclysmic events, once thought to be caused by the actions of angry gods, have since been explained by scientific data and an understanding of seismic activity. Yet, rather than discredit ancient myths, the scientific evidence offered by modern geologists and oceanographers may prove that certain legendary events did occur. Indeed, the earth did shake from time to time with deafening force, huge waves did wash ashore, and islands did rise from the sea.

Such phenomena is currently happening off the coast of Sicily, where a submerged volcanic island called Graham Bank is rising to the sea's surface due to seismic activity in the area. It last emerged in 1831 when its six-month appearance sparked a diplomatic debate among Britain, Spain and the Bourbon court of Sicily, all claiming ownership of the tiny island. This time around, in hopes of claiming this new territory for Italy the moment it reappears, Sicilian divers have planted a flag on the submerged rock, which lies about 20 feet below the surface and is located in between the coasts of Sicily and Tunisia.

Through radiocarbon dating of sediment cores, scientists can now explain phenomena from the distant past, such as the formation of the Black Sea. According to the evidence, in about 5500 BC a worldwide rise in sea levels caused the salt waters of the Mediterranean Sea to spill into the Bosporus strait and transform an existing freshwater lake into the Black Sea. This has prompted speculation that the subsequent flooding of shorelines and displacement of people may have been the basis for Noah's ark in the Book of Genesis.

Tectonic Beginnings

The Mediterranean, the world's largest inland sea, was originally a vast ocean stretching across half the globe. Its surrounding land masses emerged some 30 million years ago when collisions of the earth's crustal plates created mountain ranges and deep sea rifts, such as the Red Sea, which formed when Africa and Arabia split. The Mediterranean Sea marks the boundary of two major plates – the Eurasian and African. Much of this boundary – from the toe of Italy's 'boot' to the coast of Turkey – is a subduction zone.

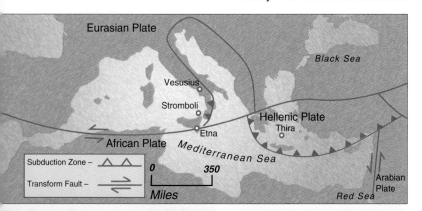

Eurasian Plate

Black Sea

Vesusius

Stromboli

Hellenic Plate
Thira

Etna

African Plate

Mediterranean Sea

Subduction Zone –	△ △
Transform Fault –	⇄

0   350

Miles

Arabian Plate

Red Sea

The world's most destructive earthquakes occur along such zones, where the leading edge of one plate is pushing beneath the edge of another. Transform faults – where the edges of two plates are sliding past one another – run along the Mediterranean's North African coastline and extend from Turkey to the Red Sea.

The biblical cities of Sodom and Gomorrah were quite likely destroyed not by 'fire and brimstone' but by earthquakes. In more recent times, an earthquake registering 6.3 on the Richter scale shook southern Turkey in June 1998, followed by two more in 1999, both in western Turkey, the latter registering a magnitude of 7.2. In February 2004, a 6.5-magnitude quake hit northern Morocco, its epicenter located beneath the sea bed near the Strait of Gibraltar. Italy has also been struck in recent years by earthquakes, including a series of quakes that battered central Italy in 1997. Increased seismic activity on Sicily in 2002 resulted in 200 small quakes which rattled the island's east side in the vicinity of **Mount Etna**, Europe's largest and most active volcano. And in January 2006, a 6.9-magnitude quake shook southern Greece, its epicenter located beneath the seabed about 125 miles south of Athens.

Volcanic Eruptions

Volcanoes form around an aperture in the earth's crust, through which gases, lava (molten rock) and solid fragments are ejected. Any mountain that is cone-shaped can be considered a potentially active volcano. A volcano's crater is formed when the cone collapses during an eruption, with steam vents left covering the crater floor.

The Mediterranean's legendary volcanoes include the Greek island of **Santorini** (Thira), which is the site of an exploded volcano, and its harbor is a flooded crater.

Stromboli is an active volcano with several craters for which the 'Strombolian' form of volcanic eruption is named. This fairly mild type of eruption consists of a continuous discharge of viscous lava which produces luminous clouds. In December 2002, after 20 years of relative quiet, Stromboli began erupting with unusual force, suggesting a new interaction between its magma and seawater. Residents of the tiny volcanic island had to evacuate when part of Stromboli's lava field slid down a steep slope into the Tyrrhenian Sea, triggering a huge harbor wave.

Sicily's **Mount Etna** also has become increasingly active, erupting more than 60 times in the first six months of 2000. Huge

Stromboli, one of Italy's Lipari Islands, is an active volcano.

'bombs' of lava, 4.5 feet in diameter, have shot from Etna's main summit cone, followed by explosions of ash from the northern vent area and slow lava flows that pour from the volcano's youngest crater on its southeastern flank. Ash has fallen on nearby villages, and trenches have been dug to divert the flow of magma away from the town of Linguaglossa. In October 2002 a stream of lava destroyed some ski lift pylons as it flowed toward Piano Provenzana, a plateau used by visitors as a starting point for mountain hikes. Scientists surmise that Etna is evolving from a predictable 'hotspot-type' of volcano to a more violent 'island-arc' variety.

Mount Vesuvius, standing on the eastern shore of the Bay of Naples, is the only active volcano on the European mainland. Its cataclysmic eruption of 79 AD buried Pompeii, Herculaneum and Stabiae under cinders, ashes and mud. Vesuvius has frequently erupted since then, including three times in the 20th century, and scientists predict another cataclysmic eruption. The height of the main cone is about 4,000 feet (1,200 meters) and is half encircled by the ridge of a second summit Monte Somma. The lower slopes of Vesuvius are quite fertile, where vineyards produce the famous Lachryma Christi wine.

A Storied Sea

The strong local winds that blow across the Mediterranean Sea – such as the hot, dry sirocco from the south, and the cold mistral from the north – were believed by ancient mariners to be controlled by gods. Inspiring several myths were the currents and whirlpools that plague the **Strait of Messina**, which lies between mainland Italy and the island of Sicily. The whirlpools in particular were attributed to the sea monster Scylla, who lived on the rocks on the mainland side of the strait, where she would seize and devour sailors. Odysseus passed through this strait in his wanderings, as did Jason and the Argonauts.

The enclosed Mediterranean is an almost tideless sea, and its currents are generally estuarine in nature. This two-way circulation is created by extensive evaporation of the surface waters, which become saltier and heavier than waters at lower levels, causing the surface waters to sink to the bottom of the seabed and eventually flow out through the **Strait of Gibraltar** where less salty (and lighter) Atlantic water flows into the Mediterranean. During World War II, German submarines that were trapped by the Allied blockade of the Strait of Gibraltar would sneak out of the Mediterranean by silently drifting seaward on these bottom currents.

The Mediterranean once supported a brilliant array of sponges, corals and fish species, and tales of dolphins rescuing people from drowning date back to Greek mythology. In recent times, the sea has suffered from overfishing and pollution. When Jacques-Yves Cousteau, in the summer of 1943, slipped into the warm waters of a cove on the

French Riviera to test the Aqualung he had developed with a French engineer, the Mediterranean teemed with life. By the early '70s, Cousteau was so concerned with the drastic decrease in marine life he founded the Cousteau Society to spread his ardent advocacy of the seas.

Military exercises in the Mediterranean also pose a threat to the sea's marine life. When a dozen Cuvier's beaked whales beached themselves on the coast of the Kyparissiakos Gulf in May 1997, a Greek researcher suggested that a NATO test using very loud, low-frequency sounds designed to detect quiet diesel and nuclear submarines may have disoriented the whales. And when the corpses of 22 dolphins washed up on the south coast of France in March 1998, naval operations were again suspect.

Another troubling trend is the rise in water temperature, with a growing number of tropical fish species now making the Mediterranean Sea their permanent home. They are arriving from the Red Sea and the Atlantic Ocean off Africa, and are thriving in part because the Mediterranean's indigenous species have been weakened by environmental stress. In the summer of 2005, a four-degree rise in water temperature created an ideal breeding ground for stinging jellyfish, their influx prompting swimming bans at beaches along the coasts of Spain, France and Italy.

When the ancient Greeks, using ropes and stone weights, began diving beneath the sea's surface in search of sponges and sunken treasure, they feared the mysterious creatures of the deep. Today we fear the threat of their extinction.

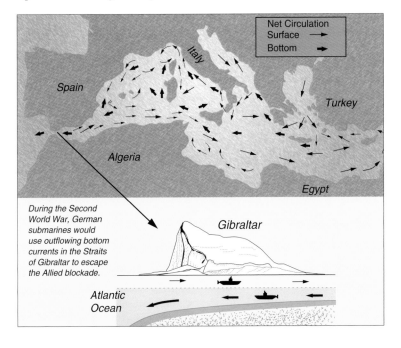

During the Second World War, German submarines would use outflowing bottom currents in the Straits of Gibraltar to escape the Allied blockade.

ANCIENT MARINERS

Since prehistoric times, shipping has determined human social development. Early civilizations formed along navigable rivers or on the coasts of warm seas, and the ideally situated Mediterranean became the cradle of maritime endeavor. As early as 3500 BC the **Egyptians** were sailing boats on the Nile, and by 2500 BC they were making tentative voyages into the Mediterranean Sea, tracing the coast by day and anchoring at night. Egypt was also the first Mediterranean nation to engage in shipbuilding. Early boats were made from bundles of papyrus reeds lashed together, their ends raised and bound, while those made of wood consisted of planks 'sewn' together with ropes. The larger boats were multi-oared and rigged with a steering oar. Over time, the Egyptians became skilled shipwrights, adept at dovetailing and scarfing hundreds of small timbers together, for there were no tall trees in Egypt from which to cut long planks.

While the Egyptians were sailing along the shores of the eastern Mediterranean, another seafaring civilization was flourishing on the island of Crete. Then several earthquakes struck, and the maritime commerce that had once been controlled by the people of Crete fell to the **Phoenicians** who, by 1250 BC, were well established as the primary navigators and traders of the Mediterranean world. The Phoenicians lived on the Mediterranean's eastern shores, their territory corresponding roughly with that of present-day Lebanon, and their main city-states were Tyre and Sidon. When Egyptian power waned in the 12th century BC, Phoenician mariners began dominating the entire Mediterranean. They sailed to the edges of the known world, and eventually ventured beyond the Pillars of Hercules at the western entrance to the Mediterranean, travelling north to England in search of tin, and south along the coast of Africa. The Phoenicians established numerous colonies along the shores of the Mediterranean, including **Carthage** on the north coast of Africa, which eventually became a powerful city-state and rival of imperial Rome.

Navigation & Chartmaking

Mediterranean is a Latin word meaning 'sea in the midst of lands.' Strong local winds blow across this inland sea, and the early sailors used these winds as a means of navigation when sailing from one port to another. Greek mariners, when out of sight of land, used four winds to determine their position. The Boreas blew from the north, the Euros from the east, the Notos from the south and the Zephuros from the west. Each wind was identified in relation to the sun's bearing or, at night, by the star Polaris. Other telltale signs were the wind's temperature and moisture content. As longer voyages were taken, four more winds, indicating the directions of northeast, southeast, southwest and northwest, were added to the wind-rose – the compass of ancient mariners. Over time the system was expanded until there were 32 winds, representing the 32 points of the wind-rose.

The first pilot books were written about 500 BC. The mouth of the Nile was a starting point from which the pilot would guide mariners, in a clockwise direction, from port to port. Tides, which are minimal in the Mediterranean, were believed to be controlled by sea monsters until a Greek navigator and astronomer named **Pytheas**, who lived in Massilia (modern Marseille) in the 4th century BC, discovered that tides were connected with the moon. Pytheas also embarked, from Cadiz, on a famous voyage along the Atlantic coast to the British Isles.

As early as the 6th century BC, the Greek philosopher Pythagoras realized that the earth was spherical. **Eratosthenes**, keeper of Alexandria's great library in the 3rd century BC, expanded on Pythagoras's theory and devised a method for measuring the earth's circumference, which incorporated existing surveys of the Nile river. He constructed a map of the known world using parallels and meridians that passed through important places, such as **Rhodes** (which was then the maritime center of the known world) and the **Pillars of Hercules**, which marked the Mediterranean's western entrance.

An important port as early as 400 BC, Rhodes was used by ancient cartographers as the central reference point on maps.

In the 1st century AD, Marinus of Tyre created the first marine charts, with Rhodes remaining the primary meridian and parallel. But it was **Ptolemy** (85-160 AD), perhaps the greatest cartographer of all, who first projected part of the spherical earth's surface onto a plane surface. A Greek born in Egypt, Ptolemy spent most of his life in **Alexandria** where he studied mathematics and astronomy. He wrote many works, the most famous of which was his *Geography* or *Geographica*, compiled into eight books and containing an atlas of the known world. This great work was lost with the fall of the Roman Empire, but it resurfaced in 1400 in Constantinople (now Istanbul). A century later, in Italy, Ptolemy's *Geography* was translated into Latin and, with the development of printing allowing for its wide distribution, *Geography* became the basis for mapping the new discoveries of the world throughout the 15th and 16th centuries.

Ship Design

In the beginning, small merchant ships plied the waters between Phoenicia, Egypt and Greece, carrying such luxury items as spices, perfumes and fine pottery for trade. Baskets filled with stones were used as anchors, but as ships grew larger, iron hooks were designed to dig into the sea bed. When the Phoenician sailors began making longer voyages, they built larger ships which carried, in addition to oars, a square sail for running before the wind.

The **Romans**, skilled engineers who both imitated and improved upon their neighboring nations' ship designs, built larger and stronger ships for transporting military supplies and troops to outlying outposts of Rome's expanding empire. These broad, full-bodied ships could carry up to 400 tons of cargo, and were used for shipping grain and other foodstuffs from their colonies. They were propelled by sails and steered by two deep oars, one on each quarter.

An innovative application of nautical know-how was used by the Romans during construction of the **Colosseum** in the 1st century AD, when a retractable sail-cloth was rigged as a sun shade for spectators. The sailors living in a camp nearby were adept at handling the wooden pulleys and ropes used to furl this cloth roof in heavy rains and winds, then unfurl it in fair weather.

Merchant ships, designed to carry cargo, were often accompanied by galleys for protection. War galleys were long, narrow vessels designed for speed and rowed by slaves and prisoners of war who were chained to benches. A beak or metal point was fixed on the bow and was used for ramming enemy vessels with the intent of piercing their hulls and sinking them. The crew of ancient warships used catapults for firing missiles and incendiaries such as Greek Fire, which

Ptolemy's famous map of North Africa was drafted in the 2nd century.

was a flammable substance of sulphur, naphtha and quicklime.

Attached to the ship's beak was a figurehead. Associated with a sea deity for protection, this figure had eyes enabling the ship to 'see' its way swiftly across the water. The Egyptians mounted figures of various holy birds on the prows of their ships; the Phoenicians used a horse's head; the Greeks favored a boar's head; and the Romans often used a centurion.

A number of superstitions and rituals still practiced by modern mariners originated in ancient times. The tradition of breaking a bottle of champagne across a new ship's bow began as a cruel ritual during antiquity when a new galley had to 'taste blood' to be successful in battle. To this end, galleys were launched by rolling them across slaves tied to the keel blocks. Their bodies, when crushed, would splash blood against the ship's hull.

Galleys were eventually rigged as sailing vessels, and by the 15th century, the caravel – a three-masted sailing vessel with a roundish hull – was being used by the Portuguese and Spanish for ocean-going exploration. The galley continued to be used in the eastern Mediterranean until the 18th century.

Traditional boats that are still in use include the felucca, a lateen-rigged sailing vessel once used in the Mediterranean and still seen on the Nile, as is the *dahabeeyah*, a large river vessel with high lateen sails. The word *dahabeeyah* is Arabic for 'golden' and was originally applied in

A felucca on the Nile (above). Traditional beaks are still seen on Venetian gondolas (below).

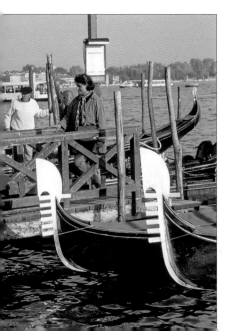

reference to the gilded barges Egyptian rulers used for river processions and ceremonies of state. Cleopatra's barge was described by Shakespeare in *Antony and Cleopatra* as "a burnished throne" with a golden poop, silver oars and purple sails "so perfumed the winds were love-sick with them".

The Venetian *bucentaur*, from the Italian *buzino d'oro* (meaning 'golden bark'), was another sumptuously decorated vessel. The state galley of the doges (rulers of Venice), it was used in an annual symbolic ceremony called 'the wedding of the sea' which commemorated Venice's victory over the Dalmatian pirates in 1000 AD. Venice's most famous vessel is the **gondola**, which dates to at least the 11th century and is still used today as a popular mode of transport for tourists transiting the city's canals. Long, sleek and efficient, its hull shape embodies the principles of the wave line theory of modern shipbuilding. With a flat bottom and a high prow and stern, it is propelled by a single oarsman – called a gondolier – positioned near the stern. The bright metal beak at the bow, called a ferro, is shaped like the ancient *rostrum tridens*.

Naval Battles

The Mediterranean's early naval fleets set off on raiding or trading expeditions, and were eventually organized for conquest and defense as naval supremacy became critical to an empire's survival. When the Athenian navy destroyed a Persian fleet off the Aegean island of Salamis in 480 BC, this great naval victory established the maritime supremacy of **Athens** and ushered in the city-state's golden age under the leadership of Pericles. The port of Piraeus, linked to Athens by a fortified corridor called the Long Walls, became an important naval center holding nearly 300 war galleys. Fifty years later, the rival city-state of Sparta, aided by the Persians, defeated the Athenian navy and tore down the Long Walls.

In the 3rd century BC, following its conquest of central and southern Italy, **Rome** began to look seaward. The North African city of Carthage ruled the western Mediterranean, and Rome's designs on Sicily drew these two city-states into a protracted conflict. Rome eventually emerged

Ancient galleys of the Mediterranean were rigged with a square sail for running before the wind.

as victor, with the Romans now referring to the Mediterranean as Mare Nostrum ('Our Sea').

Rome's first naval hero was Gaius Duillius, who led a fleet to victory in the Battle of Mylae in 260 BC, defeating the Carthaginian fleet off the northern coast of Sicily. Duillius carried boarding bridges and designed grappling irons which he used to bind his ships to those of the enemy. Thus aided, he captured fifty ships and was the first Roman to achieve victory over the naval power of Carthage. His great triumph was honored in Rome with the raising of a column adorned with the beakheads of the captured vessels. Hailed as a hero, he was attended by a torchbearer and flute player whenever he walked the streets of Rome in the evening.

Piracy & Plunder

The fall of the Roman Empire was followed by the rise of piracy, and throughout the Middle Ages pirates plagued the Mediterranean. Coastal trading ports were fortified with walls and bastions, and chains were drawn across harbor entrances during times of attack. Sacking and plundering coastal settlements was highly lucrative, and became even more so when oared galleys were replaced with sailing ships, which greatly increased a pirate's range of operation. The most

famous pirates of the Mediterranean operated from the coast of north Africa. Many were displaced Moors of Spain who had been driven into exile in the 15th century by the Catholic forces of Ferdinand and Isabella. Bent on revenge against Christians in general and the Spanish in particular, they were called **Barbary pirates** for the Berber settlements from which they embarked on their raids. These notorious corsairs, who lived by plunder, operated out of Tripoli, Tunis and Algiers, all of which were military republics that broke free of Turkish rule in the mid-1600s.

The Barbary pirates specialized in the capture and sale of slaves, with some venturing as far away as Iceland. The most feared were the Barbarossa brothers, whose names struck terror in the hearts of Christians. From 1510 to 1545, they burned, pillaged and murdered in raids along the Spanish and Italian coasts. One brother was eventually killed by Spanish troops but the other retired with vast riches to a palace he had built at Constantinople.

Piracy's promise of easy money attracted European renegades to the Barbary ranks, including an Englishman named Verney (who was from a distinguished Buckinghamshire family) and a Fleming who took the Arabic name of Murad Reise. The latter led a raid on Baltimore, Ireland, during which the town was sacked and most of its residents seized as slaves to be sold at the slave market in Algiers. Despite numerous attempts to stamp out piracy in the throne. He then headed to Asia Minor, where an easy victory over the ancient country of Pontus prompted his famous words "Veni, vidi, vici" – I came, I saw, I conquered. When a triumphant Caesar returned to Rome in 47 BC, the great leader pardoned all his enemies, then set about improving the living conditions of the people. His dictatorial powers aroused widespread resentment, however, and Caesar was stabbed to death in the senate house on March 15, 44 BC.

Antony, who gave a famous funeral address in Caesar's honor, stirred the mob into anger and drove Caesar's conspirators from Rome. Antony then formed an alliance with **Octavian**, Caesar's grand-nephew and heir, who arranged a Second Triumvirate consisting of himself, Antony and Lepidus, which ruled Rome for five years amid political turmoil and the ongoing threat of civil war. Antony, who had a notorious reputation for riotous living, met Cleopatra in 42 BC and fell hopelessly in love. Five years later, he settled with her in Alexandria to pursue a life of pleasure. Back in Rome, the growing ill will towards him culminated in the famous naval battle off Actium in 31 BC, at which Octavian's fleet, commanded by Agrippa, defeated the less-maneuverable ships of Antony and Cleopatra. The two lovers fled to Egypt where they committed suicide.

Octavian became the first emperor of Rome in 27 BC, receiving from the senate the title **Augustus**. His rule began a long 200-year period of peace, during which an extensive system of roads was built, linking Rome with its most distant provinces. Remarkably durable, these roads were generally built in four layers, the uppermost layer consisting of a pavement of stones or pebbles set in concrete. The Appian Way was one of the first of these great highways, many of which are, in part, still used today.

Augustus also patronized the arts and letters, which were largely an imitation of Greek culture. Many of the Greek gods had been adopted by the Romans, who also became influenced by Greek mysteries – secret cults based on primitive fertility rites, including the worship of Isis, the nature goddess of ancient Egypt. The mysteries, which fulfilled an individual's desire for personal salvation, created a religious climate conducive to the eventual ascent of Christianity.

Meanwhile a line of notorious emperors left their mark on the Roman Empire. **Tiberius**, stepson of Augustus, was unpopular in Rome and spent his latter years ruling the empire by correspondence from Capri. **Caligula**, a cruel and insane tyrant, was eventually murdered. His successor, **Claudius**, found by soldiers hiding behind a palace curtain when Caligula was murdered, was hauled forth and proclaimed emperor. During his reign, Claudius had one of his wives killed and he himself was eventually poisoned by his wife Agrippina, who was a sister of Caligula and a niece of Claudius. Her son **Nero**, begat from a previ-

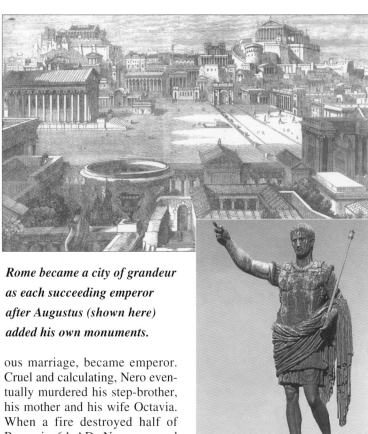

Rome became a city of grandeur as each succeeding emperor after Augustus (shown here) added his own monuments.

ous marriage, became emperor. Cruel and calculating, Nero eventually murdered his step-brother, his mother and his wife Octavia. When a fire destroyed half of Rome in 64 AD, Nero accused the Christians of starting it and thus began a barbarous persecution, with St. Peter and St. Paul among the many Christians killed. Nero rebuilt much of the city on the right bank of the Tiber, with broader streets and impressive buildings, but a series of revolts caused him to commit suicide in 68 and his memory was publicly execrated.

The death of Nero marked the end of the Julio-Claudian line. After a brief struggle, Vespasian became emperor, followed by his son **Titus** in 79 AD. A benevolent ruler, Titus completed the Colosseum and built a luxurious

bath. He also lent aid to victims of the volcanic eruption of Vesuvius, which buried Pompeii and Herculaneum. Before becoming emperor, his military campaigns had included the capture and destruction of Jerusalem in 70 AD.

Several great emperors ruled during the 1st century AD. **Trajan**, born in Spain and the first non-Italian to head the empire, pushed its eastern borders past Mesopotamia. His successor **Hadrian** pulled Roman rule back to the Euphrates, and in Britain he built Hadrian's Wall to keep out

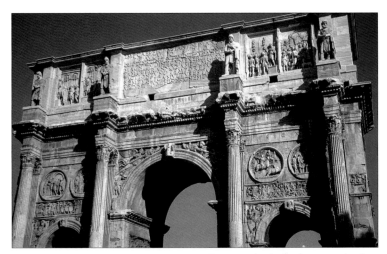

Constantine's arch was raised in 312 AD to commemorate a military victory that made him the unchallenged ruler of Rome's west empire.

the northern barbarians who were threatening Rome's developing province. **Marcus Aurelius** ruled during the Golden Age of the empire, from 161 to 180 AD. A humanitarian, he improved the living conditions of poor children and tried to curb the brutality at gladiatorial shows. He was also a man of letters, whose philosophy was based on Stoicism, a Greek school of philosophy which incorporated the Socratic ideals of virtue and self-sufficiency.

Roman law forms the basis of modern civil law, and the greatest figure in its development was the learned jurist Papinian. A close friend of the emperor **Septimius Severus**, who ruled from 193 to 211, Papian was a stern moralist whose chief works became the foremost authority in legal decisions. Under Roman law, an important distinction was established between public law, in which the state is directly involved, and private law, which addresses disputes between individuals.

As the 2nd century drew to a close, the decline of the Roman Empire began. A series of emperors ruled in rapid succession during the 3rd century and, with the capture of the emperor **Valerian** by the Persians in 260, the empire fell into anarchy. **Diocletian**, named emperor by the army in 284, divided the empire into four political sections: two eastern and two western. In 330, **Constantine I** moved the empire's capital to Byzantium and renamed it Constantinople. He also granted universal religious tolerance, which allowed Christians to worship without fear of persecution.

The Roman empire became permanently divided into East and West after the death of **Theodosius I** in 395. As the Dark Ages descended on Europe,

Rome's western empire soon foundered, and not until the 19th century did Italy recover from the fall of Rome. The eastern (**Byzantine**) empire, however, endured for a thousand years despite constant invasions, religious controversies and internal political strife.

MIDDLE AGES

The Middle Ages, between the fall of Rome and the beginning of the Renaissance, were once viewed as a thousand years of darkness. The designation of Dark Ages now refers strictly to the Early Middle Ages (c. 450-750), when the collapse of the West Roman Empire plunged western Europe into turmoil. The year 476, when emperor **Romulus Augustulus** abdicated, is regarded as the end of Rome.

The seeds of Rome's demise were sown by the emperor Constantine. Within 15 years of taking the reins of power, **Constantine** made two decisions, either of which alone would have changed the future of the world. The first was to embrace

Christianity as the official religion of the Roman Empire and the second was to transfer the capital from Rome to the city of Byzantium, which became known as **Constantinople**.

Constantine's disillusionment with Rome – its republican and pagan traditions matched with its inferior location – was confirmed on his second visit to the city in 326 AD. To him, the old city seemed decadent, tired and vulnerable. Constantine's vision was to create a New Rome where its citizens were Christian, its streets and public buildings clean and new, and its grandeur supreme in the world. In a period of just three years, he stripped cities throughout the empire of monuments, columns and artwork for his new capital, and in 330 he formally dedicated Constantinople to the God of the Christians.

Moving the capital east resulted quickly – and unexpectedly – in splitting the realm, and eventually led to a schism between the Roman (Catholic) church and the Eastern (Orthodox) church. While the Eastern (Byzantine) Empire became a military, commercial and cultural power, focused on regaining territories from the Persians, the West Roman Empire suffered waves of Germanic invaders. The emperors of Constantinople tried to hold on to the empire's western province but their attention was soon directed at a new threat to their eastern frontiers – the rise of **Islam**.

Constantine the Great, Museo dei Conservatori, Rome.

With lightening speed this new religion, founded by the Arab prophet **Muhammad** in 622, spread outward from his birthplace of Mecca. By 732 the Arabs had swept across northern Africa into Spain, threatening to add southwestern France to their conquests. Called Saracens by the Christians (Moors in Spain), the Arabs closed the Mediterranean to outside commerce, thus isolating western Europe. Amid the political and social upheaval of western Europe, in which the Germanic and Roman cultures were assimilating, Christianity became a unifying force – despite an ongoing dispute between the pope in Rome and the patriarch in Constantinople, both of whom claimed leadership of Christendom.

In 800, **Charlemagne**, the Carolingian king of the Franks, was crowned emperor of the West by the pope in Rome, and this symbolic ceremony introduced a new concept: the interdependence of church and state. Such sharing of power did not exist in the Orthodox East, where the emperors embodied both spiritual and secular authority, regularly installing patriarchs of their choice. Charlemagne's splendid court was located not in Rome but in Aachen (now part of West Germany near the Belgian and Dutch borders), and the center of civilization in western Europe shifted northward. The Mediterranean, once a great highway of commerce and cultural exchange, became a border zone dominated by the Arabs and the Byzantine Empire.

Feudalism, originating in the empire of Charlemagne, spread to neighboring countries and provided protection from attack by plundering Germanic bands. An agricultural-based system of distributing wealth, feudalism was based on a hierarchy of king, nobility and peasantry. The nobles, who held land directly from the king, provided protection to the serfs who worked the land. **Chivalry**, a fusion of Christian and military concepts, grew out of feudalism and inspired the **Crusades** – an attempt by western Europeans to regain the Holy Land from the Muslims. Monastic orders of knights were sworn to uphold the Christian ideal, and tournaments were staged in which knights

Medieval ports were entered through fortified gates. Shown here is Porta Soprana in Genoa.

could prove their chivalric virtues.

The **Holy Roman Empire**, successor state to the empire of Charlemagne, was established in 936, but its emperors, who were initially elected by German princes and crowned by the pope, were constantly struggling to assert their control over a fragmented western Europe. The papacy, surrounded by corruption, was weakened in 1083 when Rome was sacked by the Normans. In 1305, Pole Clement V moved the papal court to **Avignon**, where it came under French control until its return to Rome in 1378.

Meanwhile, the Byzantine Empire had spiralled into a slow decline upon the death of one of its greatest emperors, **Justinian**, in 565 AD. Although the empire stayed more or less intact over the next four centuries, encompass-

Paganism & Christianity

During the Middle Ages pagan rituals of ancient Rome were slowly assimilated into Christian festivals. Saint **Valentine's Day**, established by the Christians in memory of the martyrdom of the 3rd-century saint, was rooted in the Roman feast of Lupercalia. This ancient festival was held in honor of Faunus, a woodland deity who was attended by fauns (similar to the Greek satyrs), which were half man and half goat. In ancient Rome, two male youths dressed as goats (which embodied sexuality) would run around the city slapping people with strips of goat skin.

When this pagan holiday became christianized in medieval times, St. Valentine came to be associated with the union of lovers under conditions of duress. According to legend, the young priest Valentine, while imprisoned for his Christian beliefs, would pick violets that grew outside his cell window and write messages to his loved ones on the heart-shaped leaves, delivering them by dove. The modern 'valentine' appeared in England and America in the mid-19th century, establishing the popular custom of exchanging Valentine's Day cards each February 14th.

Also dating from the Middle Ages is the great Christian festival of **Christmas** (Christ's mass), which became a widely celebrated feast day in western Europe in the 4th century. December 25th was chosen as the date to celebrate the nativity of Jesus Christ, a date coinciding closely with winter solstice, traditionally a time of pagan rejoicing. Saint Nicholas, the patron of children and sailors in Greece, Sicily and other places, was a 4th-century bishop of Myra in Asia Minor, and the December 6th feast day of St. Nicholas eventually became a children's holiday in parts of Europe. Called Sint Nikolaas in Dutch, the saint was adopted by the English in colonial New York and transformed into Santa Claus, and the children's festival was moved to Christmas Day. In the mid-19th century, Christmas started to become secularized as a holiday of gift giving and good cheer.

ing the area of present-day Turkey and beyond – to the Danube, most of Greece and southern Italy – it was riven from within with political and religious intrigues Yet it remained a bulwark against waves of Arab attacks during a time when most of Europe was vulnerable and in chaos.

Then, during the 11th and 12th centuries, as the Franks and Southern Italians grew in strength and the rift between the Catholic Latins and the Orthodox Byzantines grew, Constantinople found itself fighting on two fronts and becoming progressively weaker. In 1071, the Seljuk Turks finally broke into the Byzantine heartland of Antolia (Asia Minor) in a decisive battle at Manzikert. Although this led to the fall of most of the empire's Asian possessions, the death blow was administered not by the determined Turks, but by a 90-year-old man from Venice. His name was **Enrico Dandolo** who, as doge of Venice, led a fleet of Crusaders to take the fabled city of Constantinople – the largest and most splendid city of medieval Europe. In 1204, the Crusaders breached the seawalls of the city and Dandolo, who was blind, led his troops into the 'Queen of Cities' and stripped Constantinople of its wealth. It was a blow from which Byzantium never recovered.

In the middle of the 14th century, a tribe broke away from the crumbling Seljuk Turk nation and became, under a series of strong leaders, the rapidly growing **Ottoman Empire**. In 1451, with

The famous bronze horses displayed at Venice's St. Mark's Cathedral were looted from Constantinople in 1204.

the accession of **Sultan Mehmet II**, the city of Constantinople (all that remained of the Byzantine Empire) found itself surrounded. In preparation for a siege of the great city, Mehmet bought the largest cannon the world had ever known, and in 1453, the Ottoman Turks broke through the great Theodosian land walls and seized Constantinople. The glorious capital of one of the world's longest-lasting empires had fallen.

By the late Middle Ages, feudalism was firmly entrenched in France and southern Italy, but not in northern Italy, where the rise of the city-state had begun in the 10th century. The two great

Italian seaports of **Venice** and **Genoa**, distinct in character and constantly warring with each other, enjoyed a material prosperity based largely on trade with the Middle East. The Christian crusades generated additional wealth for these and other city states, and influential banking firms came to dominate Genoa and the powerful republic of **Florence**, where the prominent Medici family rose from bankers to dukes. Although guilds perpetuated the Christian and medieval spirit of collective wealth and regulated competition, the growth of cities and the ascent of the merchant class eventually brought about the demise of feudalism, marking the end of the Middle Ages and the dawn of the Renaissance.

THE RENAISSANCE

Called the *rinascita* in Italian and the *renaissance* in French, this 'rebirth' of classical antiquity's arts and sciences not only produced an outpouring of creativity never before seen, it ultimately ushered in modern civilization. The Renaissance, which originated in Italy, did not begin with a single momentous event but began as an artistic and intellectual movement that gradually gained momentum and eventually spread across Western Europe to Great Britain, where humanist thought influenced the works of Ben Jonson and William Shakespeare.

The seeds of the Renaissance's flowering were planted during the late Middle Ages, when a rediscovery of Greek and Roman literature led to the eventual development of the humanist movement. The Italian poet **Petrarch**, who lived from 1304 to 1374, is considered the first modern poet and the father of **humanism**. By proclaiming pagan antiquity as the most enlightened stage of history, and the centuries that followed as a time of darkness, he set in motion the pursuit of learning based on a secular rather than a religious framework. This humanistic challenge to scholasticism advocated not a pre-Christian paganism but a reconciliation of classical antiquity's artistic and intellectual achievements with Christian beliefs.

The Renaissance began around 1400 in Florence, where local

The Vatican, Rome.

writers and artists cultivated an interest in the classical teachings of Greek scholars. The mid-15th century was marked by the rise of the **Medici** banking family. Politically powerful and generous patrons of the arts and letters, the Medicis founded a library and filled it with Greek and Roman books. When Constantinople fell to the Turks in 1453, Greek scholars fled to Italy with manuscripts documenting the civilizations of ancient Greece, further fuelling a thirst for knowledge and an active search for classical works. The bronze and marble sculptures excavated in Rome and other ancient sites, which had previously been treated as scrap metal or mortar, were now highly valued by collectors.

As medieval courtliness and codes of conduct gave way to a new era that focussed on expressiveness and emotionalism, the social status of the artist was elevated. Lorenzo de Medici's Florentine court became known as the **Platonic Academy** and prominent members of this circle included the artists Botticelli and Michelangelo. Stressing human values and capabilities, humanism's rejection of medieval religious authority climaxed in 1517 when the German cleric **Martin Luther** sparked the Protestant Reformation with his open attack on the doctrines of the wealthy and corrupt Catholic church. Condemning such practices as the sale of indulgences (pardons for

sin), Luther believed individuals could communicate directly with God and could seek salvation by reading the Bible, obtaining grace not through the sacraments (religious ceremonies conducted by priests) but through faith.

The growth of literacy, education and middle-class wealth provided a fertile environment for the new Protestant culture, which adopted an austere taste in Christian art, in contrast to the worldly opulence of Rome. New subject matters – landscapes, still lifes and scenes of daily life – formed part of the Renaissance taste in personal artwork, as did portraiture, and artists found new clients from wealthy townspeople. The church, however, continued to be the foremost patron of the arts, and in the 16th century the center of Italian art shifted from Florence to Rome, where

Leonardo da Vinci's Mona Lisa.

(The Louvre, Paris)

the **Vatican** commissioned Michelangelo, Leonardo da Vinci and Raphael for various projects, resulting in some of the greatest masterpieces of Renaissance art. Venetian art also came into its full glory in the 16th century. The Venetian school was known for the superb coloring of its oil paintings, created by such masters as Bellini and Giorgione, and later succeeded by Titian, Veronese and Tintoretto.

The sciences were also advanced during the 16th century, aided by the rediscovery of Galen's physiological and anatomical studies and Ptolemy's Geography. Scientific thinkers began refining the theories of classical physics, with Copernicus proposing the heliocentric model of the solar system, and **Galileo** inventing an accurate telescope for viewing the heavens. **Leonardo da Vinci**, the consummate Renaissance man, studied anatomy and astronomy, his copious notes covering everything from the curved trajectory to metallurgical techniques. In his paintings, accurate depictions of the human form were based on his anatomical observations. Other sciences that were developed during the Renaissance included botany, zoology and astrology.

The scientific and intellectual achievements of the Renaissance, along with seaborne exploration and the discovery of new lands and cultures, fostered further learning in the 17th century. The rationalism of Descartes, the empiricism of Francis Bacon and John Locke, and the ground breaking achievements of Isaac Newton, widely considered the greatest scientist of all time, reflected an intensifying belief in natural law, universal order and human reason. The Renaissance also set the stage for an emerging middle class of merchants and craftsmen which eventually spearheaded the revolutionary upheavals of the 18th century.

THE GRAND TOUR

The 18th century in Europe was called the **Age of Enlightenment** – an era marked by colonial expansion, scientific discoveries and mechanical inventions. The first geographical survey was undertaken in France, as was the first flight in a hot-air balloon. Captain James Cook and other explorers opened up new territories across vast expanses of the Pacific Ocean, while Wolfgang Amadeus Mozart entertained the courts of Europe with his musical genius. Rational and scientific approaches were now applied to all issues – whether social, economic, religious or political. Amid a stimulating atmosphere of skepticism and idealism, Christianity was questioned and classical teachings were scrutinized. The French philosopher Voltaire even dared to declare that Plato "wrote better than he reasoned.".

The most cataclysmic event of 18th-century Europe was the **French Revolution**, which began in 1789 and eventually affected the entire world as it tore down the medieval structures of Europe and made way for 19th-century liberalism and nationalism. France, not yet free of feudalism, was ripe for rebellion. The country was still ruled by two privileged classes, the nobility and the clergy, and a simmering resentment among the oppressed bourgeoisie and working classes led to widespread violence and anarchy. A Parisian mob's storming of the Bastille, a prison fortress, symbolized the revolt of the lower classes. In 1793, to the horror of other European monarchs, the king of France was beheaded, along with hundreds of aristocrats.

The army general **Napoleon Bonaparte** rose to dictatorial power in 1799 and had himself crowned emperor in 1804. Although the British navy defeated the French at Trafalgar in 1805, Napoleon soon controlled the European continent. The Holy Roman Empire dissolved in 1806, and Napoleon installed his brothers on the thrones of Europe. Napoleon was defeated by the allied forces of Britain, Prussia, Sweden and Austria in 1814 and exiled to the island of **Elba** off the coast of Italy, but he returned a year later, only to be defeated in the Waterloo Campaign and sent as a prisoner of war to the isolated British island of Saint Helena in the south Atlantic, where he died six years later. The French monarchy was restored, but unrest and rebellion continued, culminating in a bloody insurrection in 1848. The collapse of the French monarchy and the establishment of a new republic caused a chain reaction across Europe, spawning public demonstrations and a general cry for the overthrow of

A British tour group at Giza.

monarchies as an urban bourgeoisie called for constitutional, representative government.

Propelling this massive upheaval was the **Industrial Revolution**. Originating in England in the mid-1700s, it marked Europe's transition from an agricultural-based society to a modern industrialized society. The steam engine was invented in England in 1698 and by 1814 the steam locomotive was being used to power early rail travel, followed by the first steamship crossing of the Atlantic in 1819. Europe began rapidly industrializing, building roads and rail lines. A line from Marseille to Cannes was laid in 1863 and extended a year later to Nice, with Tsar Alexander II and his wife among the first to arrive by train in Nice. The railroad line was extended to Monaco a few years later, transforming the tiny principality into a gambling mecca, and by 1870 the rail line reached the Italian border. The railroad revolutionized travel, for people could now journey across the continent in a fraction of the time it had once taken. Leisure travel, formerly the reserve of the privileged wealthy, would soon become the domain of the masses.

Leisure travel to the Mediterranean originated with the grand tours of the British aristocracy. By the mid-18th century, it was commonplace for the young men of Britain's upper classes to embark on an educational tour of Europe to acquaint themselves with the famous classical ruins and Renaissance art of Rome and other Italian cities. Although politically fragmented and in a state of economic decline, **Italy** was still considered the heart of western culture. Britain had become the wealthiest nation in the world due to its colonial trade, but its privileged classes, who were schooled in Latin and the classics, felt isolated from the cultural riches of Europe. Thus, a Grand Tour was considered necessary for a person to become a fully educated member of elite society.

Italy, and the Mediterranean in general, also held a sensual allure. Escaping damp winters and the prevailing work ethic of the Protestant north, young Englishmen were understandably eager to sojourn in the sunny south of Europe where warm weather and uninhibited attitudes extended to the pleasures of the flesh.

Reaching the Grand Tour's 'must-sees' – namely Rome, Florence, Naples and Venice – entailed a lengthy and at times arduous journey by boat and stage-coach. Early tourists included James Boswell, who achieved fame with his *Account of Corsica* (1768), and Edward Gibbon, who claimed that a walk through the Forum's ruins inspired him to write *The History of the Decline and Fall of the Roman Empire*. Goethe, the German poet and scientist, was smitten with Naples and its bright colors and carefree mood. As there were no guidebooks for the early travellers, works by Vergil and other ancient classics were used as references.

The French Revolution and the Napoleonic Wars interrupted continental touring by the British, but these conflicts didn't stop **Lord Byron** from voyaging to the Mediterranean in 1809. Fresh from Cambridge, he sailed to Lisbon, then entered the Mediterranean Sea, stopping at Gibraltar, Sardinia and Malta before embarking on an overland tour of Greece and Turkey. The defeat of Napoleon at Waterloo in 1815 brought peace to the continent and one of the first postwar travellers to return was Lord Byron, who lived for three years in Venice before settling in Genoa. Other Romantic poets followed suit, including Keats, who died in Rome, and Shelley, who drowned while sailing in the Bay of Spezia on the Italian Riviera. Byron died of a fever in 1824, while working for the the cause of Greek independence. The Romantic poets' literary works spawned a fresh interest by the British in the antiquities of continental Europe, and the first modern guidebooks appeared around this time, with the Mediterranean homes of Byron joining the lists of local attractions. William Thackery, Charles Dickens and Mark Twain were among the popular writers given free passage on steamships in exchange for writing a book about their travels. By the end of the 19th century, the Americans were second only to the British in terms of numbers touring the Mediterranean.

In 1841, an English cabinet maker named **Thomas Cook** organized the first group excursion when he obtained reduced train fares for members of his temperance society, who were travelling to a regional meeting. His organizational skills soon led to a new concept – the guided tour. These packaged holidays appealed to average Britons of modest means who wanted to travel abroad and see the sights previously enjoyed only by the wealthy, who would spend months, even years, completing their grand tours.

As British and American tourists began travelling through Europe in steadily increasing numbers, the wealthy elite sought ever more exclusive and exotic destinations. Egypt became a popular winter destination, with tourists arriving by steamer at Alexandria and spending a few days in Cairo to view the pyramids before heading up the Nile aboard a hired *dahabeeya* (a river sailing craft). Cook's tours expanded into Egypt as well, when regular steamer service was introduced in the early 1870s, and within a decade Cook's Nile fleet had grown to 40 vessels.

A Middle East grand tour wasn't complete without a pilgrimage to the Holy Land, with tourists travelling by horseback across the desert accompanied by an army of servants, including armed guards, who would set up tents for sleeping each night. This was luxury camping, with meals served in dining tents on white linen and fine china, and the sleeping tents outfitted with iron bedsteads and clean sheets.

Luxury travel, in the form of Pullman rail cars, grand hotels and palatial steamships, enabled the wealthy to isolate themselves

The Grand Canal, Venice.

from the travelling masses. By the end of the industrial revolution, the 'high bourgeoisie', consisting of rich industrialists and bankers, were distinguishing themselves from the 'petty bourgeoisie', which comprised tradespeople and white-collar workers. The bourgeoisie's preoccupation with status and material gain had long been ridiculed, beginning in the 17th century with witty satires by the French playwright Moliere, who was himself the son of a merchant. Some of society's commentators rose to the defense of working men and women, including Karl Marx, who interpreted attacks on the upwardly mobile classes as an effort to subdue the wage-earning proletariat.

Archaeology, which originated in Renaissance Italy with the excavation of ancient Greek sculptures, was advanced in the 18th century by the chance discovery of an ancient Roman resort called Herculaneum, on the Bay of Naples, followed a few decades later by the unearthing of Pompeii. Both places had been buried in ash when Mt. Vesuvius erupted in 79 AD, and their discovery triggered a new wave of interest in antiquarian culture, with parties of fashionable ladies and gentlemen, equipped with shovels and picnic baskets, digging for bronze and marble statuary to add to their collections. In 1764, the German classical archaeologist Johann Winckelmann published a scholarly account of the Naples discoveries – the first such report in the field of classical antiquities.

Another movement, fostered during the Age of Enlightenment, was the construction of art museums, galleries and academies, including the famous **British Museum**, which was established in 1753 and began occupying its present buildings in 1829. The Athenian monuments of ancient Greece sparked public interest in England when Lord Elgin, the British ambassador to Turkey (which at that time ruled Greece), removed numerous marble sculptures from the Parthenon. Byron was among those critical of Elgin, who defended his actions in a pamphlet he wrote in 1820, claiming he wanted to protect the Greek sculptures from destruction under Turkish rule. In any event, the **Elgin Marbles**, currently in the British Museum, stimulated a strong interest in ancient Greece among the English Romantic poets and became the subject of a poem by John Keats entitled 'On Seeing the Elgin Marbles'.

Egypt also became a source of historical interest when the **Rosetta Stone**, a slab of black basalt engraved with hieroglyphics, was discovered at the mouth of the Nile by scientists accompanying Napoleon on his Egyptian campaign of 1798. Deciphered a quarter of a century later by the French scholar Jean Francois Champollion, the Rosetta Stone's inscriptions provided the first key to understanding the language and lives of the ancient Egyptians. Scientific findings from Napoleon's Egyptian campaign were published in 21 volumes over a 20-year period, thus launching Europe's fascination with ancient Egypt.

Museums began indiscriminately collecting Egyptian antiquities, as dozens of explorers and collectors dug through the desert sands in search of treasures. Eventually a more systematic process was enforced following the British occupation of Egypt in 1882, with all excavated objects recorded and catalogued. Meanwhile, the Egyptian government had made diplomatic gifts of several New Kingdom obelisks, presenting France with one from the Luxor temple, which now stands in the Place de la Concorde in Paris, and sending one of Cleopatra's Needles to England where it was re-erected on the Thames Embankment.

Famous archaeological treasures were also discovered in the Aegean region in the latter half of the 19th century, most notably the discovery of the ruins of Troy by German archaeologist Heinrich Schliemann, a wealthy businessman and student of Homer who used the Homeric poems for reference when searching for ancient sites and identifying the unearthed objects. Schliemann also excavated the ruins of Mycenae, Ithaca and Tiryns. As the century drew to a close, the English archaeologist Arthur Evans began devoting his time to the excavation of the Minoan ruins on Crete.

By the end of the 19th century, advancements in science, mathematics and engineering had produced the diesel and turbine engines, the electric motor, the automobile, the light bulb and the camera. The invention of photography introduced a new medium to the visual arts, and helped fuel the growth of tourism, as people were increasingly exposed to photographic images of faraway lands and exotic cultures.

The opening of the **Suez Canal** in 1869, linking the Mediterranean to the Red Sea, transformed the Mediterranean from a vast seawater lake into a direct seaway between the Far East and Europe, making it one of the most strategically important areas in the world. The British built a great naval dockyard at Valletta, Malta, as a base for its British Mediterranean Fleet, and other maritime nations maintained fleets in the Mediterranean to protect their seagoing trade. The canal, which

A group of 19th-century British tourists at the ruins of Pompeii.

is level and has no locks, is about 100 miles (160 km) long. Its construction took 10 years and was supervised by the French engineer Ferdinand de Lesseps, who later faced bankruptcy and was convicted for misappropriating funds when attempting to build the Panama Canal.

The Modern Mediterranean

The 20th century began with optimism, preceded by a long era of relative peace. However, the decaying Ottoman Empire had left the Balkan territories susceptible to diplomatic intrigue among the European powers of Austria, Britain, Prussia, Russia and France. The imperialistic, territorial and economic rivalries of these countries, along with a rampant spirit of nationalism, all contributed to the outbreak of **World War I**. Called the Great War, it was the largest war the world had yet seen. Fought chiefly in the trenches of Europe, it spread to the Middle East where Britain stopped a Turkish drive on the Suez Canal, then proceeded to

Florence's Ponte Vecchio was the only bridge left standing by retreating Germans in WWII.

destroy the Ottoman Empire. The British soldier **T.E. Lawrence** (Lawrence of Arabia) became a leader in the Arab revolt against Turkish domination, and British field marshal Edmund Allenby invaded Palestine, taking Jerusalem in December 1917.

When the First World War ended on November 11, 1918, without a single decisive battle having been fought, at least 10 million people had been killed and 20 million wounded, with additional deaths from starvation and epidemics in the war's aftermath. The face of Europe had radically changed, and a general revulsion to the destruction and suffering of war was symbolized by the creation of the **League of Nations**. Still, a fervent nationalism soon resurfaced in several countries where the hardships of the Great Depression made the masses vulnerable to the promises of demagogues. In Italy, **Benito Mussolini** and his Fascists rose to power in 1922. Mussolini gradually turned his premiership into a dictatorship, then began his imperialist designs with the conquest of Ethiopia in 1935. Meanwhile, **Adolf Hitler** had risen to power in Germany in 1933, where he began rebuilding the German army in preparation for a war of conquest. Both he and Mussolini helped the fascist general Francisco Franco win the Spanish Civil War in 1939.

When Germany invaded Poland on September 1, 1939, the democratic governments of Britain and France declared war. Soon all of the Mediterranean region was pulled into World War II, with the Axis powers (Germany, Japan and Italy) occupying North Africa, Greece and Yugoslavia. The German commander Rommel seemed about to take Cairo when British General Montgomery routed the German forces at Alamein in October 1941. Less than a week later, US troops landed in Algeria, helping to clinch an Allied victory in North Africa. Italy surrendered in September 1943, following Allied invasions of Sicily and southern Italy, but German resistance continued until Hitler's suicide in April 1945.

An Allied victory in the Pacific brought the war to an end in August 1945, but the devastation it wreaked remains horrifying to contemplate. Modern warfare had brought upon the world a barbarism of such scale that previous wars paled in comparison. The blanket bombing of cities, and Germany's systematic attempt to exterminate entire racial groups, terrorized civilians as well as soldiers and caused millions to die.

In post-war Europe, a widespread aversion to the national rivalries that had provoked such bloodshed and destruction prompted the idea of a united Europe as a way to provide strength and security to the war-torn region and prevent further hostilities. The **European Economic Community** (known informally as the Common Market and today called the European Union) was established in the 1950s as an economic and political confederation of European nations. Its original members were West Germany and France, soon joined by Belgium, Luxembourg, the Netherlands and Italy. Great Britain, Ireland and Denmark joined the EC in 1973, followed by Greece in 1981, and Spain and Portugal in 1986. A central banking system was provided by the 1992 Maastricht Treaty, and the gradual introduction of a common currency – the euro – was completed in 2002, the national currencies of 300 million Europeans replaced with 10 billion new bills and 50 billion new coins. Not since the 8th century, when Charlemagne circulated his own silver coinage throughout his empire, had Europe used a common currency. Its introduction has created the practice of 'rounding up' prices, thus making some things more expensive for locals. In Italy, for instance, people grumbled about the price of fruit and vegetables being affected by the introduction of the euro. When a cafe in a seaside town near Rome overcharged someone 23 euro cents for his cappuccino, this was too much to bear and a justice of the peace ordered the cafe to refund the price increase plus the plantiff's legal costs – a symbolic victory for Italians bemoaning the loss of the lira.

Joining the European Union

has been a hotly debated issue for the citizens of Europe, in both its member and candidate nations. Fierce national rivalries remain, as do economic disparities. Italy's government, looking to reduce its debt before joining the European single currency, considered privatizing some of its famous museums and national monuments.

In 2004, the 15-member European Union admitted 10 new members, including Malta and Cypress, thus increasing the EU's population to more than 450 million. Additional candidate nations, including Croatia, will likely be allowed to join in the following three or four years. Meanwhile, after waiting nearly 40 years, the Muslim (but officially secular) nation of Turkey has been offered a calendar for entry talks, with EU leaders monitoring Turkey's reform progress.

Western Europe's societies have become increasingly diverse in recent decades, with several countries now containing substantial Muslim minorities. The accompanying cultural and religious tensions have resulted in immigration becoming a key election issue in countries such as Italy, where conservatives want to preserve the country's Christian roots. In France, a fiercely secular nation, the government has banned the wearing of ostentatious religious symbols by workers in the public sector and by students in public schools. The ban includes Jewish skullcaps and large Christian crosses, but it was the refusal of Muslim schoolgirls to remove their head scarves – perceived by many French citizens to be a sym-

bol of militant Islam – that prompted the appointment of a presidential commission to address this controversial issue in a country containing the largest Muslim population of western Europe (about seven per cent of France's 60 million people).

According to scholars, Europe's fear of a Muslim invasion dates to medieval times, when Islam was poised to conquer Europe and three-quarters of Spain was under Moorish (Muslim) rule. For most westerners, the year 1492 marks Christopher Columbus's famous voyage from Spain to the New World, but for fundamentalist Islam this date marks the end of a halcyon age of Muslim culture and the decline of Muslim power when the Moors were driven from Spain by Christian monarchs Ferdinand and Isabella. Shortly after bombs exploded on several Madrid commuter trains in March 2004, the al-Qaida terrorist network claimed responsibility and reiterated militant Islam's goal of reclaiming its lost kingdom of Al-Andalus (Andalusia in southern Spain).

As Europe faces a new war, this time against terrorism, old scores are still being settled. Efforts to regain the spoils of Holocaust plunder have intensified, and officially neutral countries have been accused of selling vital supplies to the Nazis in exchange for gold stolen from Jews and from the central banks of conquered countries. Much of this plundered gold was channeled through Swiss banks, which have agreed to pay an estimated $1.25 billion in compensation to the tens of thousands of Holocaust survivors who launched a class-action lawsuit. Art treasures seized during the war are another bone of contention, with governments and individuals pressuring museums to return plundered artwork. The question of rightful ownership is, of course, a contentious issue, and one that existed long before WWII.

The Greek government has pleaded for decades with the British Museum to return the marble sculptures taken from the Parthenon in 1802 by Lord Elgin, British ambassador to Greece when it was under Turkish occupation. Meanwhile, Egypt has sought the return of the Rosetta Stone and a fragment of the Sphinx's beard, both of which are housed in the British Museum. But these attempts to repatriate cultural property have clashed with the mandate of museums, which is to preserve artifacts that might otherwise have been lost or damaged.

Following the sensational discovery in 1922 of King Tutankhamun's tomb by Howard Carter while under the employ of Lord Carnarvon, the Egyptian government passed a law that strictly controls excavation and allows the Egyptian Department of Antiquities to confiscate any significant finds. Other countries have established similar measures, with government permits required before archaeologists can proceed with an excavation.

During construction of a new airport and highway outside Athens prior to the 2004 Olympic Games, archaeologists unearthed enough antiquities to fill 4,000 crates. Another 30,000 ancient objects were uncovered in a 10-year dig during construction of the city's new subway system, and some of these artifacts, or their replicas, are now displayed at several subway stations. Construction projects in Rome often face delays because almost any digging there leads to the discovery of antiquities, bringing all work to a halt until study and/or removal can be completed. The past is a constant companion to the peoples of the Mediterranean.

Workers repair a cobblestone street in Rhodes, Greece.

*Michelangelo's David
Galleria dell'Accademia,
Florence*

ART
ART

&

Western civilization's vast treasury of art and architecture began with the ancient Egyptians, whose megaprojects involved the construction of massive temple complexes. These colossal creations later inspired the Athenians of Classical Greece to transform the Acropolis into a showpiece of artistic and architectural perfection. Two

Bernini's colonnade
St. Peter's Square, Rome

architecture
architect

cornice

frieze

entablature

architrave

Corinthian capital

thousand years later,
when Renaissance artists
looked for inspiration,
they turned to the classical antiquities of Greece
and Rome. In this sec-
tion, we embark on a
visual journey that covers
nearly 5,000 years of
artistic vision.

The glossary on the next two
pages contains terminology
used by artists and architects.

TALKING ART & ARCHITECTURE

arcade – a series of arches supported by piers or columns; called a 'blind arcade' when attached to a wall.

arches –

round (structural)

pier

pointed (structural)

lancet

cirquefoil

ogee

art categories – fine art is any painting, drawing or sculpture that is aesthetically beautiful. In free art, the object is purely ornamental. Decorative art adorns a useful object, such as a flower painted on a plate. The applied arts are functional and include the crafts of weaving, furniture-making, glassmaking and ceramics.

balustrade – railing supported by short pillars, called balusters.

basilica – in ancient Rome, a large rectangular building containing the law courts and serving as a public meeting place. Elements of the Roman basilica were later implemented in Christian churches. Differing from the longitudinal, basilica-plan church is the central-plan church (also called Greek-cross church) which has four arms of equal length.

Apse

Bema

Aisle

Aisle

Nave

Narthex

Atrium

Entrance

campanile – bell tower, from the Italian word for bell, *campana.*

caryatid – a sculptured female figure serving as a structural support, used in Egyptian and Greek architecture. A celebrated example is the Porch of the Caryatids atop the Acropolis in Athens.

cathedral – church in which a bishop resides. Important medieval cathedrals include those of Florence, Pisa and Barcelona.

Apse — Ambulatory

Buttress

Sacristy

Chapel

Chapel

Choir

Transept

Transept

Nave

Aisles

Baptistery

clerestory – an upper row of openings or windows that is higher than the rest of the structure. Implemented in certain Egyptian temples, this feature was later used in the great halls of Roman basilicas and became a characteristic element of Gothic churches.

colonnade – a row of columns supporting either an entablature or a series of arches.

fresco – the Italian word for 'fresh'; a technique of painting on wet plaster so that the paint becomes part of the wall.

frieze – a continuous band of painted or sculptured decoration.

gold leaf – gold beaten into very thin 'leaves' and applied to illuminated manuscripts and panel paintings.

hypostyle hall – an outer courtyard bordered with columns

icon – small panel painting of a sacred image, usually Christ, the Virgin Mary or a saint.

Iconoclasm – a movement in 8th and 9th century Byzantium to destroy all figurative religious images.

loggia – an open-air, covered arcade, either free-standing or running alongside a building.

lusterware – pottery finished with an overglaze containing copper and silver to create an iridescent effect. Initially used by Islamic potters, the technique was practiced in Moorish Spain and later adopted by Josiah Wedgwood in 18th-century England.

majolica – a technique of decorating and glazing pottery that was highly developed in medieval Italy, beginning in the 11th century, and named for the island of Majorca where the craft was first introduced by Muslim artisans during the Arab conquest of the western Mediterranean.

minaret – a tall slender tower attached to a mosque from which a muezzin calls the faithful to prayer.

mosaic – decorative work in which surfaces are covered with small pieces of colored materials, such as marble or glass, that are set in plaster or concrete.

orders of architecture – a system devised in Roman times to categorize architectural styles. The three main orders are Doric, Ionic and Corinthian. Tuscan is a simplified version of Doric, with unfluted columns. Composite combines Ionic and Corinthian. Colossal is any order with columns or pillars rising above one storey.

palazzo – stately residence or government building.

pantheon – temple dedicated to all the gods.

pediment – triangular area formed by a gabled roof. A feature of Greek temples, it later became a decorative motif as well, used chiefly over doors and windows.

peristyle hall – an inner court filled with columns

Pieta – representation of the Virgin grieving over the dead Christ lying in her lap.

pillar – general term for upright structural supports, including columns (which are cylindrical), piers (which are square or rectangular) and pilasters (which are piers that project from a wall surface and are generally decorative rather than structural).

plateresque – earliest phase of Spanish Renaissance art, combining Italian influences with Moorish and Gothic elements.

portal – a monumental door or gate.

portico – a columned porch.

relief – figures carved from a flat surface. High relief is deeply carved so that the figures are almost fully detached from their support. Bas-relief consists of low sculptures that barely protrude.

rose window – a large circular window of stained glass and ornamental stonework (tracery), frequently used in Gothic churches.

rustication – a masonry technique that creates a roughly textured surface by projecting blocks of stone beyond the mortar joints.

sarcophagus – large stone coffin, often ornamented.

stele – an upright stone slab bearing a carved illustration or inscription.

stoa – an ancient Greek portico, providing a sheltered promenade.

tempera – form of painting used before the development of oil painting, in which pigments were mixed with egg yolk and water.

terracotta – Italian word for 'baked earth'; a fired, unglazed clay of varying colour (depending on the type of clay), but often a shade of red. One of the oldest known building materials, it is used for pottery and architectural ornament.

treasury – miniature temple for storing votive gifts.

trompe-l'oeil – French for 'deceives the eye'; painting style that utilizes realism and perspective to create the illusion that what is depicted actually exists, i.e. a door or window painted on a wall.

Egyptian Art

In ancient Egypt, where religion dominated all aspects of society, art and architecture served a religious purpose. Stone construction was limited to tombs and temples while people lived in mud-brick dwellings. Even royal palaces were made of mud-brick or wood, with stone used sparingly. A diverse range of stone types were found in the deserts on either side of the Nile valley, and by 2500 BC there were hundreds of quarries scattered across Egypt. Although slave labor was sometimes used to build royal funerary monuments, most work was carried out by free laborers who lived in villages near the building sites and were paid with simple rations.

The basic post-and-lintel system – later adopted by the Greeks – was used exclusively in building temples. Their general design consisted of a massive entrance gate (called a pylon) which opened onto an outer courtyard bordered with columns, which in turn led to an inner court filled with columns. The capitals of Egyptian columns often depicted the closed bud or open flower of the papyrus and lotus flowers, symbols of Lower and Upper Egypt.

The art of ancient Egypt changed little over the centuries, and features of the highly admired Old Kingdom art were imitated by subsequent dynasties. Subjects were portrayed in a formulaic manner so they would be easily recognized and fulfill their symbolic roles. There was an emphasis on symmetry and separate components, with the human torso and an eye viewed frontally and the arms, legs and face shown in profile. Outer temple walls were decorated with shallow reliefs depicting the victorious pharaoh smiting the enemy, and those on inner walls depicted the pharaoh performing religious rituals. The colorful wall paintings inside royal tombs portrayed military, hunting and ceremonial scenes, along with domestic activities to be continued in the afterlife. Male figures were depicted with a darker skin tone than female figures, a practice introduced in 2580 BC and later adopted by, among others, the artists of the Renaissance.

Statues of pharaohs were usually huge, to represent their godlike

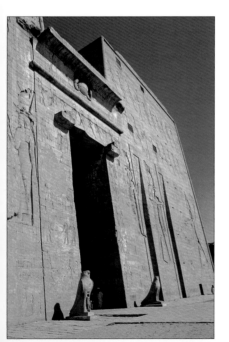

Entrance to the temple of Horus at Edfu, Upper Egypt.

stature, and often combined the human figure, which represented intelligence, with an animal, such as a lion or eagle, which represented strength or swiftness. A famous example is the Great Sphinx at Giza, with the head of a man and the body of a lion. Other colossal monuments included obelisks, often in pairs outside temple entrances. These tapering shafts of red granite, dedicated to the sun god, were covered with deeply incised hieroglyphs and terminated in a pyramidal top that was gilded to reflect the sun's rays. Obelisks became popular with other ancient cultures, and many of those erected in Egypt were later removed to imperial Rome. (For more information on the pyramids see Chapter 10.)

Greek Art

Greek art was influenced both by monumental Egyptian art and by the more sensual art of Minoan Crete, which dates from about 2000 BC and brought an Oriental opulence to Greek art. Several periods preceded the great Classical Period, including the Geometric Period (1100 to 700 BC) which produced pottery painted with angular designs. The famous Dipylon vases from this period are named for the cemetery near Athens where they were found.

The Archaic Period (700 to 475 BC) reflected an Oriental influence, evidenced by its painted vases with motifs of fighting animals and winged monsters. Greek sculptors of this period, unlike Egyptian

Minoan mural at Knossos, Crete.

sculptors, began to free their human forms from the stone by carving spaces in between the legs and between the arms and torso, creating the first free-standing statues.

The culmination of these artistic developments was reached in the Classical Period (475 to 323 BC) when Greek art reached its pinnacle of beauty and perfection. With an emphasis on physical beauty, classical Greek art idealized the human form. The marble decorations of the Parthenon included the east pediment's ensemble of deities watching the birth of Athena from the head of Zeus. Their relaxed and reclining forms reflect a complete ease of movement, both in the masculinity of Dionysus and in the flowing drapery of the three goddesses. These marble sculptures, removed by Lord Elgin between 1801 and 1803, are now on display in the British Museum.

The profound influence Classical Greek art would exert on later civilizations began in about 200 BC, during the Hellenistic age, when statues and paintings were first recognized as works of art to be appreciated for their own sake. During this period, the wealthy began decorating their homes with copies of the great works. Hellenistic sculptures were distinctly different from the Classical works in that they conveyed a more pronounced realism. Famous Hellenistic works include the Rhodian *Nike of Samothrace* (c. 200 BC) which portrays the outspread wings of the goddess lifted by a strong head wind as she stands at the prow of a ship.

Until the *Nike* was discovered in the last century, the most admired work of Hellenistic statuary had been *The Laocoön Group*, created in the 1st century BC by three Rhodian sculptors. This work depicts the horrible death of Laocoon and his two sons by a pair of sea serpents sent by Athena to punish the Trojan priest for trying to warn his people of the trick wooden horse. Found in a Roman vineyard in 1506, *The Laocoön Group* was

admired by, among others, Michelangelo, who considered it the finest sculpture ever created.

Although the Minoans of Crete began constructing palace complexes some 4,000 years ago, it was on mainland Greece where the building of temples culminated in the zenith of Classical Greek architecture. Between 480 BC and 323 BC all of the major masterpieces were created, including the famous Parthenon. By then three columnar types had evolved, called Doric, Ionic and Corinthian. The Doric order originated on mainland Greece, while the Ionic order developed on the Aegean Islands and the coast of Asia Minor. The Corinthian capital was invented as an elaborate substitute for the Ionic order and was initially used only for interiors. The Greek orders of column consisted of a shaft composed of sections, called drums, and a capital. A row of regularly spaced columns formed a colonnade that supported an entablature decorated with carved friezes. A triangular pediment atop the entablature held sculptures. The structure was built entirely of stone blocks that were carefully shaped and fitted together without mortar, although metal dowels were sometimes used. Shallow vertical grooves, called flutes, were carved the length of the column once it was erect.

The Parthenon, built atop the sacred Acropolis of Athens

The Laocoön Group (Vatican Museum). The replica shown here is displayed at the Grand Master's Palace, Rhodes.

*Pediment of the
Academy of Athens.*

Doric Column

capital

shaft

flutes

Ionic Column

Corinthian Column

between 447 and 432 BC, was a Doric temple dedicated to the goddess Athena. Designed by the architect Ictinus, this columned structure was built using a white, fine-grained marble and is consid-

*Marble sculptures from the
Parthenon's east pediment.*
(British Museum, London)

ered a perfect composition of grace and unity. Subtle adjustments were made to the colonnade's columns, and these deviations lend the structure an organic quality. For example, the columns all lean inward and their capitals are distorted to fit the architrave, which is slightly curved, so that the centre of the entablature is a bit higher than the ends. Another feature is that the corner columns are spaced more closely to their neighboring columns than are the middle columns.

The Erechtheum, built on the Acropolis between 421 and 405 BC, is one of the finest examples of the Ionic order. The Monument of Lysicrates in Athens, built a century later, is the earliest known example of exterior Corinthian columns. Greek theatres, before the 4th century, consisted simply of stone benches or wooden bleachers placed on a natural slope. These basic seating arrangements evolved into concentric rows of seats built into the hillside, with regularly-spaced staircase aisles providing seating access. The front-row seats, made of luxurious marble, were reserved for eminent public figures.

Tomb paintings, Tarquinia

The Etruscans settled in an area known as Tuscany between Florence and Rome in the 8th century BC, about the same time the Greeks were settling along the southern shores of Italy and Sicily. At their height of power in the 7th and 6th centuries, Etruscan cities rivaled Greece's city-states. The Etruscans ruled Rome for about a century, until the establishment of the Republic in 510 BC. They, like the Egyptians, created elaborate sculptures and wall paintings devoted to the afterlife, but Etruscan art also reflects a Greek influence, similar to that created during the Archaic Period.

Roman Art

The Romans were great builders and architectural engineers. They admired Greek models but Roman designs stressed power and boldness, in contrast to the Greek emphasis on harmony and beauty. By perfecting the use of brick and concrete, the Romans were able to use arches and vaults to create complex and spacious interiors with soaring roofs that could accommodate large numbers of people. The most famous example of their outstanding engineering is the Colosseum, with its miles of stairways and vaulted corridors.

The Romans created concrete by combining pozzolana (a volcanic earth) with lime, broken stones, bricks and tuff (a rock formed by the consolidation of volcanic ashes). Easily made and extremely durable, this concrete was used in the vast construction projects undertaken to sustain Rome's growing empire, including the building of roads, aqueducts and bridges. Cities and towns were laid out according to a logical plan with an emphasis on drainage, water supply and zoning. The urban center's focus was the forum, an open public square surrounded by public buildings which included temples, exchanges and basilicas (law courts). Public baths, derived from Greek gymnasia, were built on an unprecedented scale and the Romans engaged in

Vaults

Barrel   Cross   Ribbed

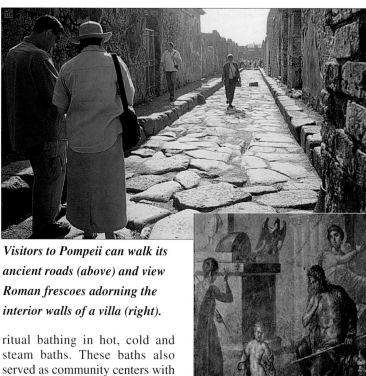

Visitors to Pompeii can walk its ancient roads (above) and view Roman frescoes adorning the interior walls of a villa (right).

ritual bathing in hot, cold and steam baths. These baths also served as community centers with libraries, shops, shaded walks and open areas for poetry reading. A typical town house consisted of rooms arranged around a central atrium with an opening in the roof. Multistorey apartment buildings were also common in the larger cities, in contrast to the spacious country villas of the wealthy which contained central courtyard gardens.

The Roman amphitheaters, unlike their Greek prototypes, were freestanding and oval-shaped. The exposed concrete of Roman ruins, which makes them today look less appealing than those of Greece, would have been covered during ancient times by a facing of brick, stone, marble or smooth plaster. The Roman imperial practice of raising free-stand-ing, commemorative columns may have originated from the Egyptian tradition of raising obelisks, but the triumphal arch was a purely Roman invention. Raised to honor an emperor or commemorate a military triumph, these monumental structures were built throughout the empire and would often span a road.

Roman roads were usually built in a straight line, regardless of obstacles, and consisted of four layers, the uppermost being a pavement of flat stones, concrete or pebbles set in mortar. Such roads still exist near Rome and elsewhere, as do some of the aqueducts. The bridge portion of aqueducts consisted of one to three tiers of arches, depending on the depth of the valley crossed. Nine aqueducts brought water to ancient Rome, three of which still supply the modern city, along with another one that was completed in 1585. Other aqueducts still exist in Italy and in France, where the famous Pont du Gard stands near Nimes.

Roman art was highly imitative and eclectic, reflecting the various cultures encompassed by its far-reaching empire. Pseudo-Egyptian statuary were popular and the low reliefs on Trajan's Column mirror the Egyptian illustrative tradition. However, it was the art and culture of Greece that thoroughly permeated Roman tastes. The Romans held Greek art and culture in such high esteem that original sculptures of every Greek period – Archaic, Classical and Hellenistic – were imported and copied by the thousands. Modifications were made to reflect the Roman emphasis on action and strength versus the contemplative nature inherent in Greek culture, and a distinct Roman style of portraiture developed which combined Greek idealism with Roman realism. The Italianate tradition of making death masks also led to the Roman style of portrait bust.

In about 200 AD, just as Roman art was fusing with Greek, the doctrines of Christianity, including denunciation of all pleasures of the flesh, shattered the synthesizing process. Eastern influences that had been introduced during the time of Constantine eventually developed into the stiff iconographic forms of early Christian and Byzantine eras. Early churches, inspired by imperial Rome, were basilican in design (an oblong interior divided into three or five aisles by rows of columns) and decorated with Byzantine-style mosaics.

The famous Portland Vase (1st century BC) was excavated near Rome in the 17th century. Made of dark blue glass overlaid with white cameo relief, the vase was widely copied, most notably in jasper ware by Josiah Wedgwood. It was eventually acquired by the Duke of Portland, who lent it to the British Museum. In 1845, a deranged museum visitor smashed the priceless vase to pieces, but it was skillfully restored and remains on display.

Medieval Art

Christian art initially declined in Europe following the fall of the Western Roman Empire in the 5th century, but continued to thrive in the Eastern Roman Empire where Byzantine art, especially mosaic decoration, flourished. Oriental influences combined with Hellenistic and Roman art forms to produce an ornate style exhibiting great pomp and dignity. Byzantine architects created a medieval masterpiece when they developed the pendentive to elevate the dome of Hagia Sophia (The Church of Holy Wisdom) in Constantinople. Built in the 6th century during the reign of Emperor Justinian I, the vaulted and domed Hagia Sophia was daring in design. With the brilliant use of piers, penditives and semi-domes to create an expansive interior, Hagia Sophia's architects successfully captured the splendor of the heavens.

Medieval cities, facing barbarian invasions and pirate attacks, were designed with security in mind and were protected by thick walls. The only open areas amid the narrow winding streets were municipal or church squares. Fortresses, castles, even monasteries were built for defense. The

(Above) Hagia Sophia in Istanbul is considered the greatest monument of Byzantine art. (Below) A medieval street in Rhodes.

Lantern

Dome

Drum

Pendentive

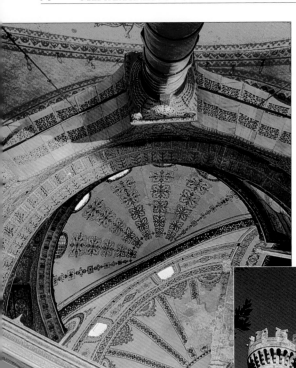

(Left) Interior view of Hagia Sophia, Istanbul, reveals its revolutionary dome and semi-dome design. (Below) The Grand Master's Palace in Rhodes is an example of medieval military architecture.

9th century's Carolingian style, so named for the Frankish emperor Charlemagne, was followed by the Romanesque style ('in the manner of the Roman') and its variants, such as Norman and Gothic. Local styles developed under the generic name Romanesque, but common features included the rounded arch and vault, as well as heavy walls and piers for structural support.

The Gothic style originated in France in about 1150 and flourished until 1450, especially in the cathedrals of northern Europe. Churches became airy and soaring, with pointed arches and vaults, slender piers and counterbalancing flying buttresses. Walls were thin and windows were large to allow a mystical and wondrous light to filter through their panes of stained glass. The sculpting of gargoyles in the form of beasts and grotesque human forms reached its peak in the Gothic period, after which the use of these ornate waterspouts was gradually replaced with lead drainpipes. In

Italy the Gothic style of architecture was tempered by Romanesque proportions, and Spanish Gothic architecture was influenced by Moorish traditions.

All other visual art forms were dominated by architecture during the Gothic period, with sculpture and stained glass integrated into the churches. The exception was in Italy where medieval painting, long influenced by Byzantine art's use of mosaics and murals, took on a new and revolutionary form in the early 14th century with the works of Giotto di Bondone. A Florentine artist, he painted lifelike scenes with a three-dimensional reality and tactile quality, which prompted some to claim that painting had surpassed sculpture as an art form. The newly elevated status of painting was symbolized by Giotto's appointment in 1334 as head of the Florence Cathedral workshop, a position formerly held only by architects or sculptors. The artistic momentum generated by Giotto was, however, temporarily extinguished when an epidemic of the bubonic plague – called the Black Death – swept across Europe between 1347 and 1350, killing about one third of Europe's population.

(Above) Clerestory of Barcelona's Gothic cathedral with 15th century stained glass windows. (Right) Mosaics adorn St. Mark's Basilica in Venice.

Islamic Art

With the Muslim faith discouraging pictorial representation, Islamic art specializes in the decoration of surfaces with patterns that are abstract or geometrical, characterized by interlaced lines and brilliant colors. Calligraphy (Greek for 'beautiful writing') is highly esteemed and used by Muslims to decorate mosques, pottery, metalwork, and textiles, as well as books. The Islamic (Moorish) presence in western Europe during the Middle Ages was reflected in such decorative arts as tile work and lusterware.

Early mosques were simple in design, based on the floor plan of the Prophet Muhammad's house. As Islam spread, a variety of existing edifices were taken over and converted into mosques. The Muslim practice of whitewashing the walls of temples and churches when converting them into mosques often resulted in the preservation of the underlying frescoes. Domed mosques were not common until the Byzantine church of Hagia Sofia became a model for mosques following the Turkish conquest of Constantinople in 1453. One famous exception is the Dome of the Rock in Jerusalem, built in 691 AD, which follows an octagonal Byzantine plan and has a wooden dome. Elements of Islamic art were often incorporated in Romanesque, Gothic and Renaissance buildings.

Renaissance Art

The Italian Renaissance, which began shortly after 1400 in Florence, ushered in a new and exciting age. Whereas medieval towns were built with moats, fortresses and city walls for protection from marauding bands, Renaissance cities were built with monumental views provided by wide avenues and long approaches to handsome buildings. New World discoveries contributed to the joy of expansion, but it was a revival of classical antiquity that formed the basis of Renaissance thought and art. The great masters studied the works of Plato and other Greek philosophers, embracing humanism and a belief in man's ability to understand the universe.

In architecture, the classical ideals of order, symmetry and unity were adopted. Rome's structural elements – arches, vaults and domes – were used in original combinations, with the dome symbolizing Renaissance

Self portrait, Leonardo da Vinci.

man's pursuit of both learning and clarity. The great Florentine architect **Brunelleschi**, who made several trips to Rome to study classical buildings, incorporated the systematic use of perspective and proportion in his designs, which included the octagonal ribbed dome of the Florence cathedral. The famous sculptor **Donatello** accompanied Brunelleschi on one of his trips to Rome, and the classical influence is evident in such works as his bronze *David*. This statue is one of the earliest free-standing nude figures of the Renaissance, and it marked the end of a medieval interdependence of architecture and sculpture.

In painting, as in the other visual arts, the Renaissance artists sought perfection. Three staggered planes – foreground, middle distance and background – were used to achieve perspective depth, and the painting's figures were harmoniously arranged, their expressive gestures achieving a heightened emotional intensity. The ideal human figure measured seven times the height of the head, and male nudes were painted with golden brown skin in contrast to the pink rose skin of a female nude.

Leonardo da Vinci best personified the ideal 'Renaissance man' with his restless quest for beauty and truth, both in his paintings and in his scientific studies, which relied on a precise observation of the phenomena of nature. Leonardo was one of several supreme artists who generated the great works of the High Renaissance between 1495 and

Florence Cathedral's dome was designed by Brunelleschi, the first great architect of the Italian Renaissance.

1520. Others included Bramante, Michelangelo, Raphael and Titian. **Bramante**, an architect and painter, designed the original plan for St. Peter's Basilica in Rome, influencing the appearance of many smaller churches. The paintings of **Raphael** (known as 'the Divine') were considered the Renaissance ideal of harmony and balance. And the Venetian painter **Titian**, celebrated for his use of color, was admired by none less than Michelangelo who apparently said, "Only he alone deserves to be called a painter."

Although the Renaissance artist was liberated from medieval convention, with pagan symbols reappearing alongside symbols of

the REDISCOVERY of LIGHT

Andrea del Verrocchio and
Leonardo da Vinci
Detail from: The Baptism of
Christ, c. 1470-75
Uffizi Gallery, Florence

Michelangelo
Holy Family, c. 1503-04
Uffizi Gallery, Florence

Titian
Venus of Urbino (1536)
Uffizi Gallery, Florence

Giovanni Bellini
*Enthroned Madonna, with
Saints, 1505
San Zaccaria, Venice*

*Raphael
Madonna with the Goldfinch, c. 1507
Uffizi Gallery, Florence*

*Sandro Botticelli
The Birth of Venus, c. 1485
Uffizi Gallery, Florence*

the Christian faith, the challenge of reconciling rational thought with religious belief was personified in the tormented genius of **Michelangelo**. A master of the three major visual arts – sculpture, painting and architecture – he transcended conventions and traditions, and is considered the first truly modern artist. Michelangelo believed that his artistic genius was a divine inspiration, and when sculpting a piece of marble he sought to free its pre-existing figures from the stone.

On the heels of the High Renaissance came mannerism, a style in which scale and spatial relationships between figures were deliberately confused. Mannerism, lasting from about 1520 to 1600, originated in Italy as a reaction to the High Renaissance's equilibrium of form and proportion. While the term 'mannerism' was coined to describe the painting of this period, the characteristics of mannerist architecture included an artificial integration of elements and an emphasis on surface effect, especially through the use of encrusted decoration. Jacopo Sansovino's Library of St. Mark's in Venice is a classic example of this lavish use of sculptural encrustation.

The mannerist schools of painting produced some outstanding artists, including Tintoretto and Veronese, both of the Venetian school. The famous mannerist painter **El Greco**, born on the Greek island of Crete in 1541, was initially trained in the Byzantine tradition of iconography, but he later studied in Venice, then in Rome, absorbing the lessons of the Italian masters, before settling in Spain. In Mannerist nativity scenes, signs of poverty were erased from the manger and the newborn Christ child was transformed into a cherub-like one-year-old perched on the lap of a rosy-cheeked Madonna. This less reverent and more intimate attitude was also reflected in the artists' penchant for painting themselves and fellow artists into scenes – positioning themselves not modestly to one side, as had been the customary position for donors of religious pictures, but squarely in the centre of the canvas. The jubilant and joyous nature of mannerist art was criticized by austere theologians, but the last glorious outburst of Christian art was yet to come in the form of baroque, the dominant art of the 17th century.

Baroque

The baroque style harmoniously united painting, sculpture and architecture. The latter became fluid, like sculpture on a massive scale, with curving forms and undulating facades. Sculptures set within this elaborate architecture seem to spill from their niches or soar heavenward. Famous baroque works include those of the Italian sculptor and architect Bernini, who adorned Rome with his fountains, statues and other monuments, including the elliptical piazza in front of St. Peter's Basilica. Baroque painters used illusionist effects to create a deep sense of space, and its masters included Rembrandt, Rubens and

Rome's Trevi Fountain, completed in 1762, is rococo in style.

van Dyck. In the late phases of baroque, the centre of the movement shifted from Italy to France, due largely to the patronage of Louis XIV.

As the vitality and force of baroque spilled into the 18th century, its final flowering became known as rococo. Originating in France and lasting from 1700 to 1750, the rococo style, with its light lines and exquisite refinement, was especially popular for interiors and the decorative arts. It was an unfettered style of excessive ornamentation and embellishment, with frescoes travelling across entire walls and ceilings, often multiplied in wall mirrors and reflected in polished parquet floors. In Venice, the painter Tiepolo won international fame with his frescoes in the doge's palace.

Modern Art

The first of a series of overlapping movements and counter-movements began in the mid-18th century. These 'revival' movements were manifested mostly in architecture and began with neoclassicism, which was inspired by the discovery of the ancient Roman ruins of Herculaneum and Pompeii on the Bay of Naples. In tandem with the classical revival was the Gothic revival, which began to dominate after 1800, its largest monument being the Houses of Parliament in London. The final revival phases were the neo-

Renaissance and neo-baroque, which dominated from 1850 to 1875 and lingered through the turn of the century. Neo-baroque buildings favored a profusion of ornament, creating an excess of opulence that appealed particularly to the newly rich and powerful of the Industrial Revolution. New materials and building techniques included the use of iron, which was used extensively in the construction of railroad stations, exhibitions halls and public libraries. The Eiffel Tower, erected at the entrance to the Paris World's Fair of 1889, became a famous symbol of 19th-century technology.

Art nouveau, a decorative arts movement lasting from the 1880s to World War I, was originally meant to produce art for the

*The ornate facade of Monte
Carlo's opera house.*

masses. As a reaction to the historical emphasis of mid-19th century art, this new style incorporated dreamlike forms which are best exemplified architecturally in the innovative designs of **Antonio Gaudi**, who lived and worked in Barcelona. Another turn-of-the-century style was associated with the Ecole des Beaux-Arts in Paris and became fashionable both in Europe and North America. Beaux-arts buildings were an eclectic mix of styles, often incorporating Greek, Roman and Egyptian elements.

Romanticism was another artistic movement that arose in the late 18th century. Inspired by ideals of the Enlightenment, the romantics revered nature and the individual's freedom to act naturally. As artists and intellectuals scrutinized classical thought and Christian beliefs, two conflicting views emerged: one supporting scientific and material progress, which was identified with the middle class; the other regarding the bourgeoisie as the enemy of culture. It was the second view that became the battle cry of modern artists, many of whom fervently challenged accepted perceptions of the world with the avant-garde, a term from French warfare meaning 'vanguard'.

After romanticism, most painters rejected traditional subjects taken from the Bible, the classics or the life of the courts, and turned instead to everyday scenes around them. No single movement has dominated modern western art for long periods of time since the 18th century, and there has been a speeding up of successive styles and ideas. The impressionist movement, originating in late-19th century France, rejected the romantics' emphasis on emotion and instead pursued objectivity when painting visual impressions, often directly from nature.

Following the impressionist movement, artists sought new inspiration in fresh landscapes. Fleeing the industrial north, **Vincent van Gogh** headed to the south of France to be 'near Africa', **Paul Cezanne** retreated to his native Provence, and **Gauguin** eventually left Europe for the tropical island paradise of Tahiti. Van Gogh's dark and somber early paintings gave way to swirling brush strokes and intense yellows, greens and blues found in his later works, which represented the archetype of expressionism's emotional spontaneity in painting.

20th Century Art

Artists in the early 20th century, attempting to express an inner vision, intensified their search into the subconscious. The French painter **Henri Matisse**, considered one of the foremost artists of the modern period, began using strong primary colors while living in the Mediterranean village of Collioure, and he became a leader of Fauvism, a style emphasizing the use of vivid color. **Pablo Picasso**, who played a leading role in 20th-century art movements, created cubism's most significant work when he painted *Les Demoiselles d'Avignon* in 1907. Surrealism, a movement founded in Paris in 1924 and influenced by Freudian theories, uses dream-inspired symbols. The paintings of **Salvador Dali**, born near Barcelona in 1904, combine dream imagery with near-photographic realism.

Umberto Primo Arcade, Naples (above). Chapelle St. Pierre, Villefranche, painted by avant-garde artist Jean Cocteau.

Preserving & Restoring Art

Art museums take extraordinary precautions to preserve their priceless works, using climate control systems that filter dust and chemical pollutants from the air, and sensors that monitor temperature and humidity. Even the wrong kind of carpet, when walked on, can produce dust and lint that settles onto paintings. When Leonardo da Vinci's masterpiece *The Last Supper* was reopened to the public in Milan, visitors were required to pass through three antechambers designed to remove dust, dirt, car exhaust and other particles from their clothes. A bubble of clean air surrounds the restored painting, which covers most of one wall in the refectory of Santa Maria delle Grazie. The original painting was applied to a dry finished wall, rather than on wet plaster, and shortly after its completion it began to deteriorate.

Art restoration is as old as art itself, with early restorers using varnishes made of animal glue to temporarily brighten fresco paintings. When modern restorers cleaned Michelangelo's frescoes in the Sistine Chapel, their painstaking methods involved washing an area with deionized water and an organic solvent, then sponging ammonium carbonate onto the area through layers of absorbent paper, which were left in place for several minutes before being removed. Any loosened dirt was wiped away and the area given a final rinse with water.

Space age technology is also used in art restoration, with a NASA researcher developing a way to use corrosive, atomic oxygen to dissolve sticky soot left on paintings after a fire. Modern laser and microwave techniques were used to clean the marble sculptures that once adorned the Parthenon in Athens, a technique approved by Greece's Central Archaeological Council only after experts spent two years practicing this method on other marbles. In Florence, a thorough cleaning of Michelangelo's statue *David* came to a halt when experts disagreed over the cleaning technique to be used.

When paintings travel to other museums, there is always the risk of damage, despite careful handling by white-gloved workers and the use of custom-designed metal cases fitted with high-density foam. Concerns include potential damage from jet engine vibrations, which can gradually shiver paint from a fragile canvas, and sudden decreases in humidity which can cause a canvas to shrink and possibly crack.

Preserving outdoor monuments is another challenge. Ancient marble monuments are threatened by air pollution, as well as microorganisms such as algae, lichens and fungi, which discolor surfaces and burrow beneath the surface. Ongoing restoration work on the Acropolis is estimated to take several more decades to complete and cost millions of dollars. Hagia Sophia has had scaffolding in place since 1995. Scaffolding is a fact of life in Europe, where restoration work by skilled marble masons is time-consuming and extremely costly.

Gardens have been cultivated since antiquity. The ancient Egyptians built walled gardens centered around a pool stocked with ornamental fish and shaded by fig and date trees. Lotus flowers (a kind of water lily) often grew in these garden pools. The revered olive tree, described by Homer as a source of liquid gold, has also been cultivated since ancient times along the Mediterranean coast, and today Italy, Spain and Greece produce 75% of the world's olive oil. Green olives are full-grown but unripened when picked, and ripened olives are purplish black and richer in oil.

Vineyards were introduced to Europe by the Greeks from Asia Minor in about 600 BC. The warm, dry Mediterranean climate was so ideal for the proliferation of viticulture that the Roman Emperor Domitian, fearing grain scarcity, had to restrict the spread of vineyards in Italy during the 1st century AD. During the days of the Roman Empire, landscape gardening was highly developed and formal gardens, designed by architects, were often terraced and adorned with statuary and fountains. The emperors in particular enjoyed retreating to their country villas, replete with formal gardens. According to Edward Gibbon, when Diocletian retired permanently to his estate on the Dalmatian coast in the early 4th century, he dismissed with a smile his former co-emperor's urgings to return by remarking that "if he could show Maximian the cabbages he had planted with his own hands at Salona, (Maximian) would no longer be urged to relinquish the enjoyment of happiness for the pursuit of power."

Early gardens were often simple plots for growing herbs and vegetables. In fact, throughout antiquity and the Middle Ages, herbs were highly valued for their medicinal and curative properties. Saffron, which is featured in Mediterranean cooking, was also a source of yellow dye in the ancient world. Thyme was used by the Greeks as a temple

(Above) Ancient olive trees grow in Jerusalem's Garden of Gethsemene, where Jesus spent his last hours before his arrest. The courtyard garden at House of Vetti in Pompeii (below).

incense, and by the Romans who put it in their bath water to energize themselves. Rosemary, a name derived from Latin and meaning 'dew of the sea', grows along coastal cliff tops where it draws moisture from the sea mists. Rosemary's aromatic leaves are used for seasoning and its small blue flowers are the source of an extract used in perfumes and medicines.

Other flowers native to the eastern Mediterranean include the tulip, hyacinth, crocus and hibiscus. Scrubby woodlands dominate the coastline, where prevalent types of trees include the umbrella pine tree, its nuts used for cakes and sauces. Cork oak is also native to the Mediterranean, which is where most of the world's commercial cork is harvested and processed. The bark of these trees is stripped off every 10 years.

During the Middle Ages, various citrus trees were introduced to the Mediterranean area by the Arabs, including tangerines oranges lemons and limes. The Crusades also introduced new plants and gardening techniques to Europe, as did the Moors of Spain and Portugal. During the Italian Renaissance the classical garden was revived, and leading artists of the day were commissioned to design elaborate hillside landscapes of fountains, waterfalls and ponds, mingled with statuary and topiary, often in geometrical designs.

(Above) Gardens outside Palma's cathedral, Marjorca. (Right) An Egyptian lotus pond.

Italian-designed gardens lie outside the Grand Master's Palace in Rhodes, Greece.

PART II

THE VOYAGE AND THE PORTS

MADEIRA

Curral das
Freiras •

Cabo
Girao   • Funchal

0   100
Miles   N

Oporto •

PORTUGAL

SPAIN

Ma

Fatima •

Lisbon ★

Costa de Lisboa

ATLANTIC OCEAN

Azores ←

Portimao   • Faro

Sevill

Gulf of Cadiz   Cadiz •

Tangier •

Casablanca   Rabat ★

MOROCCO

MADEIRA
ISLANDS
(Portugal)

Marrakech •

Canary Islands
(Spain)

PORTUGAL

In Portugal, all school children are taught the words to *The Lusiads* by Luis de Camoes. This epic poem is based on the famous voyage of explorer Vasco da Gama, the first European to journey by sea to India. He left Lisbon in 1497, rounded the Cape of Good Hope and sailed across the Indian Ocean to Calicut, returning home in 1499. The discovery of this sea route gave Portugal access to the riches of the Indies, and marked the beginning of the Portuguese Empire.

Camoes, the greatest figure of Portuguese literature, was well qualified to write his country's epic poem. Born of a poor Lisbon family, he pursued a life of romance and adventure, one that provided inspiration for his fiery love poems and vigorous narratives. In 1546 he was banished from the royal circle after falling in love with a lady of the Lisbon court. A few years later he was imprisoned for wounding a court aide in a street fight. To obtain his release from prison, Camoes served military duty in India, after which he was posted as an official to Macao, where he eventually faced charges of maladministration. When the ship carrying him from Macao to Goa in India was wrecked, Camoes managed to save the manuscript he was working on of The Lusiads.

The Portuguese people's love of poetry and song is an integral part of their culture, best exemplified by the troubadour-style fado, which is a poem or story accompanied by the guitar. Derived from the Latin word for 'fate', the fado can be heard throughout the country where it is performed in village pubs, family restaurants and the sophisticated clubs de fado in Lisbon. Listening to the fado, which speaks through its melody, is an excellent way to get to know Portugal.

Portugal At A Glance

About 11 million people live in Portugal, which includes the Madeira Islands and the Azores in the Atlantic Ocean. The country's last overseas territory, Macao, reverted to Chinese sovereignty in 1999. Roman Catholicism is Portugal's major religion, and the mother tongue is

The Tower of Belem stands at the entrance to Lisbon's port.

Portuguese, its vocabulary based on vernacular Latin but also containing words absorbed from Arabic, French and Italian. English and French are the second languages of Portugal.

The country's post-revolution constitution of 1976 established a parliamentary republic with an elected president and legislative assembly. Once the poorest country of Western Europe, Portugal has successfully reformed its economy in recent decades and held the last world's fair of the 20th century when Lisbon hosted Expo '98, its maritime theme commemorating the role of oceans in the planet's development.

Travel Tips

Currency: The unit of currency is the euro. Traveler's checks are widely accepted as are most credit cards. ATMs are located throughout the city of Lisbon and are tied to international networks such as Cirrus. Banks are open Monday to Friday, from 8:30 a.m. to 3 p.m.

Dining: Costa de Lisboa is noted for its seafood, and regional specialties include Caldeirada (fish stew) and clams cooked with garlic and coriander. For dessert, Pasteis de Belem (custard pies) are popular, as are Portugal's fortified wines. Grapes from the Douro district produce the country's famous port wines, which are blended and stored in Oporto. Vintage port, which is wine of an exceptional growing year, is kept in casks for two or three years, then matured in bottles for up to

25 years. Portugal's other classic fortified wine is produced on Madeira Island, a traditional port of call for west-bound sailing ships which would transport this wine to North America. It has been said that the signing of America's Declaration of Independence was celebrated with a sip of Madeira wine.

Opening Hours: Museums and historic attractions generally open from 10 a.m. to 12:30 p.m. and from 2 p.m. to 5 p.m., and close on Mondays. Some palaces also close on Wednesdays.

Shopping: Shops are open Monday through Saturday from 9 a.m. to 1 p.m., reopening (except on Saturdays) from 3 p.m. to 7 p.m. Shopping malls are open daily, from 10 a.m. to 11 p.m.

Locally made wares include gold filigree jewelry, azulejos (decorative tiles), ceramics, pottery, basketware and embroideries. Lisbon's central shopping area is Rossio Square and the Chiado quarter.

Telephoning: Crediphones are common throughout Portugal, and phone cards can be bought in post offices and news agents. To phone long distance from Portugal, dial 00 followed by your country code, area/city code, and the local number.

Portuguese History

Portugal's history began in ancient times. Among its early tribes were a Celtic people called Lusitanians, who came to the area around 1000 BC. The Lusitanians fiercely resisted Roman invasion until their leader, Viratus, was killed in 139 BC. Under Roman domination, the province of Lusitania thrived and Roman ways were adopted, including the Latin language from which Portuguese is derived. The title of Portugal's epic poem by Camoes is *Os Lusiadas* in Portuguese and it means 'sons of Lusus', referring to the Portuguese people.

Lusitania was overrun by Visigoths in the 5th century AD, and they in turn were conquered by the Moors, who invaded the area in 711. But it was the Christian reconquest of the Iberian peninsula that created the country of Portugal, and this process began with the arrival of Henry of Burgundy in 1095, one of a group of French nobles summoned by Alfonso VI of Leon to assist in the fight against the Moors. Henry was granted the title Count of Portugal and the territory eventually became the independent kingdom of Portugal under his son Alfsono.

Alfonso I spent much of his life embroiled in ceaseless fighting, driving the Moors from Lisbon in 1147 and styling himself as King of Portugal. The royal court – a tumultuous place for several centuries – was the scene of family estrangements, shifting alliances, power struggles against the church, and wars with kings of Castile.

The most glorious period of Portuguese history began with the reign of John I. Rising to power in 1385, he ushered in an era of maritime exploration and colonial expansion never before seen. His son, Henry the Navigator, developed an interest in Africa during a 1415 campaign to conquer Ceuta, a coastal enclave of Morocco. Henry established an observatory and a school of navigation and geography at Sagres, in southwest Portugal, and trained navigators would set off from the nearby port at Lagos. They first sailed to Madeira, then to the

The Discoveries Monument in Belem honors Henry the Navigator.

Azores, before embarking on a painstaking exploration of the African coast, pushing further south with each voyage until they reached the Far East. When the ships returned with slaves, gold and other riches, great wealth poured into the royal coffers.

This period of prosperity reached its zenith during the reign of Manuel I (1495-1521), when the Portuguese empire extended across the seas to Africa, Asia and America. Lisbon became the centre of the lucrative European spice trade, and Portuguese mariners would return home with priceless art from other cultures, such as ivory sculptures from Africa and decorated porcelain from China. A distinct style of Portuguese decoration developed, called Manueline, which reflected the country's maritime expansion. Gothic structures were embellished with shells, twisted ropes and strange aquatic shapes, these elements mixed with religious or heraldic symbols to create sumptuous ornamentation.

The seafaring trade that brought wealth to Portugal also created corruption among her government officials. In 1496,

Praca do Comercio is Lisbon's main waterfront square.

Manuel agreed to expel all Jews and Moors from Portugal as a condition for marrying the eldest daughter of Ferdinand and Isabella of Spain, and this drained the country of communities that had contributed to its learning, science and artisanship. Piracy and foreign competition began cutting into Portugal's shipping profits, and the West's centre of trade eventually shifted from Lisbon to Northern Europe.

Portugal's monarchy endured until 1910, when a revolution established a Portuguese republic. A military coup in 1926 was followed by the right-wing dictatorship of Antonio de Oliveira Salazar from 1932 to 1968. A bloodless coup in 1974 finally brought democracy to Portugal.

Lisbon

Lisbon (Lisboa) is situated on seven terraced hills that border the banks of the Tagus River where it broadens to enter the Atlantic. Ships entering this ancient trading port are greeted by the sight of the **Tower of Belem 1**, a 16th-century fortress built at the mouth of the Tagus River. It once marked the starting point for Portuguese caravels setting off on voyages of trade and conquest. Nearby is the **Discoveries Monument** , erected in 1960 to mark the 500th anniversary of the death of Henry the Navigator.

On Your Own

The cruise ships dock at Gare Maritima de Alcantara, located about two miles (3 km) east of the city center. **Taxis** are plentiful, and a standard meter fare is charged in the city (outside the city limits, the charge is per kilometer). Your ship may provide a shuttle to the city center and to the Belem district (1.5 miles west of the port).

Buses and trams charge a flat fare, paid to the driver. The Lisboa Card, offering savings on public transportation and entry to museums, is available at the Welcome Center in Praca do Comercio and the tourist booth on Rua Augusta.

Lisbon's historic core can be explored on foot, and a good starting point is **Castelo de Sao Jorge** ❸, a hilltop fort that dominates the city. Possibly built by Romans who occupied the town in 205 BC, the fort stands on the site of an earlier citadel whose inhabitants traded with the Phoenicians and Carthaginians.

At the base of the fort is **Alfama**, a maze of Moorish-built alleys surrounding the 12th-century cathedral, the **Se** ❹. Built to

Shore Excursions *Lisbon*

Ship organized tours of Lisbon focus on the city's many historic sites. Scenic drives to nearby **Sintra** and **Cascais** are also available with some cruise lines, as is a drive to **Fatima**.

The following is a sampling of Lisbon shore excursions available through the cruise lines. The selection will vary with each cruise line. For more detail, consult your shore excursions booklet (supplied by the cruise line) or log onto your cruise line's website. **Detail on attractions listed below can be found within this chapter**:
• **Lisbon Highlights**, visit Alfama, Jeronimos Monastery & Maritime Museum with stops at Belem Tower and Monument to the Discoveries (4 hrs, about $50).
• **Lisbon Walking Tour** – explore Alfama and Se Cathedral, Rua Augusta, Rossio Square and Chiado quarter, and ride the funicular up the steep hillside to Bairro Alto (3.5 hrs, about $50).
• **Baroque Art of Tiles** – visit Basilica da Estrela and the Tile Museum (3.5 hrs, $50)
• **Lisbon by Tram & Coach** – leisurely drive and narrated trolley tour of Lisbon's historic sights (3.5 hrs)
• **Lisbon by Private Vehicle** (1-3 passengers) with guide and driver (4 hrs/ 8 hrs, about $600-$1200 per vehicle)

withstand attacks from the Moors, the cathedral resembles a fortress, its twin towers supplied with arrow slits for defence. The strength and thickness of its walls saved the cathedral from total destruction during an earthquake that destroyed parts of the city in 1755. Nearby is the Museu de Artes Decorativas (**Museum of Decorative Art**) **5**, housed in a handsome four-storey mansion. About a mile to the east is the Museu dos Azulejos (**National Tile Museum**) **6**, located in the cloisters of the Madre de Deus Church, where an array of beautiful tile panels are on display. These colorfully painted tiles, called *azulejos*, are seen on buildings throughout Lisbon and are a decorative tradition traced to the Moorish presence in Portugal during the Middle Ages.

Immediately west of Alfama is the new quarter, called **Baixa**, which was rebuilt by the Marques de Pombal following the 1755 earthquake. A monumental square called **Praca do Comercio** **7** faces the Tagus River and is anchored with a massive statue of King Jose I and a triumphal arch which opens onto the **Rua Augusta**, a wide pedestrian mall running through a bustling area of small shops, sidewalk cafes and flower sellers.

Praca Dom Pedro IV (**Rossio Square**) **8**, at the top of Rua Augusta, is faced by the handsome Teatro Nacional (National Theatre) and the **Rossio Train Station** **9**, its fanciful facade a mixture of Victorian, Moorish and Gothic architectural styles. Another nearby structure of this era is the **open-work iron elevator** **10** built by a protege of Gustave Eiffel, who designed the Eiffel Tower in Paris.

North of Rossio Square is Avenida da Liberdade, a stately avenue of ornate statues and leafy trees that is lined with hotels and shops, and leads to a park named for Britain's King Edward VII. **Gloria Elevadore** **11**, a funic-

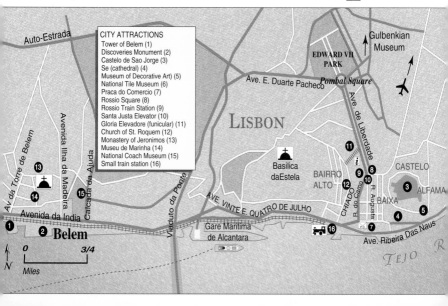

CITY ATTRACTIONS
Tower of Belem (1)
Discoveries Monument (2)
Castelo de Sao Jorge (3)
Se (cathedral) (4)
Museum of Decorative Art) (5)
National Tile Museum (6)
Praca do Comercio (7)
Rossio Square (8)
Rossio Train Station (9)
Santa Justa Elevator (10)
Gloria Elevadore (funicular) (11)
Church of St. Roquem (12)
Monastery of Jeronimos (13)
Museu de Marinha (14)
National Coach Museum (15)
Small train station (16)

Pena Palace in Sintra is an exotic mix of architectural styles.

ular, can be taken up to **Bairro Alto**, another old-quarter neighborhood of cobbled lanes which survived the earthquake and now bustles with night life at its fashionable bars and restaurants. Amid the art galleries and antique shops is the 16th-century **Church of St. Roquem** [12], its rich interior beautifully decorated with baroque mosaics, precious marbles and gold gilt.

Wedged between Bairro Alto and Baixa is the upscale **Chiado** area, featuring stylish shops and elegant cafes, including Cafe Brasileira - which was a favorite rendezvous for writers in the 1920s. A life-size bronze of Fernando Pessoa, Portugal's most famous 20th-century poet, is seated at one of its outdoor tables.

About 1.5 miles (2.5 km) west of the cruise pier is the city's **Belem** section, where some of Lisbon's most famous landmarks are located, including the modern **Discoveries Monument** in honor of Henry the Navigator. The 16th-century **Tower of Belem**, an example of Manueline architecture, was built by Manuel I to commemorate the discovery of the route to India by Vasco da Gama. The beautiful cloister of the nearby **Monastery of Jeronimos** [13] is another excellent example of Manueline ornamentation. Other attractions in this area are the **Museu de Marinha** (Maritime Museum) [14], one of the finest maritime museums in the world, and the **National Coach Museum** [15] where beautiful gilded coaches are displayed.

Out-of-Town Attractions

Trains run regularly between Lisbon and outlying towns, departing **Rossio station** for the 20-minute ride to **Queluz**, where an 18th-century palace with beautiful gardens and Rococo rooms once served as a leisure residence for the Portuguese court. Another 20 minutes further by train is the town of **Sintra**, described by Byron as a 'glorious Eden'. The National Palace stands in the cen-

The 18th-century palace at Queluz near Lisbon.

ter of town, while a nearby mountaintop is the setting for romantic **Pena Palace**, a fairy-tale, Bavarian-style castle which incorporates a variety of architectural styles, including Arab minarets and medieval battlements.

A half-hour train ride from the small station **16** near **Praca do Comercio** will take you to the seaside town of **Cascais**, which was a fashionable summer resort at the turn of the century. Further west are the windswept beaches of Guincho and the dramatic cliffs of Cabo da Roca - Europe's most westerly point.

Some 70 miles (110 km) northwest of Lisbon is the hamlet of **Fatima** where the nearby shrine of Our Lady of the Rosary of Fatima became a great center of pilgrimage after three local children reported apparitions of the Virgin Mary in 1917. Our Lady of Fatima Basilica was built in 1944, and the basilica's square drew more than a million people in 1982 to hear Pope John-Paul II.

Madeira Islands

The verdant, mountainous Madeira Islands were originally known to the Romans as the Purple Islands. Rediscovered by the Portuguese in the early 1400s, settlement took place under order of Prince Henry the Navigator. The British temporarily occupied the islands in the early 19th century, but today they are an autonomous region of Portugal. They lie closer to Africa than to Portugal, with the shores of Morocco only 400 miles away.

The archipelago's largest island is called Madeira, its steep slopes terraced with green fields and dotted with villages of red-roofed houses. Flowers such as bougainvillea and hibiscus flourish in the balmy climate, and coastal roads cling to mountainsides ribboned with cascading waterfalls. Precipitous viewpoints include the one atop Cabo Girao, the world's second-highest sea cliff.

The port of **Funchal** was a favorite winter retreat of Sir Winston Churchill, who came here on painting holidays. Situated on a beautiful harbor at the base of a mountain, Funchal has a bustling local market where fresh flowers, hand-sewn linens and wickerwork are sold. Fine local wines can be enjoyed at one of the bodegas, and afternoon tea is served at the classic Reids Hotel. A popular pastime for visitors is to take a cable car to the village of Monte, located uphill from Funchal, and from there embark on a 10-minute ride back down the steep street in a wicker sledge on runners, which is steered by two men dressed in traditional white flannels and straw boaters.

Funchal was founded in 1421 by Joao Goncalves Zarco, whose tomb lies in the local convent church. Other historic attractions are the 15th-century cathedral, the governor's house, and Parque de Santa Catarina, with its harbor views. The main tourist office on Avenida Arriaga hands out a list of scenic island drives and standard taxi fares. For about US$40, a taxi can be hired for the 30-minute drive to Curral das Freiras (Shelter of the Nuns), a spectacular valley where nuns hid in the 16th century whenever pirates pillaged the island.

(Above) Visitors to Madeira enjoy their ride in a wicker sledge. (Below) The Madeira Islands' rugged coastline.

Shore Excursions *Madeira*

Shore excursions offered by the cruise lines feature a variety of scenic island drives to mountain valleys and secluded villages, such as Camacha (center of Madeira's wickerwork industry), and along stunning coastlines.
•Scenic Island Drives (4 hrs)
•Cable Car & Botanical Gardens (4 hrs)
•4X4 Adventure along back roads and valleys (4.5 hrs)
• Visits to family-owned Blandy Gardens and Madeira Wine Lodge for a tasting (4 hrs)

CHAPTER TWO

SPAIN

Sunny Spain – land of castles and castanets – is one of the world's most popular tourist destinations. Traversed by mountains and valleys, Spain occupies most of the Iberian peninsula and is separated from the rest of Europe by the peaks of the Pyrenees. Its fertile coastal plains are cultivated with citrus groves and olive trees, while the country's fishing fleet nets sardines and anchovies. But tourism is the economy's bread and butter. Lined with golden beaches and blessed with a mild Mediterranean climate, Spain is second only to France for the number of foreign visitors it receives annually.

Spain at a Glance

Spain's population, which numbers about 44 million, is predominantly Roman Catholic. Castilian is the standard Spanish language but other languages are spoken in their respective districts, such as Catalan (akin to Provencal), Galacian (akin to Portuguese) and Basque (an independent language). Spain has had a constitutional monarchy since 1975, when King Juan Carlos I became the head of state upon the death of the military dictator Franco.

Spain consists of 17 geographic and historic regions, which generally correspond to the old Christian and Moorish kingdoms. Administratively, the country – which includes the Balearic Islands and Canary Islands – is divided into 50 provinces. This rich regional diversity has at times fermented separatist tendencies, especially among the Basques of Northern Spain and the Catalans, whose historical capital is Barcelona. In 1978 the Spanish Constitution was passed, establishing autonomous communities and granting them their own regional administrations which cooperate with the central administration. Spain's capital is Madrid, and the Spanish enclaves of Ceuta and Melilla in Morocco are remaining remnants of Spain's former empire.

Children file past Valencia's 13th-century cathedral during an annual fiesta.

Travel Tips

Currency: The unit of currency is the euro. Banks are generally open from 8:30 a.m. to 2 p.m., Monday thru Saturday, except in summer when they close Saturdays.

Dining: Spanish cuisine is as varied as the country itself. Catalania is renowned for its casseroles and sauces such as ali-oli, which is made with olive oil and garlic. Valencia, famous for its rice dishes, is where paella originated, and Andalusia is the place to order gazpacho – a spicy vegetable soup served cold. Mayonnaise was originally created in Mahon, Minorca; other celebrated specialities of the Balearic Isles include sobrasada, a sausage-meat spread, and Majorca's ensaimadas, exquisitely light pastries. The Canary Islands feature fish, tropical fruits and a hot sauce called mojo picon in their dishes. Spain's fine sherry, called Jerez, is a fortified wine. Jerez de la Frontera, the centre of Spain's sherry industry, is located in Andalusia, between Cadiz and Seville.

Restaurant hours are generally 1:00 to 3:30 p.m. for lunch and 8:30 to 11:00 p.m. for dinner, with extended hours in tourist areas. French-bread sandwiches, called bocadillos, are a popular fast food served at cafes and tapas bars. Tapas are bite-sized snacks, often served hot.

Opening Hours: Museums and historic attractions are generally open from 9:30 a.m. to 2 p.m. and from 4 p.m. to 7 p.m., Tuesday through Sunday. (Some are closed on Sundays.)

Shopping: The traditional 'siesta hours' are still common in much of Spain, with some stores closing between 1:30 and 4:30 p.m. although major shopping malls and department stores stay open without a break from 10 a.m. to 9 p.m. Spain is known for its finely crafted ceramics, colored tiles, handmade lace, Andalusian leatherwork and colorful handwoven rugs.

Telephoning: Phonecards, purchased at post offices and tobacconists, can be used in most public telephones, as can coins. To phone a number outside Spain, first dial 00 (International), then the country code, city code and number. Personal calling card access codes: AT&T 900-99-0011; MCI 900-99-0014; SPRINT 900-99-0013; CANADA 900-99-0015. For directory information, dial 11818.

A restaurant in Valldemossa on the island of Majorca.

A History of Spain

Spain has been uniquely influenced by its proximity to Africa. With the coast of Morocco lying only nine miles across the Strait of Gibraltar, it's not surprising that Spain was first inhabited by an ancient people from Africa called Iberians. Next came the Phoenicians, followed by the Carthaginians, who founded Cartagena in the 3rd century BC. This became a flourishing port and their chief base in Spain until it fell to the Romans during the Second Punic War (218-201 BC). Carthage eventually surrendered its Spanish province to Rome and the Iberian population became thoroughly romanized except for the Basques of northern Spain.

Christianity was introduced early to pagan Spain, which endured its first wave of Germanic invaders from the north in 409 AD. These included the Visigoths, who established their capital at Toledo. In 710, a nobleman named Roderick succeeded King Witiza, whose thwarted heirs turned to the Moors of North Africa for military help in overthrowing the Visigothic usurper. A Berber army, led by Tarik Ibn Ziyad, crossed the Strait of Gibraltar into Spain where it defeated Roderick. Tarik, however, did not restore the heirs of Witiza but instead sent for African reinforcements. Within a few years, he had conquered most of the Iberian Peninsula, and Moorish domination endured for nearly eight centuries, bestowing on Spain a rich cultural legacy.

The Moors, who were Muslims of Berber and Arab stock, built cities of great wealth and splendor. Their ornate palace complexes, decorated with glazed tiles and alabaster, contained open courts adorned with a multitude of low arches and marble columns. Moorish craftsmen were famous throughout Europe for their lacy wooden carvings, filigreed jewelry and fine pottery called lusterware. The Moors were also industrious farmers who cultivated the land with extensive irrigation. Amid this material prosperity was a high degree of civilization. The Moors brought Greek learning to Spain, along with advances in science and medicine. Religious tolerance was practiced, with Muslims, Christians and Jews living together in relative harmony.

Ruled by various Berber dynasties, the country's flourishing south was a constant temptation to the Christian nobles of the north who had retained a pocket of resistance in Asturias during the Moorish invasion. These nobles slowly regrouped and forged alliances through marriage. In 1137 the House of Aragon united with Barcelona (Catalonia), which had been taken from the Moors by Charlemagne back in 778. In 1212, Alfonso VIII of Castile defeated the Moors and, one by one, their strongholds fell to the Christians. By the time the kingdoms of Aragon and Castile were united under Ferdinand V and Isabella I in 1479, their predecessors had conquered most of Andalusia. Granada, the last

The hilltop Alhambra, a splendid Moorish palace, was built in Granada in the 13th century, its open courts adorned with fountains, arches and arabesque ornamentation.

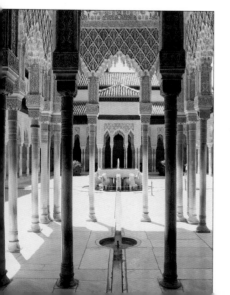

refuge of the Moors, finally surrendered to Ferdinand and Isabella in 1492.

Riding a wave of religious zeal and military vigor, the Christian rulers expelled all Jews, who took with them skills, capital and commercial connections. Muslims (called Mudejares) were forcibly converted to Christianity (and later expelled), and the infamous Spanish Inquisition – established to punish Christian converts who were deemed insincere – became so zealous in its search for heretics that soon no Spaniard was immune from its harsh censorship.

The 16th century was Spain's Golden Century, when it became the world's first superpower, with fleets on every sea and an empire encompassing most of South America and Central America, as well as the Philippines and parts of North America. Year after year Spanish galleons would return from the New World, their holds brimming with gold and silver. Yet, by the end of the 16th century, Spain's gradual decline had already begun. England defeated the Spanish Armada in 1588, marking the rise of British and other naval powers. Buccaneers preyed on Spain's treasure fleets, and centuries of war slowly weakened the once-powerful nation. The last remnants of Spain's vast colonial empire were lost in 1898 during the Spanish-American War, when Cuba, Puerto Rico, Guam and the Philippines shed the Spanish yoke and entered America's growing sphere of international power.

Following the abdication of Queen Isabella II in 1868, Spain experienced various forms of government, including a republic that was created in 1931. But civil

Christopher Columbus

Born in Genoa in 1451 to a family of wool weavers, Columbus went to sea as a lad. By 1478 he was serving as a ship's master and the following year he married a Portuguese woman, whose father was governor of the Madeira Islands. The couple settled at Funchal but, rather than pursuing a career as a professional mariner, Columbus formulated a plan of reaching the Far East by sailing due west. Finding no support in several other countries, Columbus turned to Spain.

In 1486, he presented his plan to King Ferdinand and Queen Isabella and for five years Columbus (known in Spain as Cristobal Colon) campaigned for financial support. Finally, in January 1492, upon the Christians' defeat of the Moors, Columbus secured an agreement in principle. Outfitted with three ships, Columbus set sail from Palos, at the mouth of the Rio Tinto in Andalusia, on August 3, 1492. After stopping at the Canary Islands to make some repairs and take on provisions, the fleet sailed due west on the easterly trade winds, reaching the Bahamas on October 12th.

When Columbus returned to Spain, 33 weeks later, he received a hero's welcome. Ferdinand and Isabella summoned him to the Court at Barcelona, where he was received with honors and granted the titles and privileges he had requested, including support for a second voyage. A brilliant navigator, Columbus proved to be less competent as a colonial administrator, and his third voyage to the West Indies ended with his being brought home in chains, charged with misrule of Spain's colony on Hispaniola. His last voyage to the West Indies ended in shipwreck off the coast of Jamaica, and Columbus returned to Spain in 1504, the year of Queen Isabella's death. Wracked with arthritis and nearing the end of his own life, Columbus was shunned by King Ferdinand. Outraged by the Spanish crown's lack of gratitude, the world's most famous explorer died in neglect, a disappointed man.

Columbus monument in Barcelona

war broke out a few years later, and this conflict pitted the pro-republican forces (Loyalists) against the Insurgents, who won the civil war in 1939 under the leadership of General Francisco Franco. A ruthless dictator, Franco declared Spain a kingdom in 1947 with himself regent, retaining power until his death in 1975, at which time his successor, Juan Carlos, ushered in a new and enlightened era for Spain.

Juan Carlos was the first Spanish monarch since his grandfather, Alfonso VIII, was deposed in 1931. Although chosen by Franco to be his successor, Juan Carlos surprised the world when, instead of following in Franco's footsteps, he quickly guided Spain down the road to democracy. The country's first free elections since 1936 were held in 1977, and Spain's dramatic evolution from military dictatorship to parliamentary democracy began with the election of Adolfo Suarez as prime minister. Today the future looks bright for Spain, which has thrown open its doors to the rest of the world and now receives more foreign visitors than any other European country, with the exception of France.

Barcelona

Spain's largest port and second largest city with a metropolitan population of 4.5 million, Barcelona is a fascinating mix of modern and medieval architecture. Broad avenues and modern buildings stand in contrast to the city's historic heart – the Gothic Quarter – a labyrinth of narrow winding streets and historic landmarks. In 1992 Barcelona hosted the Summer Olympics, an event that revitalized the city and the pride of its citizens.

Since medieval times Barcelona has been a stronghold of Catalan separatism, and from 1932-39 it was the capital of an autonomous government. Today, as the capital of Barcelona province and chief city of Catalonia, Barcelona remains a center of regional pride and political liberalism. It is also considered the cultural center of Spain. Modern art thrives in Barcelona, a city where Picasso began his formal art training. His famous Cubist painting *Les Demoiselles d'Avignon* is said to have been inspired by a brothel

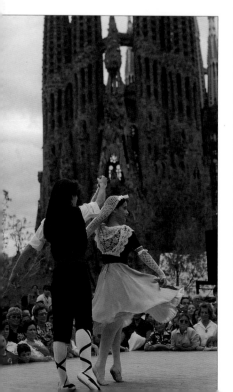

Young dancers perform near Gaudi's famous church.

that was located in the **Gothic Quarter**.

The visionary architect Antonio Gaudi has left the most visible impression on this handsome city. Famous in his day for his new and startling style, Gaudi spent most of his life in Barcelona where he was a leading figure of art nouveau. He designed fanciful buildings with undulating lines, and facades decorated with sparkling mosaics. His most famous work is the Temple of the Holy Family, a surreal creation of soaring spires and sculpted facades, which is still under construction.

Barcelona's History

Founded by Carthaginians, Barcelona's name is said to stem from the great Barca family of Carthage. Following the Roman conquest, Barcelona flourished. During the reign of Emperor Augustus (27 BC –14 AD) a fortified village was built on a small hill called Mons Taber, its streets meeting at the forum, which is now the Placa de Sant Jaume. A temple to Augustus stood on the hilltop, and four of its Corinthian columns still stand.

Barcelona declined during the Visigothic period, then fell to the Moors in the 8th century. The city was taken by Charlemagne in 801 and became an outpost of his empire. Eventually, under the influence of the powerful counts of Barcelona, the city became independent and flourished as a center for banking, cloth making and maritime trade. At its peak in the late Middle Ages, Barcelona was a Mediterranean seaport rivaling Genoa and Venice

Gaudi's Sagrada Familia (Temple of the Holy Family).

On Your Own

Barcelona's cruise port ** is located at the city's doorstep, about nine miles (14 km) from the airport. Most attractions are within walking distance of the port, and taxis can usually be hailed on the street should you get tired. Las Golondrinas (pleasure boats) provide harbor tours, and a **cable car 2 runs between the waterfront and the Montjuic area, where the Olympic stadium and other attractions are located.

One way to explore the city is by purchasing a Bus Turistic tick-

Shore Excursions *Barcelona*

The following is a sampling of escorted shore excursions offered by most cruise lines. These will vary with each cruise line. For more detail, consult your shore excursions booklet (supplied with your cruise documentation) or log onto your cruise line's website.

- Narrated motorcoach drive through the city with stops at major sites (5 hrs, about $45)
- Scenic motorcoach drive to Montserrat (4.5 hrs, about $50)
- Visit to Picasso Museum and Casa Mila (3.5 hrs)
- Bicycling tour of city (3.5 hrs)
Detail on attractions can be found within this chapter.

et which allows you to ride a sightseeing bus that runs daily from April through October. It offers two routes that stop at numerous attractions. You can get on and off at any of its stops, and a Bus Turistic ticket comes with a booklet of discount coupons to the main attractions. Tickets are sold on board the bus (18 euros for one day; 22 euros for two days) and at tourist information offices.

Dining Suggestions

Excellent restaurants are found throughout the Gothic Quarter, amid the narrow winding streets. For a casual outdoor meal of freshly prepared Catalan cuisine, try one of the eateries in La Boqueria (Barcelona's famous produce market), such as **Pinotxo Bar** and **Kiosko Ramblas**, where the fare includes garden salads and grilled seafood.

Local Attractions

The port of Barcelona is located adjacent to the city centre. A long breakwater protects the harbor area and connects with the city's waterfront at **La Barceloneta**, a tongue of land formed by accumulated sand after the port was built in the 17th century. Beaches line the east side of La Barceloneta, and beyond lies the **Olympic Port 3**, a lively spot with waterfront restaurants. More bars and restaurants are located west of La Barceloneta along **La Fusta** wharf, a long promenade connected by a drawbridge to the Espanya wharf, which is where an entertainment complex,

Las Ramblas, Barcelona's
famous pedestrian street.

including the city's aquarium, is located.

The **Columbus Monument**, which is 200 feet tall, stands near the waterfront in the center of the **Placa del Portal de la Pau**. An elevator can be taken to the top of this monument for a view of the entire city. On the west side of the square is the **Drassanes Reials** (Royal Shipyards) **4**, the largest and most complete shipyard to survive from the Middle Ages. Built in 1378, this fine example of Gothic architecture now houses the Maritime Museum, with reproductions of historical ships.

Barcelona's most famous street, **Las Ramblas**, stretches for almost a mile, from the Columbus monument to **Placa de Catalunya**, in the heart of the shopping district. A wide pedestrian promenade flanked by traffic lanes, Las Ramblas is well suited for strolling, with its outdoor cafes, flower stalls and street entertainers. Points of interest just off Las Ramblas include **Palau Guell 5**, a mansion designed by Gaudi for his patron Count Eusebi de Guell, and **Placa Reial 6**, a 19th-century arcaded square adorned with Gaudi-designed lampposts. Other attractions along Las Ramblas include the city's opulent opera house, the **Gran Teatre del Liceu 7** which was rebuilt following a devastating fire in 1994, and the bustling **Boqueria Market 8**, which is filled with delicatessens and stalls selling fruit, vegetables and seafood, and bars serving grilled prawns and other Catalan dishes made from the market's fresh ingredients. The pavement at

Columbus Monument.

nearby Pla de la Boqueria is decorated with a design by Joan Miro in 1970.

Until the mid-19th century, Barcelona's medieval city was

MUST SEE:

First-time visitors to Barcelona, should be sure to visit the **Gothic Quarter** and **Las Ramblas**, both of which can be explored on foot. Also, take a taxi (or organized tour) to see Gaudi's architectural landmarks – **Temple de la Sagrada Familia, Casa Mila** and **Casa Battlo**.

If time allows, also visit **Parc Guell**, as well as **Parc Ciutadella** (within walking distance of the port) and **Montjuic** by cable car.

BARCELONA

GOTHIC QUARTER

CITY ATTRACTIONS

(1) Cruise Terminal at 'Moll Adossat'
(2) cable car
(3) Olympic Port
(4) Royal Shipyards
(5) Palau Guell
(6) Placa Reial
(7) Gran Teatre del Liceu
(8) Boqueria Market
(9) Placa del Rei
(10) Cathedral of Santa Eulalia
(11) Adjuntament (Town Hall)
(12) Paulau de la Generalitat
(13) Placa Sant Felip Neri
(14) Placa de Sant Josep Oriol
(15) Museum Picasso
(16) Church of Santa Maria del Mar
(17) Llotja (lodge)
(18) Casa Battlo
(19) Casa Mila
(20) Temple de la Sagrada Familia
(21) Parc Guell
(22) Parc de la Ciutadella
(23) Arc del Triomf

surrounded by walls. Today the central part of the medieval city is known as the Barri Gothic (Gothic Quarter), the heart of which is **Placa del Rei** – the city's oldest square, where Ferdinand and Isabel received Columbus upon his return, in 1493, from his historic voyage to the New World. The buildings facing the square include the Chapel of Santa Agata, the Museu d'Historia de la Ciutat (The City's History Museum) and the Palau Major Reial (Royal Palace). The latter, built from the 11th to the 14th centuries, is a Romanesque building with Gothic additions.

Overlooking Placa de la Seu, where Barcelona residents gather on weekends to perform a circular folk dance called the sardana, is Barcelona's famous **Cathedral of Santa Eulalia** 10. Begun in 1291, this Gothic cathedral took 150 years to build. Its west front remained unfinished until the late 19th century, when a local industrialist offered to finance the completion of a neogothic facade based on a 15th-century drawing. Treasure-filled chapels line the cathedral's interior, which features a breathtaking display of medieval masonry with ogival ribbed vaults, slender piers, and fine cloisters surrounding a tropical garden. Noteworthy features to look for inside the hall-like cathedral include the carved choir stalls and the alabaster tomb of St. Eulalia, which is an exquisite piece of carving by a disciple of the great Italian sculptor Giovanni Pisano.

The Placa de Sant Jaume is

Barcelona's famous cathedral, dating from the 14th century, took 150 years to build. Its soaring interior is a splendid example of Gothic architecture.

flanked by the **Adjuntament** (Town Hall) **11** and the **Paulau de la Generalitat 12**, the seat of the Catalan government. The 14th century Town Hall features a Gothic facade facing the street of C. Ciutat, and the main neoclassic facade fronts the square. The Generalitat is housed in a Gothic palace with a Renaissance facade.

The **Placa Sant Felip Neri 13** is a peaceful square located in the old Jewish Quarter (or Call), while the nearby **Placa de Sant Josep Oriol 14** and adjacent Placa del Pi are lively squares featuring outdoor cafes, street musicians, and weekly art and antique markets. The church of Santa Maria del Pi features a gigantic rose window, one of the largest in the world. The quaint streets leading off these interlocking squares are fascinating to explore. Carrer de la Palla, which winds its way to the cathedral, is lined with old book and antique shops; Carrer del Pi and Carrer Petritxol both feature shops and restaurants, including granjas – eateries that serve coffee, hot

chocolate and bakery items. One of the city's oldest art galleries, the Sala Pares, is located on Carrer de Petritxol.

Separated from the Gothic Quarter by the Via Laietana, but still medieval in origin, is the Ribera Quarter, which became the centre of Barcelona in the 14th century when wealthy merchants built elegant mansions along Carrer Montcada. The popular **Museum Picasso 15** is housed here in a 15th-century mansion. Picasso, born in Malaga in 1881, was a precocious draftsman who was admitted at the age of 15 to the Royal Academy of Art in Barcelona, and a number of his early sketches are among the works on display in the museum. Nearby is the 14th-century Church of **Santa Maria del Mar 16**, considered the foremost achievement of Catalan Gothic architecture. A few blocks south of the church is the **Llotja** (Lodge) **17**, a 14th-century structure housing the Barcelona Stock Exchange Library and the Academy of Fine Arts. Remodeled in the 18th century, its interesting features include a courtyard and large Gothic hall.

In 1860, Barcelona dismantled the city walls and underwent a major expansion. The city's new section, called El Eixample ('enlargement'), was laid out in a grid pattern of streets with diamond-shaped intersections. Many

A facade decorated in the trompe-l'oeil style overlooks a square in the Gothic Quarter.

of the buildings were designed in the art nouveau style, called Modernismo in Spain, and several famous examples are located on Passeig de Gracia, near Plaza Catalunya. A block named Mancana de la Discordia (which means 'apple of discord') features three buildings of contrasting architecture, all of them built during the first decade of the 20th century. The Casa Lleo Morera presents a modernist floral facade; the Casa Ametller, in the middle, is a neogothic building, its facade decorated with polychrome ceramic; the most famous of the three, **Casa Battlo 18**, stands at the corner of Passeig de Gracia and Carrer d'Arago. Designed by Antonio Gaudi, it features a sparkling mosaic facade and a roof shaped like a dragon's tail. Another famous Art Nouveau building designed by Gaudi is **Casa Mila 19**, located a few blocks further along Passeig de Gracia. Also known as La Pedrera (The Stone Quarry), this large apartment house of cut stone appears to have been sculpted from play dough, with chimneys squeezed from a pastry tube.

Gaudi's most famous work, and a beloved Barcelona landmark, is the **Temple de la Sagrada Familia** (Temple of the Holy Family) **20**, begun in 1882 and still under construction. The church's west facade – which represents Passion and Death – is being built according to Gaudi's original design. The east facade represents the Nativity, and the Glory is planned on the south. The four towers on each of the three main facades represent the

Casa Battlo, an example of art nouveau architecture, was designed by Antonio Gaudi.

twelve Apostles. A complicated structure of inclined columns and parabolic arches, this unusual church is the ultimate example of Gaudi's artistic audacity and ingenious approach to construction, which allowed him to create his unusual building shapes.

Parc Guell 21, located about a mile northwest of the Church of the Sagrada Familia, is another showpiece of Gaudi's work. The park, named after Gaudi's main patron, is filled with fantastic and dreamlike forms, such as undulating benches and large, multicol-

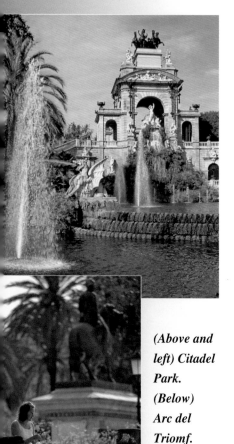

ored lizards. The house where Gaudi spent the last 20 years of his life is now a small museum.

The **Parc de la Ciutadella** (Citadel Park) **22** occupies the former site of an 18th-century fortress. Most of the buildings were demolished in 1869, but left standing was the arsenal – a baroque building which houses the Catalan parliament and the Museum of Modern Art. The park, built for an 1888 exhibition, offers a tranquil setting with a small lake and monumental waterfall featuring rocks designed by Gaudi as a young student. The nearby **Arc del Triomf 23**, a red-brick arch, was erected as a grand entrance to the exhibition.

When Barcelona hosted the 1929 World's Fair, the venue for this event was the hill of **Montjuic**, overlooking the harbor. The site was redeveloped in preparation for the 1992 Summer Olympic Games, and the 1920s stadium was remodeled into the Olympic Stadium. Accessible by funicular from the harbor,

(Above and left) Citadel Park.
(Below) Arc del Triomf.

Montjuic's attractions include pavilions, museums, gardens and a huge illuminated fountain. The assortment of buildings at Poble Espanyol (Spanish Village), from the 1929 world's fair, represents different regions of Spain.

Montserrat – Thirty-five miles northwest of Barcelona, clinging to the terraced cliffside of Monserrat mountain, is one of Spain's greatest religious shrines. Only ruins remain of the original Benedictine monastery, the present structure built in the 18th century. A guilded black image of the Virgin held in Montserrat's 16th-century Renaissance church is believed to have been carved by St. Luke and brought here by St. Peter, then hidden in a nearby cave during Spain's Moorish occupation. Montserrat can be reached by ship-organized excursion or by train from Barcelona. A cable car takes visitors up the mountainside to the monastery, church and museum, where cafes and shops are also located. Discount passes covering transportation and site admissions are available at Placa Espanya train station in Barcelona.

Tarragona – Situated 50 miles west of Barcelona at the mouth of the Francoli River, this Catalonian port flourished during Roman times, with Augustus making it the capital of the province of Tarraconensis. Ruins of the town's ancient walls, amphitheater and aqueduct can be viewed by visitors, as can the 13th century Romanesque-Gothic cathedral, which contains one of the finest cloisters in Spain.

Montserrat's celebrated monastery.

Balearic Islands

Like mainland Spain, the Balearic Islands have been inhabited since prehistoric times, and the Iberians, Phoenicians, Greeks, Carthaginians, Romans and Byzantines all laid claim to them at various points in history. In the 11th century they became a Moorish kingdom and a base for powerful pirates, until conquered by James I of Aragon in 1229. When the Spanish civil war broke out in 1936, **Majorca** and **Ibiza** were seized by Franco's insurgent forces, but **Minorca** remained in Loyalists' hands until 1939. Both Catalan and Castilian Spanish are spoken in the Balearic Islands, which has been an autonomous region since 1983.

Majorca (Mallorca)

The largest of the Balearic Islands, Majorca is a beautiful

mountainous island, with rolling hills, sandy beaches and stalagmite caves. The island's northwest coast is especially scenic, its terraced cliffsides overlooking rocky headlands and hidden coves. While living here in the winter of 1838-39, at an abandoned monastery in the village of **Valldemossa**, Frederic Chopin composed his 24 preludes. His companion was Mme Dudevant, whose pen name was George Sand. Theirs was a stormy love affair, and she later published a book about her life with Chopin, entitled *A Winter in Majorca*.

The English poet and novelist Robert Graves spent half of his life in the Majorcan village of **Deya**, not far from Valldemossa. The 1929 success of *Good-bye to All That*, an irreverent book based on his war experiences, allowed Graves to buy land and build a house in Deya, where he wrote,

among other works, *I, Claudius*. In 1936, with the Spanish Civil War looming, he left Majorca aboard a British destroyer and returned to England. Ten years later Graves and his family returned to Majorca where his house and its garden were just as he had left them.

Another famous artist who called Majorca his home was the Spanish painter Joan Miro. Considered surrealism's greatest exponent, Miro studied in Barcelona, then in Paris, before moving to Majorca in 1941 and establishing a studio in Palma.

Palma, with a quarter of a million residents, is Majorca's chief city and the capital of Baleares province. A popular holiday resort, the city stretches along the Bay of Palma and into the surrounding hills. On a hill overlooking the port is **Bellver Castle**, a former royal palace and a fine example of 14th-century military architecture, with a circular courtyard and sweeping views from its ramparts.

On the far side of the bay – about two miles from the cruise dock – is Palma's old town, once encircled by walls, a section of which still stands along the waterfront. Just inside the fortifications is Palma's splendid Gothic cathedral, begun in the year 1230, after James I of Aragon seized Palma from the Moors, and finally finished in 1601. Much of the interior was remodeled at the beginning of this century by Antonio Gaudi. The bell tower holds nine bells with the largest, which was cast in 1389, weighing four tons. Opposite the cathedral is **Castillo della Almudaina** █, originally a Moorish citadel and now a military headquarters.

Other structures of note include the 10th-century **Arab baths** █, the 13th-century **Church of San Francisco** █, and the 17th-century **Ajuntament** (Town Hall) █. **The Forn Teatro** (Theatre Bakery) █ is well known both for its photogenic facade and its delicious pastries. The nearby **Placa Major** █ is where a crafts market is held several times a week. Pedestrian shopping streets lead north from this square, and fashionable boutiques line Avinguda Jaume III and Passeig des Born, with a pedestrian promenade down the center.

Majorca's craggy northwest coast is dotted with watchtowers and spectacular viewpoints, including the one at **Son Marroig**, an estate built by

The monastery at Valldemossa where Chopin once stayed.

Shore Excursions *Majorca*

Ship-organized excursions on Majorca include sightseeing in Palma (4 hrs) and scenic island drives to Valldemossa and Son Marroig (4 hrs), La Granja (4 hrs), the wine-making village of Santa Maria (4 hrs), and the Caves of Drach (4.5 hrs). Also offered is a train ride (in wooden carriages) from Palma to Soller. The train ascends the mountains through 13 tunnels, and the return trip is by motorcoach (4 hrs total, about $65).

In addition to taking a ship-organized shore excursion, renting a car is another good way to explore the island. For about US$60, you can hire a car for the day and enjoy a leisurely drive around part of the island.

Cabo
Formentor

Puerto de Soller • Lluch

• Soller

Son   Deya •   • Alcudia
Marroig   Inca •

        • Valldemossa   Cala Ratjada

Banalbufar   Arta • •

    Palma

Paguera   Manacor •
                                • Porto
                                  Cristo

Cabo de Cala
Figuera   Lluchmayor
    Bay de Palma

        Cabo Blanco   Santany •

MALLORCA
                Isla   Cabo Salines
0   20   Conejera
                        Cabrera
Miles   N

Austrian archduke Luis Salvador,
who visited Majorca in the mid-
1800s and decided to stay. His
estate has been converted into a
museum housing his collection of
pottery and paintings. The view
from the mirador looks down
nearly 1,000 feet to a rocky headland from which the waves have
carved, over time, a huge sea arch
called Sa Foradada ('perforated').

Nearby are the villages of **Deya**
and **Valldemossa** – location of La
Cartuja, a Carthusian monastery
that was converted into lodgings
in 1835. The apartments where
Chopin and George Sand stayed
are furnished in period style and
contain a piano used by Chopin.
Other picturesque villages along
the   northwest   coast   include

Palma's Gothic cathedral.

Puerto Soller, with a natural harbor and fine beaches. Inland, the mountain village of **Lluch** is the location of a monastery set into the side of a cliff.

At the north end of the island is historic **Alcudia**, where a twice-weekly market selling handicrafts is held outside the restored remains of its Moorish city walls. A nearby Roman amphitheater was excavated in the 1950s.

On the island's east coast, near the fishing port of Porto Cristo, are the **Caves of Drach**, which contain one of the world's largest underground lakes. The pearl factory at nearby **Manacor** is another popular attraction.

The sea views at Deya (above) and Son Marroig (right) along Majorca's northwest coast.

Minorca (Menorca),

One of the Mediterranean's most desirable holiday islands, Minorca has been inhabited since Neolithic times. Several megalithic monuments of huge undressed stone stand amid the island's gentle terrain of low hills, patchwork fields and narrow hedge-lined lanes. In the 18th century, England, France and Spain all fought for control of Minorca, but the island was held mostly by the British who gave **Port Mahon** (Mao) its Georgian-style architecture. Situated at the island's east end, this strategic port and chief city was named for the Carthaginian general Mago, and its picturesque harbor is protected by two fortresses. Mahon's tourist information office is at Placa de S'Esplanada, and local highlights include the Ajuntament (City Hall) and Church of Santa

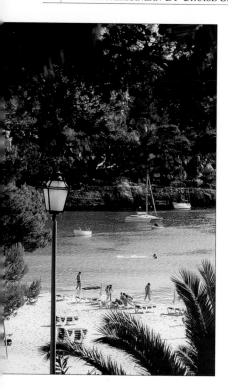

Cala Galdana, Minorca.

Maria (St. Mary's Church). The island was finally awarded to Spain in 1802, but it still retains some British flavor. **Ciutadella** (Ciudadela), at the island's west end, was Minorca's capital before the arrival of the British. A quaint city, its interesting architecture includes medieval churches and splendid palaces. Beautiful beaches line the island's south coast, such as the protected cove at **Cala Galdana** and the sandy beach at Cala 'n Porter which is sheltered from winds by cliffs.

Ibiza

A picturesque island, with terraced farmland and ancient remains, Ibiza was a popular artists' retreat in the 1960s. The island's first hippy market was located at Patio de Armas, inside the medieval town of **Eivissa** (traditionally called **D'Alt Vila**). Declared a World Heritage Site by UNESCO, the town's sights include a Dominican convent (now the Town Hall), a cathedral, episcopal palace and numerous shops, cafes and art galleries. Ship shore excursions feature a walking tour of D'Alt Villa (3 hrs) and a fast ferry ride to the unspoiled island of **Formentera** to spend time at beautiful Illetes Beach (7 hrs total).

Valencia Province

Valencia is Spain's third largest city and the capital of Valencia province – the 'garden of Spain' where the famous Valencia oranges are grown. For centuries this province's fertile coastal plain has been cultivated, and the Tribunal de las Aguas, founded in the 10th century, still meets regularly in Valencia to settle disputes over the irrigation of its outlying garden region. Valencia was a rival of Barcelona during the late Middle Ages. Its university was founded in 1501, and the city became a literary and cultural centre, with a famous school of painting. Today the city is quite striking, with narrow streets and blue-tiled church domes in the old quarter, and tree-lined avenues and promenades in the modern section. Its major landmarks include a 13th-century cathedral with a Gothic bell tower (called El Miguelete), 14th-century fortified towers (called Torres de Serranos) which were built on Roman foundations, and the 15th-century silk exchange (La Lonja), which is considered one of Spain's finest Gothic buildings.

Alicante, situated on the **Costa Blanca**, is dominated by the great Moorish castle of Santa Barbara. Perched upon a rocky peak, the fortress provides breathtaking views of the city's squares, beaches and palm-lined Explanada de Espana, which runs along the waterfront. A lift, its shaft running deep inside the mountain, transports visitors to the castle. The tourist office is located near the waterfront, in the arcaded Plaza de Ayuntamiento. Behind is Plaza Santisima Faz, an inviting square filled with out-door cafes and restaurants. Nearby is the Museum of 20th Century Art, housing a small collection of works by Dali, Miro and Picasso. Playa Postiguet is the city's main beach, while those north of the city are cleaner and less crowded.

Cartagena, a city of great historical importance, was founded by Carthaginians in the 3rd century BC. Eventually this ancient city fell to the Moors in the 8th century, and was recovered by Spaniards in the 13th century. It was sacked by Francis Drake in 1585, and during the Spanish Civil War (1936-39) Cartagena was a Loyalist naval base. No traces of the ancient city remain but the ruins of the medieval Castillo de la Concepcion, surrounded by fine gardens, command a sweeping view of the city and harbor. The city's museum

A fountain-filled square in Valencia.

holds excellent pre-Roman and Roman collections, and outside the city, near the old docks, is the National Museum of Underwater Archaeology.

Ship-organized **shore excursions** in Cartagena include a narrated city drive and walking tour, and motorcoach rides to Murcia's 17th-century shrine of Fuensanta and to the Moorish town of Elche.

Malaga and Granada

Sunny **Andalusia,** the southernmost part of Spain, is best known for its beach resorts, whitewashed buildings and Moorish castles. **Malaga**, a port of access to **Granada**, is situated on the **Costa del Sol** where a mild climate, lush vegetation and beautiful beaches attract plenty of

The port of Malaga provides access to Granada.

tourists. The birthplace of Picasso, Malaga is a mostly modern city, despite its millennia of history. Founded in the 12th century BC by the Phoenicians, the city passed from empire to empire. From the 13th to the 15th centuries, Malaga flourished as a seaport of the Moorish kingdom of Granada before falling to Ferdinand and Isabella in 1487. Its historic buildings include a 16th-century cathedral, the ruins of a Moorish alcazar, and an imposing citadel called the Gibralfaro. The Museo Picasso, which opened in 2003, is housed in the Buenavista Palace. A replica of an 18th-century Spanish battleship is moored in Malaga's harbor.

Granada, which began as a Moorish fortress, is beautifully situated at the foot of the Sierra Nevada, where the Darro and Genil rivers flow together. It became a city of great splendor with construction of its famous palace complex, the **Alhambra**. A hilltop group of buildings, the Alhambra (which means 'the red' in Arabic) was built between 1230 and 1354. This luxurious royal palace and citadel are considered the finest examples of Moorish architecture in Spain.

Shore Excursions *Malaga*

First-time visitors to **Malaga** will want to visit Granada to view the famous Alhambra palace complex (9 hrs, about $150, see description, right). Other ship-organized shore excursions in Malaga include city tours, tapa tasting, and scenic drives along Costa del Sol to Marbella (4.5 hrs), to the stalagmite caves at Nerja (4.5 hrs) and to the Andalusian village of Mijas with its square bullring (4 hrs).

The halls and chambers surround a series of open courts, including the Court of Lions, which contains arcades resting on 124 white marble columns. The palace's sumptuous interior of alabaster and glazed tile is adorned with geometric ornamentation of minute detail and intricacy. When American author and diplomat Washington Irving came to live in the Alhambra in 1829, the palace was crumbling from rot and decay. His book of Spanish sketches, called *Tales of the Alhambra*, helped revive interest in the palace's preservation and, since 1862, an ongoing program of restoration has been in effect.

Sharing the Alhambra's hilltop site are the palace of Emperor Charles V, built in 1526 on the site once occupied by the sultan's private apartments, and the celebrated gardens of the Palacio del Generalife, a summer residence of the Moorish rulers. Granada's 16th-century cathedral was built in the late Gothic and plateresque style. The adjoining royal chapel, a masterpiece of ornate Gothic architecture, contains the marble tombs of Ferdinand and Isabella.

B U L L F I G H T I N G

Bullfighting, an important part of Spanish culture, was introduced by the Moors who fought bulls from horses and killed them with javelins. This Moorish practise evolved into the sport of bullfighting, called *corrida de toros* in Spanish. A controversial spectacle, criticized by some as a form of animal torture, the bullfight is nonetheless popular not only in Spain, but in Southern France, Morocco and several Latin American countries. Held in a large outdoor arena, the modern bullfight unfolds in three ritualistic parts. First, toreros wave capes at the bull and mounted picadors thrust at it with lances. The next stage involves banderillos who, while on the run, poke short barbed sticks into the bull's withers. Finally the matador, holding a small cape and a sword, makes daring passes at the bull who eventually stops charging and succumbs to the matador's dominance. When the bull strikes a stationary stance, with its four feet square on the ground and its head hung low, this is the moment when, according to ritual and law, the matador must shove his sword into the bull's heart. Fighting bulls are specially bred, and successful matadors are highly paid and admired for their skill and courage.

Cadiz and Seville

Cadiz, once one of the world's major ports, is an ancient city rich in naval history. Founded by the Phoenicians in about 1000 BC, Cadiz became the wealthiest port in Europe after the discovery of America, when Spanish treasure ships, returning from the New World, unloaded their cargoes here. In 1587 Francis Drake burned a Spanish fleet in Cadiz's harbor, in an operation known as 'the singeing of the King of Spain's beard', and nine years later another English squadron captured and sank most of the ships in this harbor.

Attacks on Cadiz continued but its wealth, based on trade with Spain's colonies, continued to grow, especially after Seville's port – reached by river from Cadiz – became partially blocked by a sandbar. The port of Cadiz was blockaded by the British in 1797, and bombarded by Sir Horatio Nelson in 1800. Five years later, a Franco-Spanish fleet sailed from Cadiz and met its destruction at the Battle of Trafalgar. Today cruise ships pull into Cadiz's natural harbor where disembarking passengers can enjoy the palm-lined promenades of this fine old city. Its 13th-century cathedral was rebuilt in the Renaissance style, and a new cathedral was begun in 1722. In

Shore Excursions *Cadiz*

Ship-organized shore excursions from Cadiz include walking tours of Seville (9 hrs, $150) and Cadiz (3 hrs, $30), as well as sherry tasting and visting an Andalusian horse school (5 hrs, $90). A ship shuttle can be taken from Cadiz to Seville (70 miles away, $75) for exploring this fascinating city on your own.

C E R V A N T E S

Miguel de Cervantes Saavedra, the Spanish novelist, dramatist and poet, wrote his masterpiece, *Don Quixote*, while living in Seville in the late 16th century. Prior to that he was a student of Italian literature and philosophy while in the service of a cardinal. He next served in the army, and was wounded and permanently crippled in his left arm during the naval battle of Lepanto, fought between the Christians and Ottomans in 1571 off the coast of Greece. On his way back to Spain, Cervantes was captured by Barbary pirates and sold as a slave. After numerous attempts at escape, he was ransomed by the viceroy of Algiers, the price paid by his family bringing them to financial ruin. While working as a government purchasing agent in Seville from 1588 to 1597, Cervante's unbusinesslike methods resulted in his imprisonment on several occasions, during which he penned parts of *Don Quixote*, a burlesque of the popular romances of chivalry and a huge success when published in 1605 .

1980 some Phoenician sarcophagi and a Roman theatre were discovered in Cadiz.

Seville, which is connected with the Atlantic by river and canal, has been the chief city of Andalusia since ancient times. The Romans made Seville a judicial centre of Baetica province and built the nearby city of Italica, where the emperors Trajan and Hadrian were born. The city fell to the Moors in 712 AD, and eventually became a flourishing commercial and cultural centre. Two parts of its famous mosque remain, the Court of Oranges and the Giralda tower, which was built between 1163 and 1184.

After a long siege, Seville fell in 1248 to Ferdinand III of Castile, and about 300,000 Moors – the majority of the population – left. Following the discovery of the New World in 1492, Seville again prospered as a chief port of trade. A beautiful **1** **Gothic cathedral**, one of the world's largest, was completed in 1519 on the site of the main mosque, its square minaret (the Giralda tower) converted to a bell tower in 1568 with the addition of an ornate Renaissance superstructure. Inside the cathedral are invaluable works of art and the tomb of Christopher Columbus. Adjoining the cathedral is the **Alcazar 2**, built by Moorish artisans, its splendid halls and exquisite decorations rivaling the Alhambra in Granada.

In addition to Seville's numerous churches and private castles, other notable buildings include the 16th-century **town hall 3** the **Ionja** (former exchange) **4** containing archives of Spanish America, and the city's **university buildings 5** which were formerly a large tobacco factory and a setting featured in Bizet's Carmen. Seville is the country's bullfighting capital, and **La Maestranza Bullring** 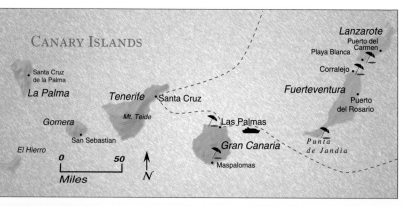, completed in 1763, is the oldest and most beautiful in Spain.

Galacia

In northwest Spain's Galacia province, the Atlantic ports of **La Coruna** and **Vigo** both provide access to **Santiago de Compostela**, one of the chief shrines of Christendom. In the early 9th century, Alfonso II of Asturias had a sanctuary built on the presumed site of the apostle St. James The Greater's tomb. The city, which grew around the shrine, became an important place of pilgrimage during the Middle Ages, second only to Jerusalem and Rome. The Moors destroyed the sanctuary in the 10th century, and a Romanesque cathedral was built on the site between the 11th and 13th centuries, with baroque and plateresque additions made during later restorations. The Hospital Real was built in the early 1500s by Ferdinand and Isabella to accommodate poor pilgrims. Today millions of Christians annually make the pilgrimage along part or all of the paths that lead to the shrine.

Canary Islands

These Atlantic isles, lying off the coast of Africa, are volcanic in origin and immensely appealing to pleasure-seeking visitors because of their subtropical climate, clear waters and expansive beaches. Starkly beautiful, the islands are a study in contrasts. Sea cliffs and craggy coves give way to massive sand dunes and vast beaches. Mountain villages with whitewashed houses and red-tiled roofs seem far removed from the resort areas' modern hotels and championship golf courses. Millions of visitors arrive annually by air, while those arriving by cruise ship pull into historic ports of cobblestone streets and Spanish colonial architecture – the same ports that greeted famous sea captains in centuries past.

The islands' original inhabitants were a cave-dwelling people called Guanches, who likely migrated from Africa. The islands were visited by Romans as early as 40 BC, and several classical writers referred to them as the Fortunate Islands. The Middle Ages brought the occasional visit by Arabs and Europeans, but no

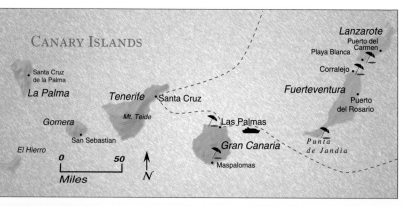

permanent settlement until 1402, when a Norman named Jean de Bethencourt arrived at Lanzarote. In 1479 a treaty between Portugal and Spain gave the latter sovereignty over the Canaries, and the Spanish conquest of the Guanches was complete by 1496.

The islands became an important base for voyages to the Americas, and they were frequently raided by pirates and privateers. England's Francis Drake attacked Las Palmas in 1595 but was repulsed; the Dutch were more successful four years later, when they ravaged the port. Two centuries later, in 1797, Horatio Nelson tried to capture a Spanish treasure ship at Santa Cruz but was repulsed, losing an arm in the battle. The Canaries, comprising two provinces, have been an autonomous region of Spain since 1982. Santa Cruz de Tenerife, whose capital is Santa Cruz on the island of Tenerife, encompasses the western islands; Las Palmas, whose capital is Las Palmas on the island of Gran Canaria, encompasses the eastern islands.

Tenerife is the largest of Canary Islands. Its northern valleys are filled with banana and pineapple plantations, and the entire island is dominated by the snowcovered summit of Mt. Teide – Spain's highest point at 12,162 feet (3,707 meters). The visitor centre at Teide National Park provides guided hikes and bus tours, and a cable car carries visitors close to the top of the volcano, where the final ascent is made on foot to the edge of the crater. Tenerife's port city of

A whitewashed village on Gran Canaria island.

Santa Cruz has several museums and historic structures, including a Moorish bell tower. The 18th-century cannons that held off an attack by Horatio Nelson are still in place, including the one that scored a direct hit on his right arm, which was so badly injured it had to be amputated that evening on board his battleship.

The cliff-edged island of **Gomera** is where Columbus made his last stop, his ships pulling into the port of San Sebastian, before sailing across the Atlantic Ocean in 1492.

La Palma, also called La Isla Bonita ('The Pretty Island'), is a verdant island of volcanic mountains, including Cumbre Vieja, which erupted in 1971 and is slowly sliding toward the sea at a rate of half an inch per year. The island's capital of **Santa Cruz de la Palma** is situated on the edge of a crater. A bustling ship-building centre in the 16th century, the port has retained its colonial appearance.

Las Palmas, capital of Las Palmas province, is situated on **Gran Canaria**, an island famous for its enormous beaches and sand dunes, such as those found at Maspalomas. The city of Las Palmas was founded in 1478, and its nearby harbor at Puerto de la Luz is the Canaries' chief port and one of the busiest in Spain. An impressive castle, Castillo de la Luz, protects the harbor, and a Gothic cathedral, dating to the early 1500s, stands in the city's old quarter. It took four centuries to complete the cathedral, hence its 19th-century exterior. The Casa Museo Colon (Columbus Museum) is housed in the palace where Columbus likely stayed in 1492. Not far from Castillo de la Luz, is a fine beach called Las Cantara.

The island of **Lanzarote**, an unusual lunar-like landscape with black and red beaches, features bubbling geysers and grottoes containing emerald-colored water. Fuerteventura offers stunning beaches, including those of powdery sand on the island's south coast.

Gibraltar

A British crown colony, Gibraltar is a military fortress perched on a narrow peninsula, called the Rock of Gibraltar, which is connected to the Spanish mainland by a low sandy area of neutral ground. In ancient times, the Rock was regarded as one of the two mythological Pillars of Hercules – the other being Mt. Acha at Ceuta in Africa. These two promontories flank the east entrance to the Strait of Gibraltar and were said to mark the end of the world by the Ancient Greeks.

The name Gibraltar is Arabic in origin, derived from Jabal-al-Tarik ('mount of Tarik'). In 711, the Moorish leader Tarik captured the Rock of Gibraltar and built its first fortifications, upon which enlargements and improvements have been made over the centuries. The Moors held Gibraltar until 1462, when the Spanish seized control of the fortress. The British gained possession of 'the Rock' in 1704 and have held it ever since, fending off several sieges by the Spanish and French in the 18th century. During the Spanish civil war (1936-39), refugees fled to Gibraltar. Most civilians were evacuated during World War II, when its fortifications were strengthened

Gibraltar is only three miles long and less than a mile wide but, as a strategic naval and air base, it has been an ongoing source of friction between Great Britain and Spain. Despite Spain's persistent claim to Gibraltar, its residents voted in 1967 to maintain their ties to Britain, and in 1981 Gibraltar's small civilian population, mainly of Spanish, Italian, Portuguese, Maltese and Jewish descent, were granted full British citizenship. In 1985 Spain reopened its border with Gibraltar, after closing it in 1969, and today many of the colony's laborers live in the Spanish border town of La Linea. A proposed plan in which Britain would share sovereignty of the colony with Spain was rejected by Gibraltarians in a 2002 referendum.

The Rock of Gibraltar is made of Jurassic limestone, and is honeycombed with caves, arsenals and a tunnel bisecting the rock from east to west. Valuable archaeological finds have been made in **St. Michael's Cave** **1** where stalagmites and stalactites create a dramatic setting for the daily sound-and-light shows. Tours are available of the tunnels leading off the cave's main chambers. From St. Michael's Cave, it's about a 20-minute walk to the **Apes' Den** **2** where the famous Barbary Apes – a breed of monkey native to Morocco – are fed twice daily. In between feedings, they pass the time snatching purses and cameras from curious tourists.

The view from the Rock's summit is spectacular, looking across the Strait of Gibraltar to Africa. This lookout, as well as the Apes' Den and St. Michael's Cave, can all be reached by **cable car** from the town **3**, where a tourist office is located in Cathedral Square. Local attractions include the Governor's Residence, the Law Courts, the Anglican cathedral and the Catholic cathedral. Main Street is lined with shops, pubs and restaurants. At the north end of town is the **Moorish Castle** **4**, its Tower of Homage dating from 1333. At the south end of town, just past the harbor, is Rosia Bay. Following the Battle of Trafalgar in 1805, Nelson's flagship *Victory* was brought here and the dead on board were transferred to Trafalgar Cemetery at the south edge of town. Nelson's body was shipped back to England, preserved in a barrel of rum.

Shore Excursions Gibraltar

While it's fairly easy to explore Gibraltar on your own, taking a ship's shore excursion is an alternative. An historical tour, which includes a 45-minute guided walk through the siege tunnels (begun by the British in 1782) and a motorcoach ride to the Trafalgar Cemetery and the Moorish Castle, takes about 3.5 hours. Other ship excursions worth considering include a boat ride across the Bay of Gibraltar where dolphins are frequently sighted (2 hrs), and a narrated drive to the major sights as well as a visit to the World War II tunnels (3.5 hrs).

the
SOUTH of FRANCE

CRUISE ROUTES

ROUTES: ----------

Rail System

N

0   20
Miles

Italy
France

HAUTES-
ALPES

ALPES-DE-
HAUTE-PROVENCE

ALPES-
MARITIMES

Mt. Ventoux
△ (6,263 ft)

Digne

VAUCLUSE

PROVENCE

Chateauneuf-du-Pape

Avignon

St-Remy

■ Chateau Du
Marquis De Sade

Les Baux

Mt. Ste-Victoire
△ (3,317 ft)

Grasse

St. Paul
de Vence

Villefranche

Eze

Monaco

Nice

Antibes

Cannes

Côte d'Azur

Arles

Pont du
■ Gard

Nimes

Sete

Rhone River

Aix-en-
Provence

Marseille

Aubagne

Cassis

Toulon

Saint-Tropez

Giens

Ile du Levant

Heliopolis

Ile d' Hyeres

CHAPTER THREE

FRANCE

French culture has been widely admired since the 13th century, when its poetry, manners and ideals of chivalry were adopted as a model by the other courts of Europe. Today it's the food, the wine and a general joie de vivre that many of us admire in the French. In a nation where dining is an art form, and where the arts are for all to enjoy, the many aspects of gracious living fall into fascinating perspective. Politics are important, but so is lunch. And for the average visitor to France, figuring out the lunch menu could well be easier than understanding the many departments, districts, cantons and communes of French government.

France has had a centralized administration since the Revolution of 1789, yet each region has retained its own distinct character. This diversity harks back to the Middle Ages when provinces were ruled by dukes and counts, and feudal power was held by nobles, guilds and the clergy. The country was first settled by Greek and Phoenician traders who landed on the Mediterranean coast in about 600 BC. The Romans began colonizing Provence in the 2nd century BC, followed by Julius Caesar's widespread conquest in 58 BC. For five centuries Gaul, as the Romans called it, was under Rome's rule. Then, in 486 AD, the Franks – a Germanic tribe – routed the last Roman emperor of Gaul and the region soon lay in ruins. The only remnant of Roman civilization was the church, which also faced ruination when Saracens invaded in the 8th century.

The Carolingian dynasty, led by Pepin the Short, rescued the region. His son Charlemagne (Charles the Great) became a legendary figure. Crowned emperor of the West on Christmas Day in the year 800, Charlemagne ushered in an intellectual renaissance. A great leader and administrator, Charlemagne also promoted the rebirth of learning and the arts with the establishment of his famous palace school, along with numerous schools for children throughout the empire.

A thousand years later Napoleon drew on Charlemagne's example when forging his own empire. One of Napoleon's generals was the father of Victor Hugo,

LE CAFÉ DE PARIS
MONTE-CARLO

AUTOMNE/HIVER 1997/98

who became a towering figure of 19th-century French literature with such epic novels as *The Hunchback of Notre Dame* and *Les Miserables*. Hugo and other members of the Romantic school revived the legend of Charlemagne, who had been immortalized in medieval poems as the champion of Christendom. The glory days of empire may be over for France, but the country's artistic, literary and culinary culture remains the envy of many a nation.

A Few Words About French Wine

France's best wines set the standard for the rest of the world. Alas, these fine vintages are losing their appeal at home, where the younger generation is showing little inclination to learn the complicated labeling system of French wines, one based on regions of origin. These regions, called appellations, vary in size from single small vineyards to large districts. The French tradition of familiarizing oneself with the appellations and, more importantly, the best growers and merchants within each appellation, can be a daunting task for the novice wine drinker who relies on identifying the type of grape when choosing a wine. The French wine industry is currently debating whether or not to modify its labels and dis-

play the varietal (variety of grape) along with the appellation.

France at a Glance

About 64 million people live in France, and Roman Catholicism is the major religion. French, spoken in a variety of regional dialects, is the major language, except in Corsica where an Italian dialect is spoken. The country is governed by a president, who is directly elected for a seven-year term, and who appoints a premier and cabinet that are responsible to the national assembly. France is divided into 22 planning regions, two of which are covered in this chapter, namely Provence-Alpes-Côte d'Azur and Corsica. France is an industrial nation and major economic power, yet more than half of its land area is still used for agriculture. Tourism is also a major industry, with France receiving more international tourists than any other country in the world.

Travel Tips

Currency: The unit of currency is euro. Traveler's checks are widely accepted, as are most credit cards. Visa is the most widely accepted and Visa card holders can receive cash advances from instant tellers. ATMs are located throughout France and are tied to international networks. Banks outside of Paris are usually open Tuesday through Saturday, from 10 a.m. to 5 p.m. (closing for an hour at 1 p.m.). Approximate rate of exchange is 1 euro = 1.30 US ($1US = .77 euros).

Dining: Fresh herbs, grilled fish, olives, garlic and goat cheese are all featured in the local cuisine of southern France. Famous dishes include bouillabaisse (a fish stew) and salad nicoise, which features tuna, tomato, hard-boiled egg and anchovies. The wines produced in the south of France include the famous white wine of Cassis. The grenache grape is used to make the fruity rose wines for which Provence has a particularly good reputation. Restaurants usually offer a plat du jour (menu of the day) featuring two or three courses at a set price, which is less expensive than ordering a la carte. Most restaurants include a 15% service charge in their prices.

Opening Hours: Museums and historic attractions generally open from 10 a.m. to noon and from 2 p.m. to 5 or 6 p.m.

Shopping: The south of France is famous for its Provencal style of country decor, which is rustic and romantic, featuring cane beds, rush chairs and tapestry throws. Handcrafted items are created in earthy textures, such as wood, pewter and wrought iron, and local specialties include ceramic pots, hand-painted dishes and colorful table linens. Stores are generally open 9:30 am to 7 p.m.

Taxi fares: Approximately 40 euros per hour, but this is negotiable. Some drivers will accept US currency. Tip 10-15% of the metered fare.

Telephone Access Codes: Telecartes (telephone calling cards), purchased at post offices

A sidewalk cafe in Aix-en-Provence.

and tobacconists, can be used in most public telephones. Personal calling card access codes: AT&T 0800-99-0011; MCI 0800-99-0019; SPRINT 0800-99-0087; CANADA 0800-99-0216.

Côte d'Azur (French Riviera)

One by one they were drawn to the shimmering colors and flickering light of the Côte D'Azur (Azure Coast). Renoir, Matisse, Picasso – these and other great figures of modern art have lived and worked along the French Riviera, a narrow coastal strip squeezed between the Alps and the Mediterranean. Sheltered

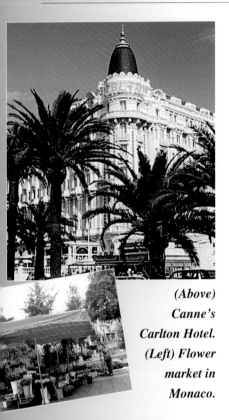

One of the first 'tourists' to the area was Lord Henry Brougham, a British statesman who served as Lord Chancellor, head of the judiciary, from 1830 to 1834. In December 1834, the British baron was travelling to Italy with his daughter Eleonore for a holiday, when he found the border closed due to an epidemic in Northern Europe. Turning back, the party headed toward Grasse and stopped for the night at a hostel located on what is now known as the Rue du Port in **Cannes**. Enchanted by the village's seaside setting, Lord Brougham decided to have a residence built there and two years later members of London's high society flocked to the opening of Villa Eleonore.

(Above) Canne's Carlton Hotel. (Left) Flower market in Monaco.

The small fishing port of Cannes quickly became a gathering place for European aristocracy. Villas and castles were built, and the bare countryside surrounding Cannes was transformed when Lord Brougham built a canal to supply water to the town and allow the planting of lawns and gardens at the palatial

from winds and blessed with a mild year-round climate, it was only a matter of time until the entire world discovered the Riviera's famed beauty and fashionable beach resorts.

Vieux Port, Antibes.

estates. The once-barren country-side, now irrigated, became a paradise of flowers and fruit trees.

A railroad line was built in the 1860s to provide access from Marseille to Cannes, Nice and Monaco. High society of Europe and America journeyed to the Riviera each winter, including Tsar Alexander II and his wife, who arrived in **Nice** a week after the railroad opened in 1864. Not all visitors were titled, however, for a new class was emerging – the recently rich and powerful of the Industrial Revolution who wanted to celebrate their wealth with opulence and excess. The often flamboyant architecture of the late 19th century is characterized by the Riviera's luxurious villas and grand hotels, such as the Victoria and Negresco in Nice, and the Carlton in Cannes, which opened in 1910, its architect reportedly modeling the palace's two domes after the bosom of a famous courtesan.

When the artist Pierre Renoir left Paris in the late 1800s to live at Cagnes-sur-Mer just east of Antibes, his style of painting had gone beyond impressionism with

the sensuous depiction of voluptuous nudes. Henri Matisse, the leader of Fauvism – a style emphasizing the use of brilliant colors – lived in Nice from 1917 until his death in 1954. And when Pablo Picasso came to the Riviera in 1946 to escape the pressures of Paris, he experienced an artistic

(Above) Place Rosetti, Old Nice. (Left) A street scene in Monaco's La Condamine.

Shore Excursions

French Riviera

When visiting the French Riviera, a leisurely day spent exploring your ship's port of call is of course very appealing. However, should you wish to visit one of the other Riviera resorts while you're there, this can be done **independently** (see 'On Your Own'). For example, if your ship stops at Villefranche, you could catch a morning train to Monaco/Monte Carlo and return on an afternoon train to stroll around Villefranche before heading back to the ship. The same applies to the other French Riviera ports: take a train or taxi to a nearby resort in the morning, returning in the afternoon to explore your ship's port of call before reboarding the ship. Lunch can be enjoyed ashore anywhere along the French Riviera, where restaurants are plentiful and most are reasonably priced (menus are posted at the entrance). **Ship-organized shore excursions** are another way to see several places along the French Riviera; cruise passengers can choose from a variety of scenic motorcoach drives along the Cote d'Azur with stops at famous beach resorts and medieval hilltop villages. Refer to your cruise line's shore excursions booklet or website for details.

rejuvenation while living in a medieval palace at Antibes.

Others have followed in the footsteps of these great artists, seeking solace in the warm sun and azure sea. Where once only footpaths led to fortified towns set high in the hills, panoramic highways now hug this rugged coastline. Back in the 1920s the renowned American writer F. Scott Fitzgerald began touting the Riviera as a summer resort and the idea quickly caught on. Today, in summer, the local population swells with visitors – from Europe and abroad – lured by the famous beach resorts and fine art museums of this scenic coast.

On Your Own

The Côte d'Azur's famous resorts lie between **Saint Tropez** and **Monaco** (a distance of about 60 miles), and are connected by roads and regular train service. Cruise passengers arriving at a French Riviera port can visit one or two nearby resorts independently by train, taxi and/or bus. For example, the train ride from Villefranche to Nice is only 15 minutes; Villefranche to Monaco is 20 minutes; and Villefranche to Cannes takes about an hour. There's no train station at Eze but the train does stop at Eze-Sur-Mer, from where it's a two-mile bus or taxi ride up to the village.

The Villefranche train station.

Buses run regularly between Nice and Saint Paul de Vence (a one-hour ride each way).

Taxis cost upwards of 40 euros per hour (this is negotiable). Some sample fares: Nice – Villefranche (20 minutes) = 20 euros; Villefranche – Monaco (30 minutes) = 45 euros; Monaco's train station to Monte Carlo's Place du Casino = 6 euros; Villefranche – Cannes (1 1/2 hours) = 77 euros. Rental cars are also available, especially in Nice. The cost is approximately 90 to 120 euros per day, depending on the size of the vehicle. The coastal highway is especially scenic along the Corniche du Littoral between Nice and Monaco. There are. no border restrictions upon entering Monaco, where the euro is the official currency.

Ports of Call

The famous resort of **Saint-Tropez** (pronounced *san-tro-pay*) lies some distance from the Côte d'Azur's other popular ports. Situated about 30 miles west of Cannes, this picturesque fishing port of 5,000 inhabitants was made famous by film personalities during the 1960s. The local Musee del'Annonciade, housed in a 17th-century church, contains works by Matisse, Dufy and others.

(Above) Ste. Maxime Beach, near St. Tropez. (Below) The beach and cruise port at Cannes.

Cannes

Cannes (pronounced *kon*), home to the famous international film festival, has long been subject to foreign invasions. Throughout the Middle Ages, Cannes experienced repeated raids by the Saracens, and by soldiers passing through on their way to battle. In the 5th century, the holy monk Honorate founded an abbey on the offshore isle that bears his name, and his sister Marguerite founded a convent on the neighboring Island of St. Marguerite where, in 1667, a man whose face was hidden behind a velvet mask was imprisoned. Immortalized by Voltaire and Alexandre Dumas, he became a mysterious figure of literature called The Man in the

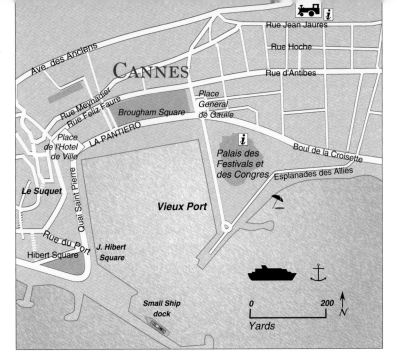

Iron Mask. His identity has long been open to speculation but he may have been a valet to Louis XIV, jailed for 34 years due to a scandalous secret he knew about the French king.

On March 1st, 1815, Napoleon landed near Cannes when returning from exile on the island of Elba and, with a handful of followers, began his triumphant march northward to Paris. Two decades later, Lord Brougham began transforming Cannes into a holiday resort. The town's seaside path, called the Chemin de la Petite Croix after a small cross that marked the gathering spot for pilgrims to the Island of St Honorat, was gradually widened into a road. Today that same path is an upscale esplanade called the **Promenade de la Croisette**, its deluxe hotels and famous blue chairs looking out over a beautiful bay where the fine sand beaches are regularly cleaned by tractor-drawn machines and the water is hydraulically vacuumed.

Cannes held its first film festival in 1939, as an alternative to the Venice Film Festival, which had fallen under the control of the Fascists and Nazis. A 'steamship of stars' arrived that September from America – Gary Cooper, Douglas Fairbanks and Mae West were among its passengers. The festival was opened under the presidency of Louis Lumiere, the inventor of cinema, only to be cancelled the next day when Germany invaded Poland. When the war ended, the festival was revived, its principles espoused in the words of writer, visual artist and filmmaker Jean Cocteau, who described the new festival as "a microcosm of what the world would be like if its inhabitants had direct contact with each other and they all spoke the same language".

Roberto Rosellini's *Open City* won the top prize among 44 international films entered in 1946 and the festival quickly became a social event. Financial difficulties, however, forced the Festival's cancellation in 1948 and 1950. In 1951 it was held in May instead of September so as not to conflict with the one held in Venice. In 1953 Brigitte Bardot appeared on the Croisette in a bikini, and in 1954 a starlet named Simone Silva bared her breasts for attentive photographers who wired the picture to newspapers around the world, dramatically increasing the festival's exposure and turning it into a major media event. The following year American actress Grace Kelly was invited to Cannes to help re-establish the artistic merit of the festival. At a press conference she met Prince Rainier of Monaco and a year later they were married at a lavish wedding held during the festival.

The Croisette Palace was eventually replaced with the **Palais des Festivals**, which was inaugurated in 1982 and is a venue for other festivals, as well as concerts, operas, recitals and ballet performances. The auditorium is named after the composer Claude Debussy (1862-1918) who, as a young boy learning to play the piano, would visit the home of his music teacher at the tip of the Croisette.

The most famous grand hotel on the Croisette is the Carlton, built in 1912. It was joined in 1926 by the Majestic, the favorite rendezvous for Film Festival stars. Excellent **bistros** line the Croisette, and prestigious restaurants include La Cote in the Carlton, La Palme d'Or in the Martinez, and La Scala in the Noga Hilton. **Shopping streets** abound, including the popular Rue Meynadier and the Rue d'Antibes. The historic heart of Cannes is **Le Suquet**, a hill mounted by winding alleys with marvellous views from the old watchtower. In addition to its restaurants and shops, attractions include the Sarrazine tower, the 17th-century church of Our Lady of Good Hope, a 12th century chapel and the Castre museum.

The highway that leads north of Cannes to **Grasse** is called the Route Napoleon, for it traces the dirt track Napoleon took after landing near Cannes in 1815. The hilly countryside through which he trekked is now a prime flower-growing region and Grasse, founded in Roman times, is the center of the French perfume industry. In addition to its numerous perfume factories, Grasse attractions include a splendid early Gothic cathedral (12th century), a town hall partially built in the Middle Ages, and a museum

Cannes viewed from Le Suquet.

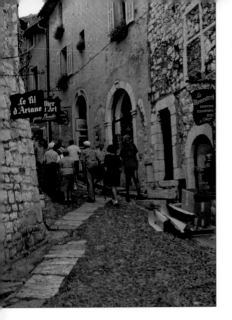

The winding cobblestone lanes of St. Paul de Vence.

containing paintings by Jean-Honore Fragonard who was born in Grasse.

The fortified seaport of **Antibes** (*an-teeb*) is another center of this famous flower-growing region. The Grimaldi chateau, built in the 14th century, houses a museum containing numerous works of Picasso, who stayed here for a few months in 1946. Fort Carre, built in the 16th century, overlooks Vieux Port. Nearby Cap D'Antibes is a fashionable resort.

The walled town of **St. Paul de Vence**, set in the hills above the Bay of Angels, is protected by 16th-century ramparts, and can be explored on foot along its winding cobblestone lanes. Near the town entrance are a park and museum, Fondation Maeght, built in 1964 by a Paris art dealer. It houses an array of modern sculpture and paintings.

Nice

Nice (pronounced *nees*), with a population of 350,000, is the major city of the French Riviera. Founded as a Greek colony (Nicea in Latin) in the 5th century BC, the city has endured numerous attacks over the centuries – from pillaging by Saracens in the 9th century to occupation by Mussolini during World War II. At the beginning of the French Revolution in 1789, Nice was a haven for Royalists. Annexed to France to 1793, Nice was restored to Sardinia in 1814, then again ceded to France in 1860 following a plebiscite. Nice became known as the Queen of the Riviera when the British aristocracy began arriving on winter sojourns.

A **Tourist Office** is annexed to the Nice train station, where detailed walking maps and other brochures are available. Nice is a treasure trove of art museums, including the **Musee Chagall** **1** on Boulevard de Cimiez, which houses a collection of 20th-century religious works by the great Russian painter Marc Chagall. **Musee Matisse** **2** (at the top of Nice's Boulevard Cimiez) houses the personal collection of Henri Matisse in a 17th-century Genoese villa surrounded by gardens and set amid Roman ruins. Nearby is the **Franciscan Monastery and Museum** **3**, which illustrates monastic life from the 13th to the 18th century, including a reconstructed chapel and monk's cell.

The four gray marble towers of the **Musee D'Art Moderne** **4**, on the north side of the Old

Town, contains an outstanding collection of works by avant-garde artists from the 1960s to present day. West of the **Old Town**, a few blocks off the Anglais Promenade, is the **Musee Des Beaux-Arts** 5, housed in a late 19th-century mansion built for a Russian princess. Its fine art collection includes paintings by Renoir, Degas and Monet, and ceramics by Picasso. The **Musee D'Art et D'Histoire** 6, with exhibits focusing on the Napoleonic era and the life of locally born general Andre Massena, is housed in the sumptuous Palais Massena, set on grounds overlooking the **Anglais Promenade**.

The Anglais Promenade follows the curving shoreline of the **Baie des Anges** (Bay of Angels), past Nice's fine pebble beach. Originally a wide path, this broad boulevard, decked with flower beds and palm trees, was constructed by an Englishman in 1820 and inaugurated in its final form in 1931 by the Duke of Connaught, one of Queen Victoria's sons. Queen Victoria herself also visited Nice, staying at the luxurious Hotel Victoria. The **Negresco** 7, another palatial hotel of that era – sometimes referred to as the Belle Epoque – was built in 1912 by an

(Above and right) The beautiful buildings of Old Nice. (Below) A beach at Nice. (Bottom) Nice's cruise ship harbor.

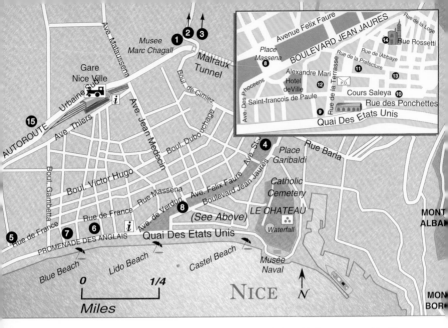

eccentric Romanian named Henry Negresco.

Avenue Jean Medecin, a busy shopping thoroughfare, leads from the train station to **Place Massena** **8**, the city's main square, where gardens lie on either side. From here the waterfront promenade leads past the **Opera House** **9**, built in 1885, to the main entrance of Nice's charming Old Town, which is a maze of narrow pedestrian streets, open-air markets, public squares and outdoor cafes. **Cours Saleya** **10** is the scene of Nice's famous flower market – a daily event except on Mondays when a flea market, complete with antique dealers, takes over this bustling strip. Two streets over, on Rue de la Prefecture, is the former **Royal Palace** **11**, built in the early 17th century to accommodate the visiting Princes of Savoy. A fine 16th century house is located at No. 18, Rue de la Prefecture.

There are also numerous churches to admire in the Old Town, including the baroque interiors of the 18th-century **Eglise St-Francois-de-Paule** **12** and the 17th-century **Eglise St-Giaume** **13**. **La Cathedrale Sainte-Reparate** **14**, built in the 17th century to honor the town's patron saint, overlooks **Place Rosetti** – the center of Old Nice, with restaurants and ice-cream parlors (see photo, page 155).

Rue Rosetti leads from the square up to **Le Chateau** – a hilltop park with an artificial waterfall overlooking Nice. A few sections of the ancient castle walls remain, and the road winds past a Catholic cemetery on its way up the hillside. More panoramic views can be enjoyed west of the Old Town, atop **Mont Alban**, with its 16th-century bastions and watchtowers, and from **Mont Boron** where the hillside homes include Chateau de L'Anglais, a pink-colored Scottish manor. Other unexpected sights in Nice include the onion-shaped cupolas of the **Russian Orthodox Church** **15**, located a few blocks west of the train station.

Villefranche

Villefranche, perfectly situated in between Nice and Monaco, is one of the most picturesque ports in the Mediterranean. Ships anchor outside its small harbor and tender passengers ashore. A tourist information office is located in the small terminal at the head of the harbor. Beside it is the 14th-century **Chapelle St Pierre** – restored and redecorated in 1957 by artist and filmmaker Jean Cocteau, a leader of the French avant-garde movement in the 1920s and author of *Les Enfants* *Terribles*. The nearby **Citadelle** was built by the Duke of Savoy in 1560 and now contains the town hall, museums and gardens. The train station is a 10-minute walk from the harbor along Quai Courbet and up some stairs.

(Above) Villefranche's colorful **waterfront and medieval citadel.**

Monaco

Monaco, an independent principality and coastal enclave within France, is only 370 acres (150 hectares) in size. This tiny kingdom has been ruled by the Grimaldi dynasty since the 13th century, when a Genoese family first seized control of the fortified medieval town, known today as 'the Rock'. When the family's male line died out, the crown's French successor by marriage assumed the name Grimaldi. In 1861 the principality was returned by Sardinia to France and until 1911 the prince of Monaco was an absolute ruler. A 1918 treaty stipulated that the French government must approve the succession to the throne and, should it become vacant, the principality would become an autonomous state under French protection.

Monaco consists of several sections. The business district, called **La Condamine**, is where the train station is located. This area is a pleasing mix of open-air markets and residential streets that lead down to the harbor. La Condamine is flanked on its northeast side by **Monte Carlo**, site of the famous casino, and on its southeast side by **Monaco Ville**, the capital, which is set upon a rocky promontory. Avenue de la Porte Neuve leads off Place D'Armes up to **Place du Palais**, where Monaco's reigning prince resides in a grand Italianate palace. Upon his death in 2005, Rainier III was succeeded by his

Monaco's neo-Romanesque cathedral.

son Albert who, like his father, governs with the assistance of a minister of state (who is traditionally French), a cabinet and the National Council, which is elected every five years. A changing of the guard takes place at the palace entrance every day at five minutes before noon. One wing of the palace, which contains the Musee Napoleon and royal apartments, is open to visitors.

In 1956 Prince Rainier married the American film star Grace Kelly. She arrived for their fairy-tale wedding on board the cruise liner *Constitution* and the famous couple were married in Monaco's neo-Romanesque **cathedral**, built in 1874 to replace the 13th-century Church of St. Nicholas. The cathedral is also the burial place of Princess Grace (Gratia Patricia on her tombstone) who died in a tragic automobile accident in 1982.

Avenue St. Martin leads from Monaco's cathedral to the **Oceanographic Museum**, founded by Rainier's great-grand-father, Prince Albert, in 1910. The underwater explorer and filmmaker Jacques Cousteau was the former head of this important research institute, which employs

(Above) Port Hercule, Monaco. (Below) A sentry at Place du Palais, Monaco-Ville (bottom).

(Above) Monte Carlo's casino.

(Below) Street in Monaco-Ville.

a staff of scientists. On display are Cousteau's diving equipment and Prince Albert's collection of seashells. Outside the museum, a small tourist train called the 'Azur Express' departs on regular circuits of Monaco-Ville and **Place du Casino** in Monte Carlo.

Monte Carlo's world-famous casino, which opened in 1858, came under the control of Greek shipping magnate Aristotle Onassis in 1954, when he became the principal stockholder of the company controlling the casino. Rainier, however, managed to thwart Onassis's efforts to gain control of Monaco's Societe de Bains de Mer (SBM), which oversees the principality's major hotels and enterprises, including the gambling casino.

By 1962 Monaco had become a tax haven for French citizens and, at the insistence of France, a new constitution was created. Only

A courtyard in Aix-en-Provence.

PROVENCE

about 2,500 of Monaco's 30,000 residents are citizens (Monegasques) and they are not admitted to the gambling casino; neither are visitors wearing improper attire, such as shorts, sandals, tennis shoes, jogging suits, jeans or beach attire. The casino opens at noon and charges an entrance fee. All hand bags and cameras must be checked, and a passport is required if you win over a certain sum of money (approximately US$400). The Casino complex, a dazzling display of gold-leaf and gilt, includes an opera house and private rooms reserved for high rollers.

The entrance to the Casino faces the gardens and fountain of Place du Casino, which is also overlooked by the palatial Hotel de Paris, where Alain Ducasse's **Louis XV** restaurant enjoys a three-star Michelin rating. On the opposite side of Place du Casino is the historic **Cafe de Paris**, a lovely spot to have lunch at a reasonable price.

Inspired by its luminous landscapes and sun-soaked colors, the Dutch painter **Vincent Van Gogh** called Provence a 'kingdom of light'. This is a land of white limestone cliffs and cobalt blue skies, of yellow sunflowers and ochre earth. The Rhone flows across Provence's western plain, its flat river delta lying in contrast to the rolling hills and mountain ridges which rise in the east and stretch northward from the Mediterranean coast to the French Alps. The countryside is clothed in vineyards and dotted with medieval villages, their winding streets too narrow for cars, their weathered stone houses adorned with painted shutters and window boxes filled with flowers.

The Romans marched through this landscape and made it a province of Rome in the 2nd century BC. They built roads and bridges, amphitheaters and public baths. By the 4th century AD, the region had become a haven for Christian monasteries. The

Middle Ages was a time of invasion – by the Visigoths, the Franks and the Arabs. Then, in 879, the Count of Arles gained control of the region and, from 933 until bequeathed to the French crown in 1481, Provence became part of the Kingdom of Arles. In the 14th century, a series of French-born popes moved the Catholic Church's headquarters from Rome to **Avignon**, on the banks of the Rhone, where a beautiful Gothic papal palace was built and fine wines were produced at the nearby village of Chateauneuf-du-Pape.

Flowers, fruits and vegetables all flourish in the fertile Rhone valley, and when Van Gogh arrived at **Arles** from Paris in 1888, he came in search of sensual beauty. Both he and **Paul Gauguin** had

(Left) The Night Cafe by Van Gogh. (Below) Marseille's city hall.

rejected industrial society and were drawn to the pastoral life of Provence. Yet, the two artists found little peace at Van Gogh's house in Arles. Their heated quarrels climaxed with Van Gogh threatening Gauguin with a razor, then cutting off his own ear in a state of deep remorse and temporary insanity.

Gauguin left Provence, but Van Gogh remained in Arles, painting his famous series of sunflowers as well as *The Night Cafe* and *The Public Gardens* in Arles. He was eventually confined in the Arles Hospital, and later in the asylum at Saint-Remy where in 1889 he painted *Starry Night*. Meanwhile, **Paul Cezanne** was living in near isolation outside **Aix-en-Provence**, his home town and the historic capital of Provence. Discouraged by ridicule from the critics, he too had fled Paris and the industrial north, returning to his place of birth. Working in seclusion, Cezanne developed his own style while painting vivid scenes of the bright outdoors. He repeatedly painted the craggy peak of Mont Ste-Victoire, showing the surrounding countryside devoid of human presence.

Both Van Gogh and Cezanne were intensely emotional painters, their art a tour de force of color and movement. They often painted scenes of the countryside, yet the nearby Mediterranean Sea was a pervasive presence. In Van Gogh's *Wheat Field and Cypress Trees*, the fields resemble a stormy sea and the hills rise like waves into a turbulent sky of swirling clouds.

Notre Dame de la Garde overlooks Marseille's Old Port.

Marseille

The sea is what brought the Ancient Greeks to the shores of Provence in 600 BC. Arriving from Asia Minor, they established a colony called Massalia, which the French now call Marseille, and this famous seaport soon dominated the Mediterranean coast for miles in either direction. It thrived during the Roman Empire and throughout the Crusades, and was incorporated into the Kingdom of France in 1481, growing steadily until the time of the French Revolution, which began in 1789. The Revolution's battle hymn originated in Marseille, where volunteer fighters marched to the army song *La Marseillaise*.

Palais de la Bourse now houses Marseille's maritime museum.

Marseille's maritime commerce eventually suffered during the long Napoleonic wars and the city rejoiced at the downfall of Napoleon at the battle of Waterloo. Prosperity returned with the French conquest of Algeria and the opening of the Suez Canal in 1869.

Today Marseille is one of the world's great seaports, its commerce fed by the rich hinterlands of Provence. The oldest city in France, and the country's second largest with a population surpassing one million, Marseille is connected with Arles and the Rhone Valley by a canal. Situated on the Gulf of Lions, Marseille forms a famous sight when approached from the sea, its gleaming white buildings nestled on a semi-circle of barren hills. The bay contains several islands, including a small rocky islet upon which the **Chateau d'If** was built in 1524 and used as a state prison, made famous by Alexandre Dumas's novel, *The Count of Monte Cristo*. Several forts protect the Vieux Port (Old Port), and the church of **Notre-Dame de la Garde** stands on a ridge overlooking the harbor, its steeple surmounted by a gilded statue of the Virgin Mary. Inside are the votive offerings of seamen for the protection Our Lady extends to mariners.

On Your Own

The cruise ships dock north of the city centre, with most providing a shuttle service into **Vieux Port**, which is situated a half mile from the train station. Notre-Dame de la Garde can be reached by bus or on foot – it's a half-mile hike up Boulevard Tellene, followed by a

Shore Excursions *Marseille*

Ship-organized excursions include city tours of Marseille and day trips to other parts of Provence, such as **Les Baux**, a medieval town carved out of white limestone atop a huge plateau, its Citadelle providing panoramic views of the valley below. Another interesting stop is **Arles**, its Roman remains including a theatre and an arena built in the 2nd century AD, that provided seating for 26,000 spectators and is now used for staging bullfights. **Avignon** is also covered by ship shore excursions, as is the fishing village of **Cassis**, east of Marseille, where the dramatic coastline consists of white-stone cliffs, craggy coves and sweeping sea views. Cassis is stunningly situated at the base of Europe's highest cliff – the 1,300-foot **Cap Canaille** – and is now a summer resort and sojourn for painters.

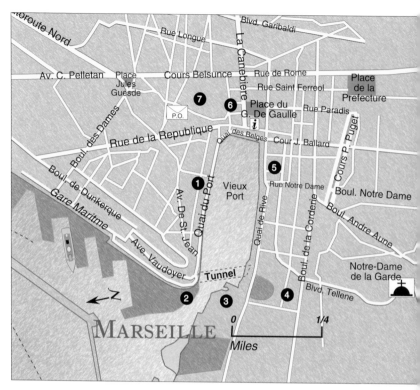

steep flight of steps. Passenger ferries run regularly from the head of Vieux Port to Chateau d'If – a 90-minute trip. Taxis are available for hire at the cruise ship pier – standard fares include 15 euros to the train station and 50 euros for a two-hour drive up to the Notre-Dame de la Garde.

Trains run regularly from Marseille to other Provencal cities and towns, one of the best-preserved being **Aix-en-Provence**, a 40-minute train ride from Marseille. First-time visitors to Marseille should consider taking the train to lovely Aix-en-Provence, where numerous attractions and inviting restaurants are within walking distance of the train station. Plan to return

by train to Marseille in plenty of time to stroll the city's historic Vieux Port before taking the shuttle back to your ship.

Marseille Attractions

Busy and brash, Marseille is first and foremost a port city, its historical heart residing in the Vieux Port – a harbor filled with fishing boats and sailing yachts. The Tourism Office is located at the head of the harbor and the 17th-century **Hotel de Ville (City Hall)** stands on its north side. Behind it, housed in a 16th-century mansion, is the Musee du Vieux Marseille.

Fort Saint-Jean and Bas **Fort Saint-Nicolas** guard the harbor entrance, which can be tra-

(Above) Place d'Albertas in Aix-en-Provence. (Below) Flower market at Place de L'Hotel de Ville in Aix.

versed by an underwater tunnel that surfaces on the north side near the city's neo-Byzantine cathedral. On the harbor's south side is the 13th-century Romanesque **church of St. Victor** [4], with 14th-century fortifications. The church's door (circa 1140) is one of the oldest in France, and downstairs the crypts include 5th-century ruins and stela, as well as sculptures dating from the 4th to the 12th century. Also on the harbor's south side is the **Place Thiars** [5] pedestrian zone, an inviting neighborhood of outdoor cafes.

The city's main avenue, running eastward from the harbor, is Rue Canebiere – named for the old ropewalks that used to operate along its length when ships' lines were made of hemp (called *cannebe* in the Provencal dialect). On Rue Canebiere's north side, housed in the **Palais de la Bourse** [6], is the city's maritime museum, which contains a fine library and a large collection of paintings, drawings and plans. Behind this large white building is the **Jardin des Vestiges** [7], a public park containing excavated ruins of Greek and Roman buildings and a small museum (Musee de L'Histoire de Marseille) featuring a 60-foot Roman boat.

Leading south from Rue Canebiere are Marseille's most fashionable **shopping streets** – Rue Paradis, Rue Saint Ferreol, Rue de Rome and Boulevard Garibaldi. Boulevard d'Athenes, leading off the

Cathedral of Saint-Sauveur.

north side of Rue Cannebiere, is a direct route to the train station (Gare Saint-Charles). About a half-mile east of the train station, at the top of Longchamp Boulevard, is the **Palais de Longchamp 8** built in 1860 by Henri Esperandieu, who also designed Notre-Dame de la Garde. This monumental palace, adorned with fountains and gardens, holds an art gallery and museum.

Aix en Provence

The capital of Provence since the 12th century (except when replaced by Arles), Aix was founded in 123 BC by the Romans near the site of some mineral springs. A popular spa town, its university was founded in 1409, after which Aix became a centre of literature and music, and a sojourn for painters. Students make up nearly a quarter of its population of 160,000, and the town's main attractions are easily explored on foot.

Avenue Victor Hugo leads from the train station to Place Gal De Gaulle, where the local tourist office is located. It overlooks **La Rotonde**, a huge traffic circle with a fountain in its center. Leading eastward off La Rotonde is **Cours Mirabeau**, the town's main avenue. On its south side are streets lined with 18th-century baroque mansions; on its north side are narrow medieval streets with shops, cafes and various attrac-

tions, such as **Place d'Albertas**
 where you can admire the
sculpted facade of the Hotel
d'Albertas (1707), and the nearby
Hotel Boyer d'Eguilles (1675),
which now houses the Museum
d'Histoire Naturelle. City hall
and a 16th-century belfry overlook the square at **Place de
l'Hotel de Ville 2** where a
bustling flower and produce market is held several mornings each
week. Other places of interest
include the 13th-century
Cathedral of Saint-Sauveur 3;
and the formal French gardens
and 17th-century mansion at
Vendome Pavilion 4.

While strolling the scenic
streets of Aix you will notice
bronze studs on the pavement
stamped with the letter 'C' –
these symbolize the footsteps of
Cezanne and mark historic places
associated with the great artist (a

brochure of this signposted tour is
available at the Tourist Office).
His studio, located off avenue
Pasteur on avenue Paul-Cezanne,
has been preserved as the Musee-
Atelier de Paul Cezanne.

Sete

The scenic fishing port of Sete,
canals crisscrossing its lower
town, is situated in the
Languedoc region of southern
France. The region's name
derives from a medieval dialect –
langue d'oc – that was spoken
throughout the south of France
back when the counts of Toulouse
ruled this former Roman
province, their brilliant court a
center of literature that attracted
troubadours.

Sete is a port of access to the
nearby medieval cities of
Carcassonne and **Montpellier**,
the latter's old quarter of winding
streets and squares dating to the
8th century. Montpellier's
famous university was founded in
the 13th century, and outside the
city are country chateaux overlooking estate wineries.

Carcassonne is home to an
impressive hill-top fortress, considered one of Europe's architectural marvels. The hill was fortified by the Romans in the 1st century BC and the towers (still
intact) were built in the 6th century, with fortifications added by
the viscounts of Carcassonne in
the 12th century. The ramparts
had fallen into disrepair when
restored in the 1800s.

A pedestrian street in medieval
Bonifacio, Corsica.

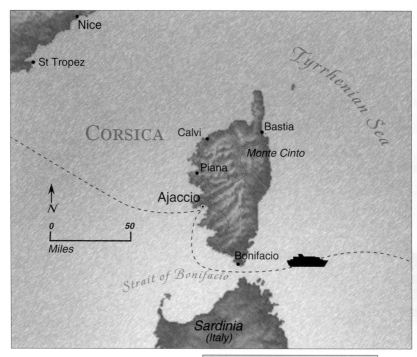

Corsica

The mountainous and sparesly populated island of Corsica was described by Balzac as a "French island basking in the Italian sun." Much of the island is wild, the ground covered with an undergrowth of flowers called Maquis. The fragrance of these wildflowers wafts far out to sea, prompting sailors to call Corsica the Scented Isle. It is also referred to as 'the mountain in the sea' with summits exceeding 6,000 feet, the peaks of which are often snow-covered much of the year. Monte Cintu approaches 9,000 feet, making Corsica the highest Mediterranean island.

The Romans first set sail for Corsica in the 3rd century BC. Their rule ended in the 5th centu-

Shore Excursions *Corsica*

Ship-organized excursions vary, depending on which port your ship pulls into. Generally speaking, these include scenic drives to various sites around the island, such as the Calanches, the megalithic ruins at Filitosa, the ancient Greek village of Cargese, and the medieval village of Sartene. One or two places are visited on a 4-hour tour, such as the Prunelli Gorges and the artificial lake of Tolla, which provides hydroelectric power to the island. Longer, 8-hour tours include lunch. Walking tours of Ajaccio and Bonifacio are each about 3 hours, as is a vist to the European Tortoises Protection Center, created in 1985 and now home to over 150 species of turtles and tortoises from all over the world.

The town of Piana overlooks Corsica's scenic west coast.

ry AD, and throughout the ensuing centuries the island changed hands numerous times. By the mid-15th century the island was under Genoese control and the port city of **Ajaccio** was established in 1492. But public unrest, fueled by the harsh and unpopular Genoese rulers, led to rebellions and often bloodshed.

In 1755, Pasquale Paoli led a successful revolt and became president under a republican constitution. By this time Genoa was weary of battling the Corsicans and in 1768 the island was sold to France. Soon defeated by the French, Paoli fled to England where his friend James Boswell introduced him into the circle of Samuel Johnson. That same year, 1769, Napoleon Bonaparte was born of a middle class family in Ajaccio. The outbreak of the French Revolution brought Paoli back to Corsica, where he was appointed governor in 1791. Accused of counter-revolutionary activities and summoned to Paris in 1793, Paoli drew on British support to expel the French from Corsica. Declaring itself a British protectorate, the Corsican national assembly bypassed Paoli for another Corsican when choosing a chief of the council of state. Paoli made his final departure for England in 1795 and the following year Corsica was recovered by the French under Napoleon.

World War II brought more invasions, this time by Italian and German troops, who were expelled in 1943. A post-war exodus prompted the French government to stimulate economic development, but the island's separatist sentiment carried on into the 1970s and '80s with occasional bombings and protests.

Attractions in Ajaccio, the capital, include the Maison Bonaparte, where Napoleon was born and raised; the Salon Napoleonien (in the Hotel de Ville), which displays memorabilia of the emperor; and the Musee d'Histoire de la Corse,

THE BONAPARTES

Napoleon's father, Carlo Bonaparte, was a nobleman and lawyer who lived with his wife and large family in Ajaccio and sent his sons to be educated in France. Initially a supporter of the Corsican patriot Pasquale Paoli, Bonaparte changed sides in 1769 and became a leader of the pro-French party in Corsica. When civil war broke out in 1793, Carlo and his family were condemned for opposing Corsican independence and they fled the island. Upon becoming emperor of France, Napoleon named his brothers and sisters as titled heads of Europe and arranged politically advantageous marriages for them. But his siblings resisted many of Napoleon's wishes and resented being left out of the line of succession, their bitterness fostering ongoing scenarios of intrigue, exile and reconciliation.

Napoleon Bonaparte

with exhibits on Corsica's military history. The 16th-century cathedral contains the marble font used for Napoleon's baptism. The Fesch Museum displays works by Botticelli, Veronese and Titiano.

North of Ajaccio, near the coastal towns of **Porto** and **Piana**, is the UNESCO-protected site of the **Calanches**, which takes its name from *calanca* – the Corsican word for inlet. Unusual patterns of erosion here have created fantastic cliffs and pinnacles of red granite rock. Hour-long boat excursions depart daily from Porto to view the Calanches, and cost about 18 euros.

Bonifacio, the oldest town of Corsica, is medieval in character. Founded in 828 on the site of a citadel built by Boniface I, Count of Tuscany, the town is situated atop a limestone cliff overlooking the harbor, and is surrounded by a rampart complete with drawbridge. The 12th-century Pisan-style church dates from Pisa's ownership of Corsica before losing the island to Genoa. The coast of Sardinia lies just seven miles across the Strait of Bonifacio.

Bonifacio began as a clifftop citadel overlooking the harbor.

CHAPTER FOUR

NORTHERN ITALY

I taly lies in the heart of the Mediterranean. The north of the country is rooted in Europe while its southern shores stretch, like a bridge, toward the coast of Africa. Many an ancient mariner has landed on Italy's rugged shores, and the eventual rise of Rome turned the Mediterranean into a Roman lake which they called Mare Nostrum ('our sea'). When Rome fell, the northern cities of Genoa, Pisa and Venice emerged as great sea powers and rival city-states. Then came the Italian Renaissance, born in Florence in the early 1400s, and beauty became the byword of Italy. Glorious churches, grand palaces and landscaped gardens were built. Marble fountains and statues soon adorned the squares, and a sense of style became an Italian birthright.

The outpouring of artistry that began with the Renaissance spilled over into all areas of Italian life. Opera flourished in the 19th century, followed by film making and high fashion in the 20th century. Italy is also a leader in cruise ship design and its famous Fincantieri shipyard near Venice is one of the busiest in the world, launching ships that are technologically advanced and stylishly appointed.

The country's creative force, fuelled throughout the centuries by political turmoil and military conflicts, has been described by the art historian Bernard Berenson as "the intensification of life." Visitors come to Italy to see the ancient ruins and famous works of art, and soon find all of their senses awakened. While pausing to enjoy a glass of Chianti wine or a freshly brewed cappuccino, they find themselves listening to animated conversations spoken in a language that rolls eloquently off the tongue, and they begin to notice the touches of beauty around them – whether it's a flower box beneath a baroque window or the pleasing arrangement of umbrella tables at an outdoor cafe. This sense of living each moment in a state of beauty, this is the Italian style.

Italy at a Glance

About 58 million people live in Italy, and the faith of the majority is Roman Catholic, the state religion. Italian, spoken in regional dialects, is the major language and English is widely understood. The country, proclaimed a republic in 1946, consists of twenty diverse regions which were unified in 1870. Vatican City and San Marino are independent enclaves. The industrial north has always been more prosperous than the agricultural south which, for centuries, languished under French and Spanish rule. Much of Italy is mountainous or hilly and the country's combination of striking scenery, mild climate, ancient ruins, artistic treasures and a vibrant culture makes it one of the world's most popular tourist destinations.

Travel Tips

Currency: The unit of currency is the euro. American currency is widely accepted but local currency is needed for trains, buses, casual dining, museums and other tourist attractions. Most shops and formal restaurants accept credit cards.

Dining: Italian food and wine is highly touted and can be enjoyed in a variety of settings. Bars, open all day, serve alco-

A trattoria in Venice.

holic drinks, rolls, coffee and small sandwiches. There is a service charge for sitting at a table, which is why patrons often stand at the bar. Other casual eateries are: *panineria* (sandwich bar); *tavola calda* (fast-food restaurant); *pizzeria* (specializing in pizza); *rosticceria* (take-out) and *gelateri* (ice-cream parlor). A *trattoria* is an informal restaurant while a *ristorante* offers formal, unhurried dining. Most restaurants serve lunch from noon to 2:30 p.m.; dinner is from 7 p.m. to 10 p.m. or later.

Opening Hours: Museums, galleries and historic sites are often closed on Monday, sometimes Tuesday, but this can vary from region to region, and from museum to museum. Daily hours are generally 9 a.m. to 1:30 p.m., although some stay open longer. Most churches are open daily for non-religious visits from 10 a.m. to 5 p.m. except on Sunday when the public is welcome from 1:30 to 4:30 p.m.

Shopping: Stores are generally open from 9 a.m. to 1 p.m. and from 4 p.m. to 8 p.m. Many stay open late on Saturday evening, and are closed on Sunday and Monday morning. Stores catering to tourists often stay open all day, every day. Bartering is not acceptable, except at open-air markets.

Taxi fares: Rates are approximately 27 euros (US$35) per hour. Some taxi drivers will accept US currency.

Telephone Access Codes: AT&T 172-1011; MCI 172-1022; SPRINT 172-1877; CANADA DIRECT 172-1001.

Italian Riviera

The Italian Riviera, extending from La Spezia to the French border, is an international playground of fashionable resorts, hotels and villas. It was once a secluded coast of craggy coves and tree-clad hillsides where medieval monasteries and tiny fishing ports, their colorful houses built by fishermen and lace makers, led a quiet existence. Today these hidden harbor are among the most picturesque ports of the Riviera.

Best known is **Portofino**, where summer villas, tucked among the umbrella pine and cypress trees, overlook a harbor filled with luxury yachts at the height of the season. The small cruise ships pull right into port, but the larger ships anchor out in the bay and tender their passengers ashore. A haunt of the rich and famous, Portofino is notoriously expensive, but a very pleasant place to stroll and soak up the atmosphere. From the main square overlooking the harbor it's an easy hike up to the **Castello di**

Cruise ships anchor off Portofino (above and below), a resort town on the Italian Riviera.

San Giorgio (Fort of St. George), built in the mid-1500s, where you can enjoy excellent views. Just beyond the fort is the church of San Giorgio, said to contain relics of St. George brought back from the Holy Land. Another path leads from the village to the lighthouse at **Punta del Capo**.

A charming way to visit Portofino's neighboring seaside villages is by boat. In addition to **ship-organized boating excursions**, a network of **local ferry** services connects these small ports. They include the resort of **Camogli**, founded by seafarers, and the medieval Benedictine monastery of **San Fruttuoso**, which is situated on a secluded cove around the headland from Portofino. In the other direction from Portofino is the resort town of **Santa Margherita Ligure**, with its elegant shops and lively cafes, and nearby **Rapallo**, another charming resort with a beach promenade, boutiques and cafes.

Trains run regularly between Camogli, Santa Margherita Ligure and Rapallo. The rail line bypasses Portofino, which is located two miles from Santa Margherita (about a US$15 taxi ride).

About 25 miles south of Rapallo is **Cinque Terre** national park, where five villages cling to coastal cliffs and are accessible only by boat, with tours departing regularly from **La Spezia**.

Genoa

Italy's chief seaport, Genoa is one of the busiest in the western Mediterranean with its fine natural harbor and modern port facilities. Historic attractions are concentrated in the city center, and can be **explored independently** on foot. The nearby **Italian Riviera** ports of Camogli, San Fruttuoso and Portofino can be reached by **mini-cruises** from Genoa's harbor.

Via XX Settembre and Via Luccoli, with their range of boutiques, are two of Genoa's most exclusive **shopping** streets. Via Orefici is lined with goldsmiths, and the market in Piazza Banchi is a good place to buy leather, silver and ceramic handicrafts.

A seaport since ancient times, Genoa's powerful navy drove the Arabs from Corsica and Sardinia, with the aid of Pisa, in the 10th century. Pisa and Genoa then battled one another over control of Sardinia, with Genoa eventually triumphing in 1284.

Genoa's wealth and power continued to expand until the city,

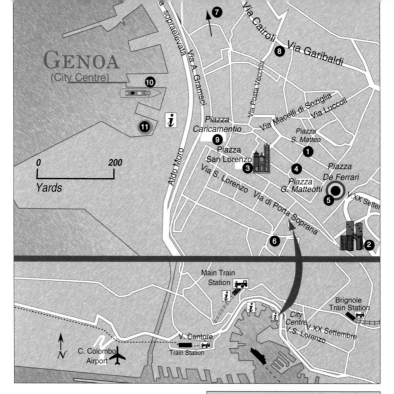

GENOA
(City Centre)

0   200
Yards

called *La Superba* (The Proud), clashed with the trading interests of Venice. Subsequent wars with Venice led to a weakening of Genoa until, in the early 1500s, the naval hero **Andrea Doria** set up a republican state and established the Doria family as rulers of Genoa. His family home is located in the lovely **Piazza San Matteo** (1), in the heart of Genoa's medieval quarter and his tomb is in the church of San Matteo, which dates from the 12th century.

The other famous mariner associated with Genoa is **Christopher Columbus**. Born Cristoforo Colombo in 1451 to a family of wool weavers, he grew up illiterate and helped his father at the loom before heading to sea as a young lad. He served as a seaman in the Mediterranean but his ambi-

Shore Excursions   *Genoa*

Ship excursions include:
• A city walking tour (3-4 hours) which includes a visit to the 16th-century Palazzo Ducale and Columbus's House
• A tour of the art galleries housed in elegant palazzos along Via Garibaldi
• A boat or bus ride to Portofino (4-5 hrs, about $75)
• A motorcoach drive to Milan (about 10 hrs)
• Harbor cruise and visit to the Aquarium of Genoa (4 hrs)

tions would eventually take him far away from his childhood home, located at the base of **Porta Soprana** (2). This medieval gate, built as a defensive rampart in the 12th century, stands at the old entrance to the Roman road that led through Genoa.

Other historic highlights in Genoa's medieval section of steep, narrow alleys (called *caruggi*) are the 12th-century **Cathedral of San Lorenzo** (3), built of black and white marble, and the nearby **Palazzo Ducale (palace of the doges)** (4), built in the 16th century. The Teatro Carlo Felice and Academy of Fine Arts overlook **Piazza De Ferrari** (5).

Churches of note include **San Donato** (6), a 12th-century Romanesque building, and the 16th-century baroque church of the **Santissima Annunziata** (7). **Via Garibaldi** is lined with Renaissance palaces built by

Genoese nobility, their frescoed rooms now housing several art galleries, including the collection in **Palazzo Rosso (Red Palace)** (8), which displays works by Titian, Veronese, Rubens and the Flemish painter Van Dyck, who once lived there.

The **Palazzo San Giorgio** (9), overlooking the harbor and now housing the Genoa Port Authority, was built in part with masonry taken from Venice. When 7,000 Venetians were captured at the naval battle of Curzola in 1298, among them was Marco Polo, who dictated his book *Il Milion* while a prisoner in this palace. A large and modern **aquarium** (10), which opened in 1992, is located on the harbor, along with the **Bigo elevator** – a lift which takes visitors to the top of a mast-like structure (erected in 1992 for Columbus Quincentennial events) for great views of this seafaring city.

Savona, 25 miles west of Genoa, is a base port for Costa Cruises, which began as a shipping company founded in the 1800s by the Costa family of Genoa.

Childhood home of Christopher Columbus (left). Bigo elevator in Genoa's harbor (below).

Venice (Venezia)

The view of St. Mark's Square as your ship pulls into port.

Venice, one of world's most beautiful and unique cities, is a living watercolor. Built on 118 alluvial islets within a lagoon in the Gulf of Venice, it began as a small fishing settlement in the 5th century AD, when refugees of the Roman Empire, fleeing the Lombard invaders of Northern Italy, sought safety on these uninhabited islands. The first settlers built huts on the mud banks and dug deep ditches for mooring their boats – the origin of Venice's modern canal system which now includes more than 100 narrow canals crossed by some 400 footbridges. In 697, these fishing communities organized themselves under a doge (derived from the Latin word *dux* = leader) and began to engage in seaborne trade.

The port grew rapidly and by the 9th century it had become the city of Venice, its prosperity making it a target of Dalmatian pirates. This prompted the Venetians to build castellated houses for protection and guard the canal entrances with chains. However, as the pirate attacks increased in frequency, the Venetians responded by arming their ships. The newly born Venetian Navy defeated the Dalmatian pirates in the year 1000, and this important victory was thereafter commemorated with great pomp on Ascension Day, with the doge's gilded galley participating in the 'wedding of the sea' ceremony, which symbolizes the marriage of the doges with the Adriatic.

The Crusades brought great wealth to Venice, her fleet transporting Christian armies to the Holy Land. In 1204 the doge Dandolo led the Fourth Crusade's storming of Constantinople, looting it of treasures. By 1216 the Venetian empire included strategic islands in the Ionian, Aegean and eastern Mediterranean, and the city's native son and world traveler Marco Polo embodied the enterprising spirit of the

Venetians. As wealth poured into Venice, its patrician merchants formed an oligarchy that maintained a tight hold on its political power through a secret police and Council of Ten, instituted to punish those who committed crimes against the state.

Venice became the envy of Genoa, a rival republic, and the two maritime powers battled for supremacy with Venice eventually emerging victorious in the late 1300s to become the Christian world's leading maritime state. It controlled all of Venetia on the mainland and, with a mighty shipbuilding arsenal, was known as the Queen of the Seas. Venice's slow decline began in the mid 15th-century when its lucrative eastern trade was threatened by the fall of Constantinople to the Turks and by the discovery of an all-sea trade route to India and China around the Cape of Good Hope. Much of

Venice's seagoing trade fell into the hands of the Portuguese, Dutch and English, but the city remained a force to be reckoned with, and it reached its artistic glory during the Renaissance with large-scale construction of churches and palaces. Venice became a city of color and light, its buildings designed by famous architects and embellished by artists such as Titian and Tintoretto.

Venice also shone musically. Monteverdi, the first great figure of opera, was appointed choirmaster of St. Mark's in 1613 and Venice's first public opera house opened in 1637. Antonio Vivaldi, whose father was a violinist at St. Mark's, also lived in Venice in the early 1700s – teaching, playing the violin and writing music.

The 18th century was a period of economic and political decline for Venice, the city's decadence personified in the Venetian adventurer Casanova who supported himself by writing, gambling and seducing women. Venice's upper class indulged in a social life of nightly theatergoing and gambling at the casino, their sexual dalliances often taking place in private boxes at the opera or inside parked gondolas.

In 1797, Venice fell without a fight to Napoleon's forces and was transferred by treaty to Austrian rule under which the city chafed for several decades. Meanwhile, opera continued to thrive, with Rossini premiering the first of a string of comic operas in Venice in 1810. Italy's foremost composer of opera, Giuseppe Verdi, also premiered a number of his works in Venice amid an atmosphere of

Marco Polo
Tessera Airport

Burano

Mestre

Murano

Venice

Lido

Alberoni

Laguna Veneta

Gulf of Venice

Venice
and
Area

0   12

Miles

N

Choggia

tolerance and freedom of expression, and the great German operatic composer Richard Wagner spent his final days in Venice, where he died in 1883. By then Venice had expelled the Austrians and was united with the new kingdom of Italy.

Some Venetians still long for a return to their city's golden era of independence. Calling themselves Soldiers of the Most Serene Republic of Venice, this fringe political group staged an extraordinary, predawn separatist stunt in May 1997, when eight men stormed the bell tower in St. Mark's Square. A few people were still sipping wine and chatting at one of the square's cafes when a canal ferry docked at the piazzetta and disembarked a ramshackle truck carrying armed men wearing ski masks. They headed straight for the doors of the bell tower, reappearing minutes later on its balcony near the top, where they unfurled the golden pennant with the lion of Saint Mark. The incident ended without a shot being fired when police arrived to recapture the landmark tower.

Secessionist politics are likely the least of Venetians' concerns. Venice, as everyone knows, is slowly sinking. The city is built on sand, silt and hard clay (which tend to compact over time) and some mainland industries have exacerbated the problem by lowering the area's underground water table, as well as polluting the lagoon. Meanwhile, a shortage of affordable housing has prompted residents to move out of Venice. Thousands of workers commute each day to the city, which is con-

Narrow, winding canals criss-cross the enchanting city of Venice

nected to the mainland (2-1/2 miles away) by a rail-and-highway bridge. Many worry that Venice no longer belongs to Venetians, but to tourists and absentee owners who spend little time in their vacation palazzos. Yet, despite the summer tourists and winter floods, this golden city of the seas will no doubt endure, as it has for more than a thousand years.

On Your Own

Venice, compact and free of motor vehicle traffic, is an intimate city and a delight to explore **on foot**. Narrow lanes (*calles*) lead to hidden squares (*campos*) and across the arched footbridges that span the side canals (*rios*). It's easy to become momentarily lost amid the maze of back streets and winding waterways that lead off the Grand Canal, but the bell tower of St. Mark's Square is usually visible above the surrounding roofs. Most ships dock overnight in Venice, so passengers have the opportunity to explore the city at their leisure.

By water is an ideal way to see Venice, and there's nothing more romantic than a **gondola ride** – especially at night when the city's timeless magic is enhanced by the watery reflection of dancing lights and voices echoing down quiet side canals. Hiring a gondola is fairly expensive, with a half-hour ride costing about US$50. Less expensive is a *traghetto*, a two-man gondola that ferries people across the Grand Canal at various, sign-posted places. The most popular and reasonably priced mode of transport is to hop on and off the motorized river boats (called *vaporetti*) that are part of the city's water bus service. They run the length of the Grand Canal, making frequent stops along the way. It's a short walk from the cruise terminal to **Piazzale Roma** where a ticket

An intriguing aspect of Venice is found along the back streets and small canals of the city.

can be purchased at the ACTV booth for a ride along the complete length of the Grand Canal to St. Mark's Square. (A map and water bus schedule is available at the Tourist Information Office located just west of the St. Mark's Piazzetta.) The cruise ships usually provide their passengers with a reasonably-priced shuttle service that runs regularly between the ship and a drop-off point east of St. Mark's Square. Private water taxis can also be hired.

The city's water bus service also provides transport to other islands in the lagoon, such as **San Michele** (the city's cemetery), **Murano** (famous for glass making since the 13th century) and **Burano** (a colorful fishing village and lace-making centre).

Venice's main **shopping** area lies between the Rialto Bridge and Piazza San Marco, where shops and cafes border the square. Fine shops featuring handcrafted carnival masks can be found on **Calle dei Fabbri**. Other local crafts include glassware and lace

Venice Attractions:

St. Mark's Square (Piazza of San Marco) is the central meeting place of Venice and one of Italy's most beautiful squares, dominated by the splendor of **St. Mark's Cathedral** ■. Begun in 1063 and modeled after the Church of the Holy Apostles in Constantinople, this 'Golden Basilica' is an outstanding example of Byzantine architecture. It follows the Greek cross plan, with each arm of the cross

---

MUST SEE:

St. Mark's Square – view it from the ship as you enter Venice, then return by boat for a close look at its famous buildings.
The Grand Canal – board a vaporetti at Piazzale Roma and ride the canal's entire length to St. Mark's Square.
Explore **Venice's back streets** and narrow waterways – on foot and (briefly) by gondola.

---

emphasized by a dome encased with gilt copper sheet and topped with an ornate lantern, making it visible from a distance and serving as a landmark for seafarers. The church's ornate facade consists of clusters of marble pillars and arches containing golden mosaics which glitter in the late afternoon sun. Gold is the dominant decorative element inside the cathedral, its walls completely

---

Shore Excursions *Venice*

Ship excursions feature gondola and canal boat rides, as well as visits to various churches and art galleries. Boat tours to the neighboring islands of Murano and Burano (4-5 hrs, about $75) to their highly regarded glass and lace factories are also featured. These tours often include a gondola ride and tours of the Doge's Palace or St. Mark's Basilica. Special evening excursions include a serenaded gondola ride or a boat ride along the Grand Canal to St. Mark's Square for a special guided tour of the Basilica (which is closed to the public in the evening). For detail on specific shore excursions offered by your cruise line, visit its website or refer to the booklet provided with your cruise documents.

VENICE

ST. MARK'S SQUARE

St. Mark's Square

1, 2, 3, 4, 5, 6, 7, 8, 9, 10

WC

WC

i

CITY ATTRACTIONS

(1) St. Mark's Cathedral
(2) Doges' Palace
(3) Bridge of Sighs
(4) Clock Tower
(5) Old Law Courts
(6) Napoleonic Wing
(7) New Law Courts
(8) Campanile (Bell Tower)
(9) Old Library
(10) Piazzetta
(11) Church of San Giorgio Maggiore
(12) Santa Maria Gloriosa dei Frari
(13) San Zaccaria

(14) Santa Maria della Salute
(15) Palazzo Loredan
(16) Ca' d'Oro (House of Gold)
(17) Palazzo Vendramin-Calergi
(18) Palazzo Grimani
(19) Ca'Pesaro
(20) Palazzo Rezzonico
(21) Gallery of the Academia
(22) P. Guggenheim Art Collection
(23) Scuola di San Rocco
(24) Rialto Bridge
(25) Harry's Bar
(26) Gritti Palace

N

Miles
0   1/2

San Michele

San Marco Canal

Is. S. Giorgio Maggiore

Basin of San Marco

Giudecca Canal

Isola della Giudecca

Grand Canal

San Polo

San Marco

Dorsoduro

Santa Croce

Rialto Bridge

Accademia Bridge

Calle dei Fabbri

St. Mark's Square

See above

Stazione di S. Lucia

Piazzale Roma

Cruise Terminal

MAINLAND

covered with mosaics from the 12th to 18th centuries. Entrance to the church is free but there is a fee to enter the Sanctuary, which contains the tomb of St. Mark and the gem-encrusted Golden Altarpiece, and the Museum, which houses four gilded bronze horses. These Greek sculptures from the 4th and 3rd centuries BC were brought to Venice from Constantinople in 1204 and were originally displayed on the church's outside gallery, where replicas now stand.

The **Doges' Palace (Palazzo Ducal)** , begun in 814, was destroyed four times by fire and each time rebuilt on a grander scale to become a magnificent example of Italian Gothic architecture. The Palace, as residence of the doge and seat of justice, exudes wealth and power in its majestic halls, famous Golden Staircase and elegant rooms with their frescoed walls and ceilings. The **Bridge of Sighs** (c. 1600) leads from the Doges palace to the former prisons, a hellish place where prisoners were held either in humid, above-ground cells that were subject to flooding, or in underground cells lined with strips of lead to make them unbearable in the summer heat. Casanova made his famous escape from the latter in 1756.

Other buildings in St. Mark's Square are the **Clock Tower** (built near the end of the 15th century), the **Old Law Courts** (Procuratie Vecchie) which were begun in the 15th century, and the **Napoleonic Wing** (or New Building), built in 1807, which houses the Correr Museum, its

collection of paintings, sculptures and precious objects tracing the history and art of Venice. The **New Law Courts** (Procuratie Nuove) were completed at the beginning of the 18th century. Beneath the portico is the famous Caffe Florian, which was frequented by Casanova, Wagner and Proust.

The **Campanile (Bell Tower)** was built in the 10th century and stands 325 feet (99 metres) high. The Loggetta, at its base, was designed by Renaissance architect Jacopo Sansovino in the early 16th century and is decorated with bronze statues and marble ornaments. The tower collapsed in 1902 and was rebuilt a few years later as an exact replica of the original. Inside, visitors can reach the balcony near the top by climbing the spiral staircase, or by taking the lift.

The **Old Library (Libreria Vecchia)**, its construction started in 1537, was designed by

Prisoners were led across the Bridge of Sighs to their cells.

St. Mark's Square

The golden facade of St. Mark's Cathedral (above). The Doges Palace reflects the wealth of Venice when it was a great sea power (left).

The Campanile (right) soars above the other buildings of St. Mark's Square.
The Italian Gothic facade of the Doges' Palace (below).

A colorful carnival mask (right). A young Venetian promotes an upcoming classical concert (below).

(Below) The view from the Piazzetta of St. Mark's Basin and the distant church of San Giorgio Maggiore.

PIGEONS

Pigeons have become a problem for the city of Venice. With an estimated population of 100,000, they now outnumber Venetians and anyone (including tourists) caught feeding the pigeons in St. Mark's Square could face a fine of US$850. This might seem severe, but the pigeons — many of them diseased — have been put on a strict diet of feed laced with anti-fertility drugs in an attempt to reduce their numbers, as well as the 74 tons of droppings they currently produce per year.

Sansovino as a structural counterpoint to the Doges' Palace – the former an educational institute, the latter the political centre of power. The Library became the prototype of Venetian classicism, with its double arcade and lavish use of decorative sculptures. It faces the **Piazzetta 10**, which leads from the square to the busy waterfront of St. Mark's Basin. The two columns standing here are from the 12th century – one holding a statue of the Lion of St. Mark, the other a statue of St. Theodore. When standing in the Piazzetta and looking across the water of St. Mark's Basin, you can see an island containing the church of **San Giorgio Maggiore 11**, begun in 1566 and designed by Andrea Palladio, who introduced elements from ancient temples to Venetian church architecture.

Venice contains many splendid churches, including **Santa Maria Gloriosa del Frari 12** with paintings by Titian, **San Zaccaria 13** with the *Enthroned Madonna* by Bellini, and the 17th-century **Church of Santa Maria della Salute 14** which stands on a point of land at the entrance to the Grand Canal.

The Grand Canal

The main thoroughfare of Venice, the Grand Canal is lined with residential palaces (called *palazzi*), their ornate and rippling patterns reflected on the water. The earliest palaces date to the 12th century and their basic features were carried through the centuries. A ground floor portico (for loading and unloading merchandise) led to a large hall where business was conducted; the family's living quarters were upstairs where a large drawing room overlooked the canal. Each palace was marked by a post, painted with the owner's heraldic colors. Their styles range from early Veneto-Byzantine to Baroque, and Eastern influences are evident in such Oriental touches as delicate lattice work. Because there was little internal strife in Venice, the homes of wealthy Venetian families were built not like fortified castles but as lavish palazzi with fairy-tale facades designed for reflection in the waters of the Grand Canal.

One of the earliest palaces is **Palazzo Loredan 15**, now the seat of the City Council, dating from the 13th century and built in the Veneto-Byzantine style. By the early 1500s the Grand Canal was astounding foreigners with its opulent palazzi, such as the late Gothic **Ca' d'Oro (House of Gold) 16**. Now housing the Galleria Franchetti, this splendid structure was built by a leading Venetian family in 1420, its lavish stone-carved ornamentation once colored with red and blue pigments and glistening gilt.

With the arrival of the Renaissance came modifications to some of the designs such as that of the **Palazzo Vendramin-Calergi 17**, completed in 1509, which introduced classical elements to the traditional Venetian facade. This famous palazzo, now a casino, is where the composer Richard Wagner died in 1883 and it became a motif in Thomas Mann's *Death in Venice*.

Ever more and imposing palaces were built along the Grand

Canal, including the 16th-century **Palazzo Grimani** , home of today's Appeal Court, and the baroque **Ca'Pesaro** 19, built in 1710 and now housing an art gallery. The **Palazzo Rezzonico** 20 contains beautifully decorated and furnished rooms which are open to visitors as the Museum of the Venetian 18th Century. Plans are underway to open more of the building to the public, including a mezzanine where the poet Robert Browning lived.

Art galleries of note along the Grand Canal include the **Gallery of the Accademia** 21, its 24 rooms containing five centuries of Venetian paintings, with a large number of works by Giovanni Bellini. The **Peggy Guggenheim Art Collection**, housed in the Palazzo Venier Dei Leoni 22, is one of most important collections of contemporary art in the world. The **Scuola di San Rocco** (Great School of San Rocco) 23, on Campo San Rocco, houses a series of painting by Tintoretto. The Grand Canal is crossed in the center of the city by the **Rialto Bridge** (Ponte di Rialto) 24, a single marble arch built between 1588 and 1591, to connect Rialto and San Marco islands. The bridge's arcades are lined with shops and nearby open-air cafes are a good place to watch the constant flow of activity in the Grand Canal.

Dining in Venice

Famous (and expensive) restaurants in Venice include **Harry's Bar** 25, which was once patronized by Ernest Hemingway, Somerset Maugham and Orson Wells; and the dining terrace of the **Gritti Palace** 26, where former guests have included Queen Elizabeth, Winston Churchill and Greta Garbo. **St. Mark's Square** is lined with outdoor cafes, as is the waterfront area beside the **Rialto Bridge**.

A ship departing Venice heads past the mouth of the Grand Canal and the Church of Santa Maria della Salute.

GRAND CANAL

Motorboats not so swell

When Venice police issue speeding tickets, these go not to heavy-footed motorists but to mariners exceeding the speed limit on the Grand Canal. Supporting local speed limit enforcement are the city's gondoliers, skilled oarsmen who find it increasingly difficult to manoeuvre amid the wash caused by passing motorboats. The graceful gondola has been used by Venetians for nearly a thousand years, but Venice's gondoliers are threatening to bring this seafaring tradition to an end by motorizing their fabled craft if the motorboats on the Grand Canal don't slow down and reduce the wash that not only jeopardizes the gondola but also sends swells slapping against the palazzi lining the canal, which could contribute to their deterioration.

A gondola wedding party (above). Regata Storica is held each September on the Grand Canal (right).

Rialto Bridge (right). Palazzi on the Grand Canal (below and bottom). Gondolas are widely available for hire (below right).

Ravenna

South of Venice is the port of Ravenna, which rose to prominence under the Romans who stationed their North Adriatic fleet at the nearby seaport of Classis. The city's political prominence endured throughout the centuries, and Ravenna also became the Western center of mosaic art in the 5th and 6th centuries, its masterworks including the decoration of San Vitale, a Byzantine church consecrated in 547.

Italy's Interior

A land tour of northern Italy is an enticing proposition for passengers beginning or ending their cruise at Venice or Genoa. To the north are the majestic Italian Alps, beautiful lakes and Italy's second-largest city, **Milan**. This prosperous city's historic landmarks include the Church of Santa Maria dell Grazie (1465-90), which contains Leonardo da Vinci's famous fresco, *The Last Supper*, and the famous opera house, Teatro alla Scala, which opened in 1778.

The city of **Verona**, a centre of trade since Roman times, reached its apex of power in the late 13th century when ruled by Ghibelline lords. The ongoing strife between the Ghibellines and the Guelphs eventually weakened Verona, a bloody rivalry that was embodied in Shakespeare's play *Romeo and Juliet*, with Romeo's family belonging to the Guelphs and Juliet's being members of the Ghibellines. The 14th century Casa di Giulietta (House of Juliet) is one of Verona's top tourist spots.

Padua, connected by canal with the Po and other rivers, is home to Italy's second-oldest university (after Bologna's) which was founded in 1222. Galileo taught here, and Dante and Petrarch were students. Other famous landmarks in Padua include the six-domed basilica of St. Anthony, its high altar adorned with bronzes by Donatello.

Bologna has been known as a centre of learning ever since the founding in 425 AD of its Roman law school. The city's famous university was established in about 1088 and, over the years, its faculties were expanded to include medical and theological faculties, and courses in the liberal arts. Bologna's Renaissance architecture includes palazzos, churches and an art gallery featuring works by Bolognese artists.

Nestled in the Appenines near the Adriatic Sea is **San Marino**, the world's smallest republic. A Christian stone-cutter from Dalmatia was said to have taken refuge on Mount Titano in the 4th century, and a community soon formed around the mountain's three peaks. Only 24 square miles in size with a population of approximately 25,000 Italian-speaking inhabitants, San Marino has renewed and expanded several times an initial treaty of friendship and economic cooperation signed with Italy in 1862. The Italian patriot and soldier Garibaldi was granted refuge in San Marino in 1849, and in 1861 Abraham Lincoln accepted an honorary citizenship of the republic.

In **Umbria**, the town of **Orvieto** is famous for its beautiful cathedral, begun in 1290, its black-and-white marble facade decorated with colorful mosaics. **Todi** is another Umbrian town of note, containing Etruscan remains, Roman ruins and Gothic palaces.

TUSCANY

Tuscany is one of Italy's most scenic regions, its gently rolling and verdant hills dotted with stone farmhouses. Vineyards of the Chianti wine region lie between Florence and Siena, and the northwest part of Tuscany is where the famous Carrara marble is quarried. The greatest artists and architects of the Renaissance spent time in Tuscany, which became a center of art and learning in the late Middle Ages when Dante, born in Florence in 1265, established Tuscan as the literary language of Italy with publication of his masterpiece, the *Divine Comedy*.

Tuscany, called Etruria in ancient times, was home to the Etruscan civilization before it was conquered by the Romans in the mid-4th century BC. The northern Lombards controlled the region next, followed by the Franks who, in the early 12th century, bequeathed Tuscany to the papacy, which set up a longstanding strife between the pro-papal Guelphs and pro-imperial Ghibellines. Amid the political turmoil and bloody battles, the towns of Tuscany prospered as commerce, industry and the arts flourished. **Pisa** initially emerged as the most powerful city of the region, but **Florence** eventually gained control and Tuscany became a grand duchy of Florence's ruling Medici family.

The small city of **Siena**, despite frequent wars with Florence, retained its independence and today draws visitors to its rich array of art and architecture. Gracing the fan-shaped main square are the Gothic Palazzo Pubblico and slender Mangia tower, and adorning the city's Italian Gothic cathedral is a striped marble facade by Giovanni Pisano, the adjoining library containing famous frescoes by Pinturicchio.

Throughout the Renaissance, Tuscany was a center of learning and art. Florence overflowed with

A stone farmhouse set amid the rolling hills and vineyards of the Tuscan countryside.

famous artists such as Michelangelo and Leonardo da Vinci, both of whom were born in the hill towns surrounding Florence. Other famous Tuscans included Petrarch, Galileo, Machiavelli, Puccini and Carlo Collodi, the 19th-century author of the children's classic *Pinocchio*.

Livorno, port for Florence, is one of Italy's most important sea ports and home to the Italian naval academy. The port evolved from a fortified castle in the Middle Ages into a flourishing city when developed by Florence's powerful Medici family in the 16th century. Livorno was considered the ideal Renaissance town, until it was bombed during World War II. Parts of its 17th-century city wall still remain and the 16th-century cathedral was restored after the war.

On Your Own

Pisa is about 14 miles north of Livorno (40 minutes by car), and Florence is about 62 miles distant – an hour-and-a-half drive through the rolling hills of Tuscany. Trains run regularly to both cities (Pisa is a stop along the Livorno-Florence route). The Livorno train station is about three miles from the cruise ship pier, but some cruise lines offer a shuttle service into town with a drop-off about one mile from the Livorno train station. The train ride to Florence varies from one to two hours; the train trip to Pisa takes about 15 minutes. Motorcoaches and cars are not allowed in the main center of Florence, which is ideal for exploring on foot.

Approximate **taxi fares** (in US$): Full-day to Florence – $280-$300; half-day to Pisa – $100; cruise ship pier to Livorno train station – $10.

Lunch in Florence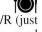

Roses at Via Parione 26/R (just off Via Tornabuoni) is a good spot to pause for lunch, as is Il Francescano at Largo Bargellini 16 (near Piazza Santa Croce).

Pisa

Pisa was at the height of its power when the tower for which it's now famous first began to lean. This well-known bell tower was meant to complete the city's splendid ensemble of ecclesiastical architecture, begun in the

Lunch can be enjoyed at a cafe in Piazza della Repubblica.

mid-11th century. Pisa was then a city on the ascent, its growing empire based on naval and economic power. Over the span of two centuries, Pisa's magnificent cathedral, baptistery and campanile ('Leaning Tower') were built at an open-air site north of the city. Called the Field of Miracles, the site proved to be a field of unstable subsoil, for Pisa is situated on the banks of the Arno River, where the ground consists of layers of sandy mud and clay. A former sea port, Pisa now lies six miles inland, its decline as a trading port caused by the silting of the river. Before its decline, Pisa was a powerful maritime republic. When its navy defeated the Arab forces at Palermo in 1062, Pisans built their Romanesque cathedral from Saracen plunder, the facade's elaborate lace-like ornamentation reflecting Islamic influences.

The Baptistery was modeled on the Holy Sepulcher in Jerusalem, and the entire complex of monuments was an attempt by the Pisans to create their own Holy City. All three buildings are clad in white marble, inlaid with horizontal stripes and ornate patterns in dark-green marble. They contain some of Pisa's greatest art treasures – including bronze panels by Bonnanno Pisano and marble pulpits by Nicola Pisano and his son Giovanni. Soon after construction began on the campanile in 1174, it began to lean. By the time it was closed to the public in 1990, the tower was 16 feet (4.9 meters) out of perpendicular alignment. So close was the 13,050-ton tower to toppling, an earthquake or storm could have demolished it. Upon being closed, the tower was temporarily supported with a steel belt and cables while engineers studied the structure, then began stabilizing it by placing 800 tons of lead weights at the tower's base on the side opposite the tilt. This was followed by the removal of tons of subsoil from beneath the tower in an area away from the incline, prompting the tower to bear down and slightly straighten itself. After 11 years of stabilization work, the bell tower was reopened to the public in late 2001, its lean now back to where it was in 1838. Visitors can once again climb to the top of the structure, but only 30 people are allowed inside at a time.

Pisa's medieval cathedral and its leaning campanile.

Florence

The Italians call her *Firenze*, the flowering city, named by Romans when this early Etruscan settlement became a town along the Cassian Way. It was a prophetic choice of name because, centuries later, Florence did indeed flower as the birthplace of the Italian Renaissance, which began here in the early 1400s. Lying at the foot of the Apennines, in the broad valley of the Arno River,

---

MUST SEE:

There are several must-see attractions for first-time visitors to Florence. Here is a good starter list:

Michelangelo's David, either the original housed in the Galleria dell'Accademia, or the replica standing in Palazzo Vecchio.

The Duomo, Florence's celebrated cathedral.

Church of Santa Croce, containing the tombs of Michelangelo and Galileo.

Church of San Lorenzo's Medici Chapel.

Ponte Vecchio, beautiful, busy, with a 15th-century atmosphere.

Florence is a small city. Her beauty is subtle, her colors muted, and just as that famous Florentine, the Mona Lisa, leaves you wondering what's behind her mysterious smile, so too does Florence, with her narrow medieval streets and fortress-like buildings, their austere exteriors offering few clues to the artistic treasures awaiting inside.

After Rome fell, Florence was controlled by various invaders until gaining autonomy in the 12th century. Then, in the 13th century, the pro-papal Guelphs and the pro-imperial Ghibellines fought for control of the city. By the end of the century, the Guelphs had captured the city but they then split into warring factions called the Blacks and the Whites. The poet Dante, a White Guelph and member of the losing side, was banished in 1302. Florence also warred against other cities, such as Pisa, and gradually grew as it absorbed neighboring towns and villages. Bankers and merchants made

Ponte Vecchio bridge spans the Arno River in Florence.

both themselves and the city wealthy by selling Florentine silks, tapestries and jewelry.

The Black Death of 1348 struck a terrible blow to the city, killing more than half the population. But Florence's most glorious days still lay ahead, her golden age ushered in by the rise to power in 1434 of a man named Cosimo de' Medici. A wealthy and powerfully connected merchant banker, Medici and his descendants would determine the destiny of Florence for the next 300 years. Despised by their enemies and denounced as tyrannical, the Medicis were initially a tolerant and positive force in Florence. Through their passionate patronage of the arts, literature and learning, the early Medicis financed Florence's growing concentration of archi-

The Bargello, built in 1255, later became a Renaissance prison.

tectural monuments and artistic masterpieces, the likes of which had not been seen since the Athens of Pericles.

Shore Excursions *Florence*

The following is a sampling of excursions from Livorno. These are usually a combination of motorcoach ride and walking tour, with a mid-day lunch stop. For more detail, consult your shore excursion booklet (provided with your cruise documents) or the cruise line's website.

• Florence & Pisa – guided walking tour of Florence and Pisa's Field of Miracles (10 hrs)
• Best of Florence – full-day walking tour of Florence (9 hrs – about $165)
• Florence & Chianti Region – time in Florence plus a tour of Chianti wine district (10 hrs)
• Tuscan Countryside – visit two medieval towns (9.5 hrs)
• Small-group tour of Uffizi Gallery and other sites (10 hrs)
• Scenic drive to Cinque Terre on Italian Riviera (9.5 hrs)

Excursion Suggestion: One of the best ways to see Florence is to take a ship-organized motorcoach ride from Livorno to Florence, where you are dropped off at a central location within walking distance of the city's highlights. After exploring the city on your own, you reboard the coach at a pre-set time and place for the return drive to Livorno. This excursion allows you to maximize your time in Florence, with no concern about getting to or from the city. A tour guide provides informed commentary during the drive into Florence and answers any questions you may have. On the return drive, you can lean back in your seat and relax from a full day of sightseeing.

Cosimo de' Medici, a generous supporter of such artists as Brunelleschi and Donatello, and the founder of the Medici Library, was an astute business-man who managed to double his personal fortune while investing in the city and spending lavishly on the arts. His grandson, Lorenzo de' Medici (il Magnifico) became a towering figure of the Italian Renaissance, and was a patron of Michelangelo, Botticelli and others. An astute politician, he held no official title but tactfully wielded power and conducted the affairs of the Florentine state. He was also a scholar and a poet who spent huge sums of his own money to advance the arts and literature of Florence. In 1478 he survived a bloody conspiracy by the rival Pazzi family, in which his brother was stabbed to death during Mass at the cathedral. A wounded Lorenzo managed to escape.

The Florentine republicans also tried to drive the Medicis from power. Each attempt was, ultimately, a failure because the early Medicis enjoyed popular support among the Florentines. There were, however, serious challengers. In 1494, Lorenzo's son and successor, Pietro, was expelled from Florence, and Girolamo Savonarola, a zealous religious reformer and enemy of the Medicis, became the spiritual leader of the city, his impassioned sermons inspiring Florentines to toss their offensive secular artwork into a huge bonfire that was lit in the Piazza della Signoria. However, his incessant preaching and rigid moral demands eventually got on people's nerves, and his attacks on the corrupt Borgia pope resulted in his being excommunicated in 1497. Savonarola was hanged a year later for heresy and the Medicis were eventually restored to power.

The Medici dynasty became affiliated with the royal houses of Europe through marriage, and produced two queens of France and three popes. However, in the process, the Medicis gained a reputation as arbitrary and ruthless rulers. Alessandro, who governed from 1532 to 1537, was so generally hated that his cousin Ippolito was sent by the people of Florence

The cloister of the Church of San Lorenzo, its series of round arches a typical feature of Renaissance architecture.

Florence's massive cathedral (the Duomo) is the focal point of the city, its dome a symbol of the Italian Renaissance.

to complain to the Holy Roman Emperor. Alas, Ippolito died en route and many believed he was poisoned by order of Alessandro. Another member of the Medici family finally murdered the despised Alessandro but his successor, Cosmo I, was no better liked, although he did expand Florence's territory to include most of Tuscany and he became the first grand duke of Tuscany.

The Medicis were influenced by Niccolo Machiavelli, author of *Il Principe* (The Prince), a famous work describing the amoral, calculating and tyrannical means by which an 'ideal' prince may gain and maintain political power. Machiavelli was born in 1469 to an impoverished branch of a distinguished Florentine family and he rose, in the aftermath of Savonarola's death, from obscure bureaucrat to high-profile republican. His fall came with the return of the Medicis in 1512. Briefly imprisoned and tortured for allegedly plotting against the Medicis, Machiavelli later retired to his country estate to write his chief works.

The decline of the Medici family began in the late 1500s, although the city continued to flower. The Accademia della Crusca was established in 1582, and in 1610 Galileo was appointed court philosopher and mathematician by Cosimo II de' Medici. However, by the late 1600s the Medicis had descended into bigoted and corrupt despotism. The family continued to rule the grand duchy of Tuscany until 1737, when the last male member of the line died. Eventually, Tuscany was annexed by the house of Hapsburg-Lorraine to the kingdom of Sardinia in 1860. When the new kingdom of Italy was formed, Florence was its first capital from 1865 to 1871.

Few of Florence's famous art treasures were damaged in World War II, but Ponte Vecchio – built in the 14th century – was the only bridge to survive. A major disaster struck in November 1966 when the River Arno flooded its banks. Art experts from around the world came to help repair the buildings and statues damaged by water and mud, and beauty was restored to the city in which the Renaissance first flowered.

Florence Attractions:

Most of Florence's monuments are located within walking distance of one another but be prepared for a wait when visiting some of the popular galleries and museums. Their opening hours vary; many are closed by 2:00 p.m. (especially on Sundays) and remain closed on Mondays.

No tour buses are allowed into the town centre and passengers (including those on ship-organized excursions) are dropped off a few blocks east of the **National Library** **1** in the vicinity of Piazza Piave. The train station is located on the other side of the town centre, next to the **Church of Santa Maria Novella** **2**, built by Dominicans in the late Middle Ages (1278-1350). Its patterned marble facade was remodeled in the 15th century by Leon Battista Alberti, which is why the lower part reflects the Gothic style while the entablature is of Renaissance design. The church's Italian Gothic interior contains numerous art treasures, including a famous wooden crucifix carved in 1410 by Filippo Brunelleschi – the first great architect of the Italian Renaissance.

Brunelleschi began his career as a sculptor and goldsmith but, after failing to win a commission

to design the bronze doors of the Florence baptistery, he switched to architecture. He went to Rome to study classical buildings and, upon returning to Florence, he launched a new style of architecture based on the systematic use of perspective and a mastery of construction. His elegant designs can be seen all over Florence. Construction of the **Ospedale degli Innocenti** (Foundling Hospital) **3** began in 1419 and its motif – a series of round arches supported by columns – became a prototype of Renaissance architecture. The perfect proportions of the hospital arcade were repeated by Brunelleschi in the **Church of San Lorenzo** **4** which he designed in 1421 for the Medicis, who were so impressed with his plans for a burial chapel they were adding to the existing Romanesque church that they asked him to newly design the entire church.

The structure for which Brunelleschi is best known, however, is the soaring dome of the city's Gothic cathedral of **Santa Maria del Fiore (the Duomo)** **5**. Of revolutionary design, Brunelleschi's dome is one of the most celebrated and original in architectural history. Constructed from 1420 to 1434, this massive dome is the focal point of the city. Its daring structural technique consisted of building the dome in two separate shells, the stronger inner shell supporting the lighter outer shell. An ingenious interlinking of the bricks helped make the counter-balanced dome self-supporting, which allowed

Brunelleschi to dispense with the expense and delay of wooden scaffolding and centering.

Brunelleschi also designed the lantern atop the dome. The cathedral itself, the fourth largest in the world, was built between 1296 and 1375. The original unfinished facade was torn down in 1587 and not until 1871 was a design by Emilio de Fabris approved for the new facade. White, green and pink marble – consistent with the rest of the building – was used. The slim campanile (known as 'Giotto's Tower') was designed by the great Florentine artist Giotto di Bondone and begun in 1334. It stands 269 feet (82 metres) high.

The octagonal **Baptistery** , originally built in the 4th and 5th centuries when Florence was a Roman town, was considered a classical temple by medieval Florentines. Its current appearance dates from the 11th to 13th centuries, and the panels of its famous bronze doors were designed by two sculptors: Andrea Pisano, whose stories of the Baptist embellish the South

The nave (above) and dome (right) of the Duomo.

The marble facade of Florence's famous Duomo and, in the foreground, part of the Bapistery.

Door (1330-1336), and Lorenzo Ghiberti whose submissions won him commissions to design the North Door (1404-1424) and the East Door (1425-1452). The stunningly beautiful East Door became known as the 'The Gates of Paradise' when thus described by Michelangelo.

A copy of the Gates of Paradise now hangs in the east portal, the original being restored for exhibition in the **Museo dell-Opera dell Duomo 7** which houses works of art removed from the Duomo, the Campanile and the Baptistery. Works on display include Donatello's *Mary Magdalen* and an unfinished *Pieta* (1550-53) by Michelangelo that was intended for his tomb.

Michelangelo lived with the Medicis from 1490 to 1492, and the family employed him both in Florence and in Rome under the Medici popes Leo X and Clement VII. In between his painting commissions at the Sistine Chapel in Rome, Michelangelo was summoned back to Florence to design a chapel and library, attached to the family's parish Church of San

CITY ATTRACTIONS

(1) National Library
(2) Church of Santa Maria Novella
(3) Ospedale degli Innocenti
(4) Church of San Lorenzo
(5) Santa Maria del Fiore (the Duomo)
(6) Baptistery
(7) Museo dell-Opera dell Duomo
(8) Medici Chapel
(9) Church of Santa Croce
(10) Church of S. Spirito
(11) Church of Santa Maria del Carmine
(12) Palazzo Medici-Riccardi
(13) Palazzo Rucellai
(14) Palazzo Strozzi

(15 Dante's House
(16) Orsanmichele
(17) Palazzo Vecchio (Town Hall)
(18) Loggia dei Lanzi
(19) Uffizi
(20) Galleria dell'Accademia
(21) Bargello
(22) Archaeological Museum
(23) Monastery of St. Mark museum
(24) Pitti Palace
(25) Belvedere Fortress
(26) Piazzale Michelangelo
(27) Ponte Vecchio (Old Bridge)
(28) straw market

Lorenzo (4). The **Laurentian Library** was built to house the Medici family's huge collection of books and manuscripts. Michelangelo strived to challenge classical ideals and create new architectural forms, and an example of his daring is reflected in his design of the library's vestibule, which contains what has been described as a 'nightmarish' stairway appearing to flow downwards and outwards, defying anyone to mount the steps.

The Church of San Lorenzo's **New Sacristy (Medici Chapel)** **8** was conceived as an architectural-sculptural ensemble and is Michelangelo's only work in which his statues are in the setting specifically designed for them. The plans were changed while work was underway, with Michelangelo completing only two of the four planned tombs, before returning to Rome in 1534. One tomb was for Lorenzo de' Medici, who died at 27, and his statue atop the tomb depicts the young man in a pensive attitude, flanked by the statues *Dawn* and *Dusk*. The opposite tomb of Giuliano de' Medici is watched over by the statues *Night* and *Day*. The meaning of these allegorical figures is described in some notes found on one of the artist's drawings: "Day and Night speak, and say: We with our swift course have brought the Duke Giuliano to death." The statue of Giuliano, set in a niche, bore no resemblance to the deceased but Michelangelo was said to have remarked, "A thousand years from now, nobody will know what he looked like."

Michelangelo's own tomb is in the **Church of Santa Croce** **9**, positioned immediately to the right as you enter. He reportedly chose this spot so that on Judgment Day, when the dead are raised, the first thing he would see through the opened doors of Santa Croce would be Brunelleschi's dome. The tomb of Galileo is situated on the left side of the church, opposite Michelangelo's. Machiavelli's tomb is halfway down the nave on the left, and the composer Rossini's tomb is at the end of the nave. The interior of this Gothic church (with a 19th-century facade) also contains early 14th-century frescoes by Giotto, who departed from the Byzantine style

Church of Santa Croce holds the tombs of Michelangelo, Galileo and Rossini.

The Pazzi Chapel, annexed to the Church of Santa Croce, was designed by Brunelleschi.

of depicting religious symbols to create, instead, dramatic biblical scenes. Works here by Donatello include his *Annunciation* and *Crucifix*. Donatello, an innovative sculptor who freed sculptures of their architectural setting, was interested in ancient monuments and he travelled to Rome in 1430 with Brunelleschi. The **Pazzi Chapel**, annexed to Santa Croce, is a Brunelleschi design and was begun about 1430. He also designed the **Church of S. Spirito** 🔟 begun in 1434, which was about the same time he was designing the **Church of Santa Maria del Carmine** 1️⃣1️⃣ – a domed, central-plan church and the first of its kind for the Renaissance.

The **Palazzo Medici-Riccardi** 1️⃣2️⃣ built from 1444 to 1459, became the model for other private Florentine palaces, such as **Palazzo Rucellai** 1️⃣3️⃣ and **Palazzo Strozzi** 1️⃣4️⃣. The Medicis rejected Brunelleschi's model for their new palace, considering it too grandiose, and went instead with a design by Michelozzi, one that did not outwardly flaunt their wealth and power. Its austere Tuscan Gothic exterior of rusticated masonry contrasts sharply with the interior's elaborately decorated salons and the central courtyard's classical arcades, which imitate Brunelleschi's Foundling Hospital. Other buildings of note include **Dante's House** 1️⃣5️⃣ and the **Orsanmichele** 1️⃣6️⃣, a granary that was transformed into a church in 1336. The nearby **Piazza della Repubblica**, a 19th-century square dedicated to Vittorio Emanuele II (first king of a united Italy), is situated on the site of the Roman town's ancient forum.

Florence's main square is **Piazza della Signoria**, over-looked by the fortress-like **Palazzo Vecchio (Town Hall)** 1️⃣7️⃣ where elected members of the Signoria would temporarily live while serving their term of office. Begun in 1298 and built to with-stand armed assault in an era when political turmoil and social tensions often led to bloodshed, the building's tall tower was both a symbol of civic pride and a watch tower, with the two marble statues flanking the doorway designed for holding chains. Under the arches of the gallery are the coats of arms of the Tuscan communes ruled by

Florence. Inside the palace the grand Salone dei Cinquecento (Room of the Five Hundred) is richly decorated with frescoes by Vasari and sculptures by Michelangelo.

The statues standing in front of the Palazzo include a copy of Michelangelo's *David* (1501-1504), one of his greatest sculptural achievements. When commissioned, the statue was supposed to depict a biblical shepherd boy and occupy a pier buttress of the Duomo, but Michelangelo's interpretation of David produced instead a heroic Renaissance man whose masculine nudity made the statue unsuitable for an ecclesiastical site. A committee decided to erect it in front of the Palazzo Vecchio, and it took five days to move the colossal statue (which stands over four meters) to this site. The statue was stoned by citizens offended by its nudity, and David's private parts were covered with gilded leaves until 1545. In 1873 the statue was removed to the Academy, with a copy placed on its original site.

The statue to *David*'s left is *Hercules and Cacus* (1525-1534) by Baccio Bandinelli, whose sculptural talents were widely ridiculed by his contemporaries. When the marble block for this statue fell off the transport into the River Arno, the joke was that the stone had thrown itself into the river rather than endure mutilation by Bandinelli. The *Fountain of Neptune* (1560-1575) to *David*'s right was the work of Bartolomeo Ammanati who, soon after its completion, experienced

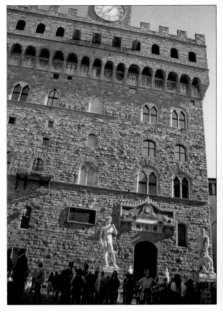

A replica of Michelangelo's David (detail below) stands outside the Town Hall (above).

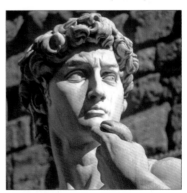

a religious crisis prompted by the counter-Reformation and disowned his works because of their nudity. The Florentines call this sculpture the 'White Giant' because of the enormous size of the white sea god standing in the center of the fountain. Statues on display in the **Loggia dei Lanzi** include *Perseus* (1533), a masterpiece in bronze by Benvenuto Cellini, and the *Rape of the Sabines* (1581-1583) by Giambologna.

The famous **Uffizi Gallery** is housed in a Renaissance palace that was built to house the administrative offices (*uffizi*) of the Medicis. This U-shaped building was designed by Giorgio Vasari, a favorite portrait artist of the Medici family. When the family installed their art collections here, it became Europe's first modern museum. The gallery, located on the second floor, consists of 45 rooms divided into sections. The famous artists represented in this vast collection of paintings include Leonardo da Vinci, Michelangelo, Raphael and Giotto, with numerous works by Sandro Botticelli.

Other art museums of note are the **Galleria dell'Accademia (Academy)** , which houses the original *David* by Michelangelo, as well as his unfinished *Slaves*. The **Museo Nazionale** in the 13th-

century **Bargello** , a former Renaissance prison, contains an outstanding collection of Renaissance sculpture with works by Donatello, Michelangelo and Cellini, and the bronze panels submitted by Brunelleschi and Ghiberti in 1402 when they competed for the commission to decorate the north doors of the Baptistery. The **Archaeological Museum** houses Etruscan and Graeco-Roman art, and the **Monastery of St. Mark Museum** contains some of the best works of Fra Angelico, a Dominican monk.

The **Pitti Palace** , originally built for the Pitti family in the 15th century, was expanded after it was bought by the rival Medici family. Works by Titian and Raphael are displayed in the Palatine Gallery, which is housed in the Royal Apartments on the right-hand side of the courtyard. Behind the Pitti Palace, which served as the Royal Palace of a united Italy from 1865 to 1870, lie the terraced Boboli Gardens (1550). A back entrance leads to the **Belvedere Fortress** , its grounds a popular picnic site for Florentines, with views

Fountain of Neptune in Piazza della Signoria.

overlooking the city's medieval maze of churches, squares and red-tiled roofs. The **Piazzale Michelangelo** 26, (farther up the hill) is where the tour buses stop to give their passengers an overview of Florence, the River Arno and its many bridges.

Ponte Vecchio (Old Bridge) 27 was built in 1345 and was the only bridge not blown up by the retreating Germans during World War II. It is lined with jewelers and goldsmiths' shops and is topped with a corridor designed by Vasari for Cosimo I de' Medici (1537-1569). Used by successive Medici grand dukes when crossing the bridge, the Vasari Corridor is lined with paintings and, although not open to the general public, the corridor is accessible as part of a recently introduced city tour called the Prince's Route. The elegant **Ponte Santa Trinita**, the next bridge downriver and the pride of Florence, was designed by Bartolemeo Ammannati in 1567 and was painstakingly rebuilt after the war.

Shopping: Florentines are renowned for their skilled craftsmanship, especially in leather work, glassware, ceramics, art reproductions and high fashion. Boutiques selling fine leather goods and designer clothing are found on Via de'Tornabuoni and Via della Vigna Nuova. More leather shops are found near Santa Croce. For antiques, including paintings, ceramics and sculptures, try Borgo Ognissanti or cross the river to Via Maggio (one block west of the Pitti Palace). The Ponte Vecchio is a

The Uffizi Gallery houses a vast collection of Renaissance art.

good place to shop for jewelry. Souvenir shoppers might try the straw market located in an open-air loggia 28 on Via Calimala.

Elba

Lying off the coast of Tuscany, the island of Elba is well known as Napoleon's place of exile from 1814 to 1815. Its principal north coast port of Portoferraio, strongly fortified by Florence's Medici family from the 16th to 18th centuries, is today a seaside resort. Napoleon's house, the Villa dei Mulini, where he resided as sovereign of the island, is now a museum. Shore excursions in Elba feature scenic drives to Porto Azzurro (a fashionable resort) and to picturesque fishing ports.

ADRIATIC SEA

Brindisi

Bari

IONIAN SEA

Golfo Di Taranto

A P P E N N I N I

Reggio di Calabria

Taormina

Strait of Messina

Mt. Vesuvius

Pompeii

Sorrento

Messina

Milazzo

Catania

Syracuse

Capri

Stromboli

LIPARI ISLANDS

Mt. Etna

Naples

Cefalu

SICILY

Malta Channe

Palermo

Segesta

Monreale

Erice

TYRRHENIAN SEA

MEDITERRANEAN SEA

Strait of Sicily

CORSICA

Porto Cervo

SARDINIA

Alghero

Cagliari

SOUTHERN ITALY

CRUISE ROUTES

ROUTES: -------

N

Miles

0   60

Tunis

TUNISIA

CHAPTER FIVE

SOUTHERN ITALY

Italy's southern states, while rich in natural beauty, have long been the poor cousin to the country's industrialized north and central regions. Centuries of exploitation by European dynasties and powerful feudal lords had kept the south in a state of backwardness, hindered by superstition and ignorance, when Italy – which hadn't been a unified political entity since the fall of the Western Roman Empire back in the 5th century – began its long struggle toward reunification.

Called Risorgimento (Italian for *resurgence*), this period of cultural nationalism and political activism was inspired by several 18th-century writers. It gained momentum in the early 1800s when the southern states, long dominated by foreign rulers, began to revolt against their repressive regimes. In 1820 there were uprisings in Naples and Sicily, followed by insurrections in Sardinia in 1821. Despite severe reprisals, the uprisings continued, led by different factions. One of these revolutionary groups favored a united Italy under the leadership of Sardinia's King Victor Emmanuel II, and it eventually gained control of the movement. Its cause, supported by the military hero Giuseppe Garibaldi, was ultimately triumphant and in 1861 the kingdom of Italy was proclaimed with Victor Emmanuel as king.

The newly declared kingdom encompassed Italy's northern and southern states, but Rome, situated in central Italy, remained part of the independent Papal States, which were protected by the troops of Napoleon III. The reunification of Italy was finally completed in 1870 when the Papal States were seized by Italian troops. A year later, Rome – the ancient capital of the Roman Empire – was once again the capital of a united Italy.

Victor Emmanuel Monument, Piazza Venezia, Rome.

For general information and travel tips on Italy, please see pages 179 and 180.

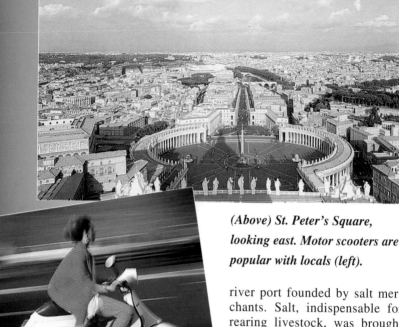

(Above) St. Peter's Square, looking east. Motor scooters are popular with locals (left).

Rome (Roma) – The Eternal City

One of the world's most exciting cities, Rome is the intellectual, cultural and religious center of Italy. Nearly three million people live in Rome, yet no buildings are built higher than the dome of St. Peter's. From hotels' rooftop gardens, sweeping views can be enjoyed of this fascinating city, its famous squares brimming with beautiful churches, fountains and monuments to history.

In ancient times, Rome was the center of one of the world's most successful empires. Long believed to have originated as a pastoral settlement on seven hills bordering the banks of the River Tiber, Rome likely began as a river port founded by salt merchants. Salt, indispensable for rearing livestock, was brought there from the nearest seaport lying downriver, and a local labor force soon gathered to unload, warehouse and trade this valuable commodity. Several tribes lived in the area – the Sabines to the north, Etruscans to the northwest, and the Latins to the southeast.

Palatine, a fortified hill of Rome, was taken in the 8th century BC by the Etruscans and, although the founding of Rome is shrouded in myth, historians traditionally set the date at 753 BC. The Etruscans, skilled engineers, built a defensive wall around the seven hills and transformed the existing group of villages into a city, draining the swampy plain of the Forum and building a temple on Capitoline Hill. According to legend, Romulus, son of Mars, was the city's founder. He and his brother, abandoned at birth in a royal plot, were suckled by a she-wolf and raised by a shepherd couple. Romulus eventually

(Above) The Spanish Steps.
(Right) Piazza Della Rotonda.

killed his brother and populated his new city with fugitives. These early Romans, in search of wives, seized women from the neighboring Sabine tribe.

In about 500 BC, the Romans overthrew their Etruscan rulers and established a republic that lasted four centuries. As the city grew, so too did its political structure. The ruling patrician class slowly ceded legislative power to the assemblies, and they in turn were eventually controlled by the senate which, as supreme power of the state, led Rome in her quest for empire and world supremacy. This expansion began with the conquest of central and southern Italy, then the defeat of Carthage to gain control of Sicily, Sardinia, Corsica, Spain and the northern shores of Africa. Macedonia was next, followed by Greece and Egypt.

However, as the empire grew, so too did turmoil back in Rome, where corruption, class dissension and barbarism threatened the republic's survival. Pompey emerged as master of Rome and, upon his return from a victorious foreign conquest, he allied himself with **Julius Caesar**, a popular democratic leader of patrician ancestry. Their allegiance, always tentative, dissolved with the death of Caesar's daughter Julia, who was married to Pompey. The two leaders led their mutual armies into battle against each other and Caesar, a military genius, emerged victorious – the new master of Rome.

Under the leadership of Caesar, a brilliant orator and patron of the arts, Roman culture thrived and was permeated by Greek thought, literature and language. Caesar's assassination in 44 BC marked the end of the Republic and the beginning of the Empire. Initially there was anarchy, until Octavian, Caesar's nephew and protege,

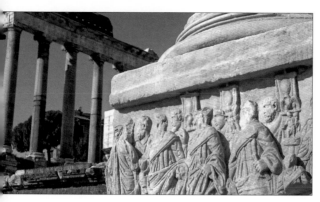

The Forum was the center of republican Rome and the scene of Julius Caesar's assassination.

emerged as leader. He defeated Antony and Cleopatra, and became the first emperor of Rome, receiving from the senate the title 'Augustus'. Peace reigned for the next two centuries

and imperial Rome grew into a city of over two million inhabitants. The city boasted a police force, fire brigades and a postal system. Aqueducts supplied water to public baths, and the wealthy had running water piped right into their villas. Efficient transportation was provided by an extensive system of roads and bridges. Indeed, at the height of Roman imperialism, all roads did lead to Rome for it was the center of the western world.

Rome's decline came quickly as the West sank into anarchy and Italy was ravaged by invaders. Rome was sacked twice and finally fell in 476, its last emperor deposed by the Goths. However, amid the political disintegration of Rome there rose a new power – that of Roman Catholicism. The grandeur that once epitomized imperial Rome would eventually return with the splendor of the Italian Renaissance, patronized by the powerful papacy, which ruled a swath of central Italy – from Rome to Ravenna – for more than 11 centuries. The Papal States were defeated in 1870 by patriot forces determined to create an Italian nation, but not until

MUST SEE:

Rome wasn't built in a day, and it's impossible to see all of Rome in a day. First-time visitors arriving by train at Terminal Railway Station could plan to visit the **Colosseum** and **Roman Forum** in the morning, pause for refreshment in **Piazza Venezia**, then take a taxi to **St. Peter's Square**. After viewing St. Peter's Basilica, walk to fountain-filled **Piazza Navona**, pausing there or at nearby **Piazza Della Rotonda** (location of the **Pantheon**) for refreshment. Then carry on to the **Trevi Fountain** before catching the train back to Civitavecchia.

If your cruise is beginning or ending in Rome, you should try to stay an extra day or two to view the **Vatican Museums**, **Sistine Chapel** and **Capitoline Hill**, and to soak up the atmosphere at the **Spanish Steps** and nearby shopping streets of chic boutiques and famous hotels.

the Lateran Treaty of 1929 – which made the pope sovereign within Vatican City – did the papacy recognize the secular state of modern Italy.

On Your Own

Civitavecchia, the chief port of Rome, is a 1.5-hour drive from Rome. Independent travelers can hire a **taxi** (a full day in Rome costs about US$250 to $300) or take the **train**. The Civitavecchia train station is a 20-minute walk or US$10 taxi ride from the cruise ship dock, and it's an hour and a quarter train ride to Termini station in downtown Rome (US$22 each way).

If you're touring Rome on your own, plan your itinerary ahead of time and don't try to see too many attractions – decide before-hand what your priorities will be. Taxis are plentiful, especially at Piazza Venezia and St. Peter's Square.

Places to pause for refreshment include **Cul de Sac** (a wine bar off Piazza Navona) and **Matricianella** (a trattoria at 2/4 Via del Leone, near the Spanish Steps) which is closed Sundays and all of August.

Rome Attractions:

The **Colosseum** ❶, completed in 80 AD during the reign of Titus, is a huge concrete amphitheater containing miles of stairways, and tier upon tier of marble seats which accommodated more than 50,000 spectators. A masterpiece of engineering, the stadium's efficient flow of people in and out of the building was achieved by utilizing 80 ground-floor entrances, each numbered to direct people to the staircases leading to their seats. Entertainment was provided by hundreds of rigorously trained gladiators (Latin for *swordsmen*), who were slaves or prisoners forced to perform exhibition combats in which they were paired off and would fight to the death – unless the crowd indicated to the victor that he spare the life of the defeated gladiator.

Gladiators were also forced to fight wild beasts, and those who revolted against this barbaric treatment were brutally killed by their Roman masters. The famous slave **Spartacus**, who died a century before the Colosseum was built, escaped from a gladiators' school at Capua (near modern Naples) and fled into the mountains, where he organized an army of fugitives who defeated several Roman forces before they were finally crushed. Spartacus was killed in battle and 6,000 of his followers were crucified even though 3,000 Roman prisoners had been found, unharmed, in his camp.

Southwest of the Colosseum stands the **Arch of Constantine**, a triple-arcaded triumphal arch raised in 312 AD to celebrate Constantine I's victory over Maxentius at the Milvian Bridge near Rome, making him the unchallenged ruler of the West. The road heading south from the Arch led to the Circus Maximus where chariot races were held.

The race-track was overlooked by the **Palatine 2**, one of Rome's seven hills and the site of the city's original 8th century BC settlement. During the city's republican period, notable citizens built homes atop the Palatine, and various emperors built palaces there during the imperial period.

Lying along the Palatine Hill, in a shallow valley between the Colosseum and Capitoline Hill, is the **Roman Forum** – the centre of republican Rome where the senate met, citizens strolled the basilicas and famous speeches were delivered by such famous orators as Caesar and Cicero. Victorious generals would ride in triumphant procession along the Sacred Way, the most famous

---

Shore Excursions *Rome*

Full-day excursions involve a motorcoach ride from the port to Rome (about a 1.5 hr drive) and an escorted walking tour upon reaching the city center. Places visited vary (depending on which excursion you book) but usually include three or four famous sites as well as lunch. The following is sampling of Rome shore excursions. For details, consult your cruise line's website or the shore excursion booklet provided with your cruise documentation.
• Full-day motorcoach and walking tour of Rome, complete tour of major sites, includes lunch (10 hrs, $130 – $200)
• Imperial Rome, tour focuses on historical sites (10hrs, $175)
• Narrated city drive, sites viewed from coach, little walking (5-6 hrs $75)
• Rome & Villa Borghese (10.5 hrs, about $180)

• Etruscan Countryside (9 hrs)
• Tarquinia by Bicycle (4 hrs, about $75)
Recommended: One of the best ways to see Rome is to take a ship-organized motorcoach ride from Civitavecchia to Rome, where you are dropped off at a central location (usually near St. Peter's Square) within walking distance of the city's highlights. After exploring the city on your own (for about 5 to 6 hrs), you reboard the coach at the same spot at a set time for the return drive to Civitavecchia. This excursion allows you to maximize your time in Rome, with no concern about getting to or from the city. A tour guide provides informed commentary during the drive into Rome and answers any questions you may have. On the return drive, you can lean back in your seat and relax after a full day of sightseeing (9 hrs, $80).

street in ancient Rome, which runs the length of the Forum.

The restored **Arch of Titus** (commemorating his conquest of Jerusalem in 70 AD) stands at one end of the Sacred Way, not far from the Colosseum, and the **Arch of Septimius Severus**, raised in 203 AD, stands at the other end. Beside it are the ruins of the rostrum (raised platform) where Mark Antony delivered the funeral address in Caesar's honor. On the other side of the Arch of Septimius Severus is the **Curia** **3**, a large brick senate hall dating from the 3rd century AD. Other important monuments in this large complex of ruins include: **The Temple of Antonius and Faustin, 4**, erected in 141 AD to commemorate the emperor and his wife; and the **Basilica of Maxentius 5**, completed by Constantine in 312.

As the empire grew, the Roman Forum could not accommodate additional structures, so certain emperors – following Julius Caesar's example – built along its outskirts. The remains of these

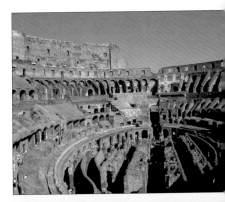

(Above) Arch of Constantine. (Below) The Colosseum's interior, missing its arena floor, and an exterior view.

Rome

N

0 1000
Yards

CITY ATTRACTIONS

(1) Colosseum
(2) Palatine
(3) Curia
(4) Temple of Antonius and Faustina
(5) Basilica of Maxentius
(6) Victor Emmanuel Monument
(7) Piazza del Campidoglio
(8) Piazza Navona
(9) Piazza Della Rotonda
(10) Piazza Campo dei Fiori
(11) Palazzo Farnese
(12) Ponte Sant' Angelo
(13) Vatican Museum
(14) Sistine Chapel
(15) Trevi Fountain
(16) Spanish Steps

imperial forums can still be seen along Via dei Fori Imperiali, a busy main street which leads to **Piazza Venezia**, the hub of central Rome. In the northwest corner of the square is the Palazzo Venezia, an early renaissance palace from which Mussolini, standing in the balcony over the main portal, would deliver speeches to the crowd-filled piazza below. Dominating Piazza Venezia is the **Victor Emmanuel Monument 6**, the huge marble 'wedding cake' commemorating the first king of a united Italy. Begun in 1885, it took forty years to complete. The ceremonial staircase leads to the Altar of the Nation which contains the Tomb of the Unknown Soldier, guarded by two sentinels. Above the shrine stands a statue of Romas flanked on both sides by celebratory reliefs. In the centre of the monument is a colossal equestrian statue of Victor Emmanuel.

Behind the Victor Emmanuel Monument, on **Capitoline Hill**, is the **Church of Santa Maria d'Aracoeli**. One of the oldest Christian churches in Rome, officiated by the Franciscan Friars Minor since 1250, its unadorned

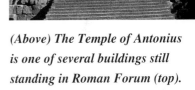

(Above) The Temple of Antonius is one of several buildings still standing in Roman Forum (top).

brick facade is reached from street level by a long stairway that was built in 1348. Another broad stairway right beside it leads to the **Piazza del Campidoglio 7**, an architectural complex designed by Michelangelo in the 1530s, at the request of Pope Paul III, and completed long after the artist's death. This complex occupies the most famous of Rome's seven hills – the Capitoline – which was

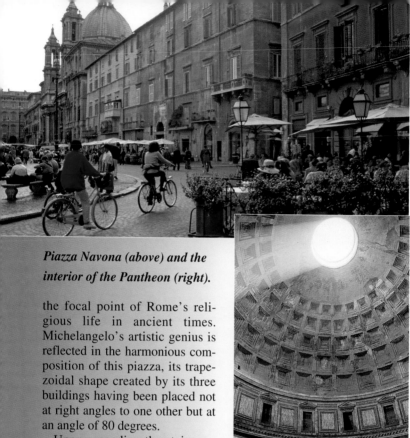

Piazza Navona (above) and the interior of the Pantheon (right).

the focal point of Rome's religious life in ancient times. Michelangelo's artistic genius is reflected in the harmonious composition of this piazza, its trapezoidal shape created by its three buildings having been placed not at right angles to one other but at an angle of 80 degrees.

Upon ascending the staircase, visitors face the **Palazzo Senatorio** (Senators' Palace), now the Town Hall, which dominates the piazza. To the right is the **Palazzo dei Conservatori** (Conservators' Palace) which displays works of art, including the famous Capitoline Wolf – a 5th century bronze statue of the she-wolf (symbol of Rome) suckling the infant Romolus (founder of Rome) and his brother Remus, figures added by a 15th-century artist. To the left is the Palazzo Nuovo, which houses the **Capitoline Museum**, its works of art including a 2nd century equestrian statue of the emperor Marcus Aurelius, the only bronze equestrian statue to survive from imperial Rome. It had stood in the center of the piazza atop a pedestal until it was removed in 1981; an exact replica was mounted in its place in the spring of 1997.

The main thoroughfare of Corso Vittoria Emanuele II runs through the centre of Old Rome, where narrow, winding streets lead to such famous attractions as the cafe-lined **Piazza Navona 8** , considered one of Rome's most beautiful squares with its baroque fountains and churches, and the **Piazza Della Rotonda**

(Above) Ponte Sant' Angelo.
(Below) St. Peter's Basilica.

9 which is dominated by the Pantheon, a domed temple from the early 2nd century AD, its impressive interior the best preserved of imperial Rome's surviving structures. **Piazza Campo dei Fiori** (Field of Flowers) **10** is the scene of a colorful outdoor market each weekday morning, and the nearby **Palazzo Farnese 11** is a beautiful Renaissance palace now housing the French Embassy.

The elegant **Ponte Sant' Angelo 12** leads across the River Tiber to Castel Sant'Angelo. Three of the bridge's arches are original – built by Hadrian's successor – and in 1688 the bridge was extended and embellished with ten angels designed by Bernini. **Castel Sant'Angelo**, built in 139 AD as a mausoleum for the emperor Hadrian, was eventually used as a fortress for popes seeking refuge in times of peril. It later served as a prison, and is now a museum containing beautifully decorated papal apartments and prison cells.

Vatican City

A tiny sovereign state in the heart of Rome, Vatican City contains some of the world's most famous buildings and works of art. **St. Peter's Basilica**, the world's largest church, stands on the site of an early shrine to St. Peter. In the 4th century, Emperor Constantine built a church over the grave of St. Peter, and it was in this wood-roofed basilica that Charlemagne and other emperors

(Above) Bernini's baldachino.
(Below) The nave (with its barrel vault) inside St. Peter's Basilica.

and popes were crowned. In 1506, Pope Julius II decided a new church should be built to replace the dilapidated original, and Bramante was commissioned to design it. A succession of architects worked on St. Peter's, including Michelangelo who took over in 1547 and added the gigantic dome. The church was finally completed in 1626 and its sublime interior of creamy marble and glittering gilt is filled with masterpieces. Michelangelo's famous *La Pieta* (sculpted when he was 24) is in one of the side chapels. Bernini's *baldachino* – a bronze canopy – stands above the high altar from which only the pope may read mass.

Piazza San Pietro (**St. Peter's Square**) was designed by Bernini in the 1650s at the request of Pope Alexander VII. He called for a grand approach to St. Peter's that wouldn't obstruct the view of the faithful who gather in the square when the pope makes an address from the church's central balcony or from a window of the adjacent Vatican Palace. Bernini met this criteria with a sweeping colonnade that curves along both sides of the square. The Egyptian obelisk in the centre of the square was brought to Rome in imperial times by the Emperor Caligula, and the monumental avenue leading to the piazza was added by Mussolini.

The **Vatican Museums** **13**, next door to the Vatican Palace, are a complex of eight museums and five galleries containing one of the world's most extensive art collections, including ancient Egyptian artifacts, Roman statues and paintings by Raphael. The ceiling and altar wall of the **Sistine Chapel** 14 where the cardinals meet to elect a new pope, were painted by Michelangelo. Considered works of unsurpassed grandeur, the ceiling frescoes depict biblical scenes and the altar wall was selected for Michelangelo's painting of the *Last Judgment*. A major restoration of these works was undertaken from 1980 to 1992, which entailed cleaning away a layer of dirt to reveal the original vibrant colors of the frescoes. Amid the spectrum of colors used by Michelangelo, the two that stand out are green and violet – the liturgical colors of the Mass.

(Above) Michelangelo's Creation of Adam, Sistine Chapel, and (below) La Pieta, St. Peter's.

THE VATICAN SWISS GUARDS

Since the 15th century, Swiss mercenaries have fought in various European armies. Called Swiss Guards, these mercenaries were put at the disposal of foreign powers in return for money payments. In 1874 the Swiss constitution forbade all recruitment of Swiss soldiers by foreign powers, with the exception of Vatican City. Founded in 1505 as the personal guard of the pope, the Swiss Guard in the Vatican carry on a centuries-old tradition of swearing to serve the pope. Recruited from Switzerland's Catholic cantons, the guardsmen on sentry duty are garbed in colorful costume of Renaissance design and wear ceremonial armor. A 100-member force, its members live in Vatican City and must observe strict rules, including a midnight curfew.

FOUNTAIN FROLICKS

Trevi Fountain

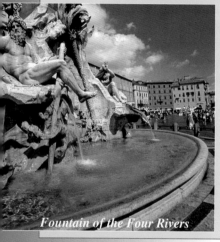
Fountain of the Four Rivers

Completed in 1762, the **Trevi Fountain** 15 is one of Rome's most popular attractions. Its centerpiece is a statue of the god Oceanus riding in a sea chariot drawn by two Tritons. The fountain was used for a scene in Fellini's famous film *La Dolce Vita*, in which characters played by Marcello Mastroianni and Anita Ekberg go wading in it. Such behaviour is, in real life, frowned upon because of the risk of vandalism, both deliberate and accidental, and the city of Rome imposes a stiff fine on anyone caught bathing in a public fountain. The fine was increased in the summer of 1997 after a 43-year-old Roman and his two companions went for a dip in the Bernini-designed *Fountain of the Four Rivers* in Piazza Navona. When the Roman climbed onto the marble tail of a water creature, a piece broke off and fell into six pieces. Romans were indignant, with film director Franco Zeffirelli even suggesting corporal punishment, but the vandal himself was unrepentant, not only refusing to apologize but also threatening to sue the city for damages because he hurt his foot in the incident.

Rome's main shopping area lies between Via del Corso and the **Spanish Steps** 16 – Rome's most fashionable gathering place. Artists and writers have long been attracted to this area, including the Romantic poet Keats, who lived and died in a house next to the Steps, his residence now a museum. The 18th-century Steps were built by the French to connect the Spanish Quarter at the bottom to the French Quarter at the top. A 16th-century church, built for France's King Louis XII, stands at the top of the Steps, and a boat-shaped fountain designed by Bernini is at the bottom. Famous **shopping streets** lead off Piazza di Spagna, namely Via Condotti and Via Borgognona, both lined with sophisticated boutiques. Less expensive shops are found on Via Frattina.

Not far from the Spanish Steps are some of Rome's most luxurious hotels, including the famous Hotel Excelsior on legendary **Via**

Veneto, where movie stars and deposed royalty held court at sidewalk cafes in the late 1950s, their antics captured in candid photos by a new breed of photographers called paparazzi. The elegant **Hotel Eden** on Via Ludovisi, with sweeping views from its rooftop bar and restaurant, was the favorite haunt of Hemingway, Fellini and Ingrid Bergman.

Tarquinia

While most passengers arriving in Civitavecchia head straight to Rome for a full day of sightseeing, some choose an excursion to Tarquinia. In 449 BC the Etruscans, whose kings had founded and ruled Rome for about a century, established the ancient city of Tarquinni. These people (possibly from Asia Minor) had first settled in the Tuscany area of Italy in the 8th century BC, about the same time the Greeks began to settle along the southern shores of Italy. The Etruscans, their commercial empire rivaling those of Greece and Phoenicia, didn't form a unified nation, but rather a network of city-states, each of which succumbed, one by one, to the Romans in the 5th and 4th centuries BC. Such was the fate of Tarquinni, but its large necropolis of tombs remained intact and today visitors can gaze at their unique murals, inspired perhaps by Egyptian wall art and painted around 500 BC. The **Etruscan National Museum**, housed in a 15th-century castle in the nearby town of Tarquinia, contains an extensive collection of Etruscan artifacts.

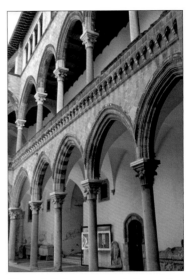

Tarquinia's museum is housed in a 15th-century castle.

Naples (Napoli)

The beautiful Bay of Naples had lured many a visitor to its scenic shores when British admiral **Horatio Nelson** pulled into port during the summer of 1798. Nelson joined a long list of illustrious guests, including Goethe, who were graciously entertained by Sir William Hamilton, the British ambassador to Naples from 1764 to 1800. Sir Hamilton, after years of scholarly pursuits, had embraced the Neapolitans' carefree attitude to life and thrown himself with gusto into the pursuit of pleasure. His beautiful young wife and former mistress, **Lady Emma Hamilton**, was a confidante of the Queen of Naples – whose court was a center of scandal and intrigue – and it was through this friendship that the British fleet, under the command of Nelson, was allowed access to the Spanish-controlled ports of Naples and Syracuse to take on provisions when all other Mediterranean ports had been shut off by the French. Nelson went on to destroy the French fleet off the mouth of the Nile River and, upon his return to Naples, he was given a hero's welcome and was bestowed with a British peerage. He also fell deeply in love with Lady Hamilton, and so began their notorious love affair.

Such is life in southern Italy, a land of sunshine and song, idyllic islands and fragrant breezes. In ancient times, wealthy Romans built themselves country villas at Herculaneum and Pompeii, situated at the base of **Mount Vesuvius**, and the tiny island paradise of Capri, in the Bay of Naples, became a holiday retreat for the early emperors Augustus and Tiberius. The cataclysmic eruption of Mount Vesuvius in 79 AD brought a thunderous end to the good life when Herculaneum and Pompeii were buried under cinders, ashes and mud, then long forgotten until they were redis-covered in the 18th century.

When the Englishman **Thomas Cook**, the world's first tour opera-tor, brought a group of British

Mount Vesuvius looms above the Bay of Naples.

tourists to Italy in 1864, the exca-vated site of ancient Pompeii was perceived as a somewhat shocking, pleasure-seeking city brimming with bars, brothels and priapic stat-uary. Some Victorians believed the eruption of Vesuvius was a fire sent from heaven to punish Pompeii for its wickedness, a belief that only added to its attrac-tion. The Romans did like their wine strong, but the presence of lead in the water pipes had dead-ened their taste. As for the Priapus figure displayed at the entrance to their homes, this Roman god of male generative power was meant to ward off evil influences. And, although the Romans' favorite form of entertainment was the cir-cus-like spectacle of gladitorial contests, there was also a refined side to Pompeii, preserved in the luxurious and lavishly decorated villas of the wealthy.

A trip to the top of Mount Vesuvius to peer into the smolder-ing volcano's crater was part of a 19th-century Cook's Italian Tour, and the company eventually bought the Italian-built funicular which carried visitors up the final ascent of the cone. A further sec-tion was added to connect the funicular with the main line, and those who rode the Vesuvius rail-way included Edward VII and Ulysses S. Grant. The line was

A wedding couple crosses a busy street in Piazza Trieste e Trento.

completely destroyed in 1944 when the volcano erupted for the third time that century. The volcano's smoldering presence has made Neapolitans somewhat superstitious, and twice a year they gather by the hundreds with their archbishop at the Cathedral of San Gennaro to pray to a 4th-century saint and witness a 'miracle' in which his blood, kept in gold vials, liquefies – a sign that disaster will not strike the city. Scientists have confirmed that the substance is blood, but they have yet to explain why it regularly liquefies.

When Antonio Bassolino was elected mayor in 1993, Naples had become over-populated and run down, and was best known for giving the world pizza and the actress Sophia Loren, who grew up in its slums. The new mayor decided to revitalize his city's cultural heritage by cleaning up the historic piazzas and restoring neglected churches, museums and palaces. In the process, he rekindled Neapolitans' pride in a city founded as Neapolis (New City)

Maritime Station was built during Mussolini's dictatorship.

by the Ancient Greeks and later the glittering capital of the Kingdom of Naples.

On Your Own

Naples is not a pedestrian-friendly city. Simply crossing some of the busy streets is challenging, for no one seems to take any notice of whether a traffic light is red or green. Fortunately, many historic buildings are located a short distance from the **Maritime Station** (Stazione Marittima) **1** where the cruise ships dock. Further afield is the Archaeological Museum, about a US$10 taxi ride away.

The **train station** is on Corso Garibaldi, about one mile from the cruise dock – a US$10 taxi ride. Herculaneum, Pompeii and Sorrento can all be reached by train, and tickets are sold in euros. A train runs every 20 to 30 minutes from Naples to **Pompeii** (disembark at the Pompeii Excavation site); the ride takes about 30 minutes and costs US$12 each way. The train ride

from Naples to **Sorrento** is an hour and 20 minutes.

Several companies operate jet boats, hydrofoils and ferries from Naples to Capri and Sorrento. Fastest and most expensive are the jet foils; slowest and cheapest are the ferries. A terminal is located beside the Maritime Station, with numerous departures by **hydrofoil** to **Capri** (approx. US$25 round trip, 40 minutes each way), and to **Sorrento** (approx. US$20 round trip, 45 minutes each way). The **ferry** from Naples to Capri takes about 75 minutes each way and costs about $10 round-trip. Boats also run between Sorrento and Capri. Tickets are sold in euros.

Shopping: Naples-area artisans are known for their fine craftsmanship in cameos (carved from shells), ceramics, wood inlay and embroidered goods. Galleria Umberto I and Via Chiaia both offer upscale shopping.

Naples Attractions

The city's medieval past is evidenced by several Neapolitan castles overlooking the harbor, including the 12th-century **Castel dell'Ovo** 3 which stands on a rocky islet, and **Castel Nuovo** 4 a symbol of power and the scene of fierce battles between the French and Spanish. Surrounded by a moat, the castle was originally built in 1279 by Charles I of Anjou, then rebuilt by Spanish and Tuscan craftsmen following the bloody wars of the 15th century. Naples became a centre of sculpture under the rule of Alfonso of Aragon, who captured Naples in 1442. His admiration of classical antiquity is reflected in the triumphal arch he had built between the two towers that flank the castle's west entrance.

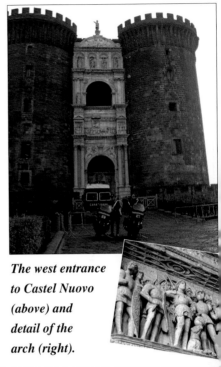

The west entrance to Castel Nuovo (above) and detail of the arch (right).

(Above) Galleria Umberto I.
(Below) Gates to Royal Palace.
(Bottom) Piazza Plebiscito.

Dozens of Renaissance sculptors worked on its complex design from 1451 until its completion 30 years later.

The Palazzo Reale (**Royal Palace**) **5**, built in the early 1600s, has been damaged, restored and remodeled over the centuries. The past home to various Neapolitan royal families, including the Spanish Bourbons, its sumptuous interior of frescoed walls and grand staircases is filled with baroque furniture, period mirrors and chandeliers, Chinese porcelain vases, gilt bronzes, and paintings by celebrated artists.

Naples is famous for its music, both classical and popular, some well-known Neapolitan songs being *Funiculi Funicula* and *O Sole Mio*. The great tenor Caruso was a Naples native, and numerous works – including *La Sonnambula* by Bellini – have premiered at the Teatro di S. Carlo (**San Carlo Opera House**) **6**, second in Italy only to La Scala in Milan. It first opened in 1737, then was reconstructed following a fire in 1816. The red and gold interior, which seats 3,000 and provides perfect acoustics, is also a visual feast, with its seven levels of private boxes, each row adorned with gilt balustrades.

Galleria Umberto I **7**, named for King Umberto I, is an iron- and glass-roofed gallery constructed in the late 1800s, which today is filled with elegant shops and cafes. More fine shops are located on Via Chiaia, off **Piazza Trieste e Trento** **8**, a lovely square with a fountain in its centre that connects with **Piazza Plebiscito** **9**, which opens to the sweeping facade of the Chiesa di S. Francesco di Paola (Church of St. Francis).

Completed in 1847, the church was modeled on the Pantheon in Rome, while the curving colonnade arcade is reminiscent of the one in St. Peter's Square. A large and majestic square, it is a popular photo shoot for Neapolitan wedding parties.

The highly acclaimed **National Archaeological Museum** **10**, housed in a 16th-century building, contains one of the world's largest collections of classical antiquities, including the historic riches recovered from Herculaneum, Pompeii and other sites. Paintings, mosaics, statues, busts, vases and domestic implements are among the discoveries on display.

Pompeii & Herculaneum

Nestled at the foot of Mount Vesuvius, the Roman centers of Pompeii, a prosperous walled city, and Herculaneum, a seaside resort town, were both recovering from the earthquake of 63 AD when disaster struck on an August day in 79 AD. The day began like any other, the residents of Pompeii going about their business as bakers, merchants, artisans, prostitutes and

CLASSIC CUISINE

Pizza is a Neapolitan dish that many people – including the president of the Italian Pizza Academy – consider to be classic cuisine. To meet the certification standards for 'genuine pizza' (set by the Italian Standards Institute), a restaurant must dice the tomato a certain size (8 mm), use mozzarella cheese made from buffalo milk, and bake the pizza at 390 to 453 degrees Fahrenheit. In Naples, where chefs have been making pizza for more than two centuries, the thick-crust style is used, but some chefs in Rome are insisting they will stick to their thin-crust style. Pizzeria Trianon, located at Via Colletta Pietro, 46 (near the central train station at Piazza Garibaldi) is one of the most famous pizzerie in Naples, baking about 1,000 pizzas a day in its three wood-burning ovens.

The basilica and antiquarium of Pompeii. (Below) Cast of man caught in final moment of life.

slaves who were in service to the wealthy owners of fine villas. The public baths were busy, as usual, and the city's shops and streets were filled with people, many pausing to read or add to the graffiti written on public walls. Chariots and carts rolled by, following the worn ruts in roads.

Then, suddenly, the ground began to shake. Instantly everyone knew they were in the grip of another devastating quake, but there was little time to react before catastrophe struck. A thunderous cloud of ash and lava

exploded from the summit of Mount Vesuvius, erupting with such force that it blew away part of the mountain. As people ran for their lives, they were suffocated by gaseous fumes, while those still inside their homes were buried beneath a torrential downpour of cinder and ash. The residents of Herculaneum made a desperate rush for the town exit but there was no escaping the darkness that descended on them. When it was all over, in a space of a few hours, Pompeii lay buried under 20 feet (7 metres) of ash and Herculaneum was sealed under a 40- to 100-foot layer of rock that formed when the ash was hardened by falling rain.

Entombed for centuries, the ancient townsite of Herculaneum was first discovered in 1706, when a well was being dug, and systematic excavations began in 1738. The larger site of Pompeii was discovered in 1748, providing the world with a detailed look at everyday Roman life as it existed in 79 AD. Archaeologists discovered hundreds of personal items in the city's private residences, including furniture, ornaments and beautifully preserved wall paintings in the villas of the town's patrician class. By pouring liquid plaster into hollows left by disintegrated bodies, they were able to make hauntingly life-like 'impressions', of the people caught in their final moments – embracing, fleeing, retrieving valuable objects from their homes.

Today's visitors to Pompeii enter through the main gate (Porta Marina) near the forum, or through a back gate near the amphitheater. A restaurant and shop carrying books and maps is located just north of the forum on Via del Foro (Forum Street). Areas of interest include the remains of the civic forum's public buildings, such as the Temple of Apollo and the Basilica, and the forum baths with a hot-water boiler and cold-water pool.

Just wandering the streets of Pompeii is a fascinating experience. The raised sidewalks and stepping stones were designed to keep pedestrians' feet dry when rainwater collected in the streets, and cat's eyes – small white marble stones – were set in the streets (and villa floors) to illuminate them at night. The villas and other private homes have been given descriptive names, and at the entrance to the House of the Tragic Poet is a 'Beware of Dog' sign, written in Latin with an accompanying mosaic of a guard dog. The best preserved villa is Casa Dei Vetti, where visitors can admire the home's atrium, frescoed walls and garden courtyard.

Mount Vesuvius, its sides scarred by lava flow, is visible from Naples, but reaching its crater takes some effort since a chair lift is no longer in operation. The mountain's fertile lower slopes are cultivated with vineyards which produce the famous Lachryma Christi (Tears of Christ) wine. The base of the volcanic mountain is encircled by a railroad and a trail can be hiked to the crater's rim.

For more information on Pompeii and ancient Roman towns, see pages 92 to 94 and page 107.

(Above) The Amalfi Coast and picturesque port of Amalfi (left).

Capri town overlooks Marina Grande, where the passenger ferries dock and a visitor information office is located. A charming town of narrow lanes and tiny squares, Capri is reached by funicular, bus or taxi. Anacapri, which is quieter than Capri, can be reached by bus from Capri. The island's footpaths provide spectacular views of a cliff-edged sea, where coastal attractions include the Blue Grotto (a sea cave bathed in iridescent blue light) which can be reached by boat from Marina Grande. Car traffic is light on the island and restaurants are numerous.

Capri

The tiny island paradise of Capri, with its lush vegetation and delightful climate, has been an exclusive retreat since the days of the Roman Empire, when Emperor Tiberius owned 12 villas on the craggy island. Twentieth-century residents have included Gracie Fields, Rudolph Nureyev and the Swedish physician and writer Axel Munthe, who built Villa San Michele, now a museum, at **Anacapri**, one of two towns on the island which are set atop limestone cliffs where herds of *capra* (goats) once roamed.

Amalfi Coast

The Amalfi coast, from Sorrento to Salerno, is one of the most scenic in the Mediterranean, with its cliff-clinging roads and spectacular views. One seaside resort after another lies along this enchanting stretch of coast, including **Sorrento**, home of the

Sorrento and (right) Positano.

legendary sirens who tried to lure Odysseus onto the rocks. Some cruise ships anchor off Sorrento and tender their passengers ashore. A tourist shuttle runs between Sorrento and **Positano**, where John Steinbeck, in 1953, lived in one of its multi-colored houses connected by hillside stairs above a crescent bay. In the hills above Positano is a gem of a restaurant called **La Tagliata**, with spectacular views and excellent local cuisine. A family-run establishment, it is located at Via Tagliata, 22, Montepertuso (about a $20 taxi ride from Positano).

Amalfi, a small fishing port and picturesque resort overlooking the Gulf of Salerno, was founded by Romans. It became, in the 9th century AD, an Italian maritime republic rivaling Pisa, Venice and Genoa in wealth and power. Its Sicilian-Arab cathedral, built in the 11th century with later additions, reflects the influence of Arab invaders who had seized Sicily in 917 and raided the mainland, until they were driven out by the Normans.

Salerno flourished during the Middle Ages, establishing a medical school in the 9th century and erecting a Sicilian-Norman cathedral in the 11th century. During World War II, allied forces landed on the beaches near Salerno, where fierce fighting forced the Germans to retreat toward Naples.

Sicily (Sicilia)

The largest of the Mediterranean islands, Sicily's mountainous terrain includes **Mt. Etna**, an active volcano and the island's highest point at 10,700 feet. The island, with its fertile soil and long, hot growing season, was a granary of the ancient world. Agriculture remains the major industry – wheat, barley and maize as well as olives, citrus fruits, almonds and wine grapes all grown here. The per-capita income is low and unemployment is high on this densely populated island of over five million people.

Sicily's first inhabitants were tribes named Sicani and Siculi. The island's east coast was colonized by the Greeks who founded Syracuse, Catania and Zancle (now Messina). Syracuse emerged as the leader of these flourishing Greek colonies, which eventually rivaled the city-states of Greece itself. By 400 BC Sicily was a battleground between the rival empires of Carthaginia and Greece, a situation that would be repeated time and again as foreign powers fought for control of Sicilian soil. During the Punic Wars, Rome and Carthaginia battled for possession of Sicily, and when the Romans eventually seized control of the island, it became the 'Breadbasket of Rome'. Sicilian culture was enriched with Hellenization, which Romans expanded, but they also exploited the island and established large estates that would eventually hinder its economic development.

After the fall of Rome, the island eventually passed to the Byzantines in 535 AD. The Arabs raided the island for two centuries before it finally fell in the 9th century. Next came the Norman conquest of Sicily in 1060, led by Roger I, whose son Roger II became the first king of Sicily, his brilliant court introducing Arab learning to western Europe. The Kingdom of Sicily came under Spanish rule in 1282, after it rebelled against Charles I of Naples, a brother of the French king. This would be the first of many times Sicily would struggle for independence from foreign rule, including revolts in 1820 and in 1848, when the bombardments of Messina and Palermo by Ferdinand II prompted Sicilians

to call him 'King Bomba'.

Sicily finally voted to join the kingdom of Sardinia after being conquered in 1860 by Giuseppe Garibaldi, a popular Italian patriot and leading figure in the Risorgimento. Sicily's most recent invasion came during World War II when, in July 1943, Allied forces staged a large-scale amphibious landing from North African bases and, following a month of heavy fighting, Sicily was once again conquered.

After centuries of exploitation by outsiders, Sicilians today are trying to rid their island of the Mafia – a name that came into use during the 19th century when it was applied to groups of brigands.

Palermo

The capital and largest city of Sicily, Palermo began as an ancient Phoenician seaport and a Carthaginian military base when it was conquered by Romans in 253 BC. It was during the Arab occupation of 831 to 1072 AD that the city prospered, rivaling Cairo with the Oriental splendor of its palaces, mosques and minarets. An important trading port between East and West, the city continued to flourish under the Normans – most notably during the reign of Roger II, whose court was a centre for the arts, letters and sciences.

Today's Palermo, plagued by poverty and heavy traffic, contains some unique and resplendent works of art which are located within walking distance of one another. Most notable is the Cappella Palatina (**Palatine Chapel**), located inside the

Norman Royal Palace, which is the seat of the Sicilian parliament. This Arab-Norman chapel, built in 1132 by Roger II, is an artistic treasure containing glittering mosaics and a honeycombed ceiling. The pink-domed San Giovanni degli Eremiti (**Church of St. John of the Hermits**) was built in 1132 on the site of an old mosque, and its lovely cloister is filled with palm and citrus trees. Other historic buildings are the 12th-century cathedral; the 15th-century Palazzo Abbatellis; and the Gothic Palazzo Chiaramonte, built in 1307. Shoppers in search of Sicilian handicrafts should visit the flea market on **Via Papireto**, behind the cathedral.

Shore excursions include a narrated drive through Palmero, a walking tour of a Norman fortified village, exploring the ancient ruins at Segesta and visiting the seaside town of Cefal.

Messina/Taormina

Situated on the Strait of Messina across from the Italian mainland, Messina is a busy seaport and the gateway to Sicily, with passenger ferries regularly pulling in and out of the harbor. Messina is a modern city that was rebuilt following a devastating earthquake in December 1908 which claimed 80,000 lives and destroyed 90 per cent of the buildings, including fine churches and palaces.

On Your Own

The main attraction for passengers arriving by ship at Messina is the nearby medieval town of Taormina with its Graeco-Roman theatre. **Taormina** is located 27 miles south of Messina, and can be reached by ship-organized shore tour, by train or by taxi. A return taxi ride from Messina to Taormina, with a two-hour wait

The Messina lighthouse (below).
The Sicilian coast viewed from Taormina (bottom).

Messina's Norman-Romanesque cathedral was rebuilt following the 1908 earthquake. The bell tower's rare clock mechanism sets statues in motion at mid-day.

at Taormina, costs about US$140. The **train station** (6) is about half a mile from the ship, and the train ride to Taormina takes from 45 minutes to one hour and 20 minutes; the fare is US$16 each way. The Taormina-Gardini train station is situated below Taormina at the base of a hill and from there you can embark on a steep hike up to the town or hire a taxi (about US$20). A cable car, based about one mile from the train station, costs approximately US$2 each way. All tickets are sold in euros.

Shore excursions from Messina include full-day tours of Taormina and Mount Etna. A unique tour is the one that visits two Sicilian villages - **Savoca** and **Forza d'Agro** – where Francis Ford Coppola filmed scenes for *The Godfather* films.

Messina Attractions

There are several interesting sights right in Messina, within walking distance of the pier. The main **shopping** area is along Via Garibaldi, Piazza Cairoli and Viale San Martino.

The **Norman-Romanesque cathedral 1**, was originally built by the Norman king Roger II in 1197. Modified over time, it was damaged by earthquakes in 1638 and 1783, then almost entirely destroyed by the 1908 earthquake. It has been recon-

The Sanctuary of Christo Re.

structed to its original Norman appearance, including most of the mosaics and works of art. The bell tower houses an astronomical clock, one of the largest and most complex of its kind, which was brought from Strasbourg in 1933, and which springs into mechanized action at mid-day.

The church of the Annunziata dei Catalani (**The Most Holy Annunciation of the Catalans**) **2** was founded in the 12th century on the ruins of an ancient temple of Neptune. Reflecting both Byzantine and Arab influences, the church today stands several feet below street level because of the city's progressive raising due to earthquakes and reconstructions. Two of the original Quattro Fontane (**Four Fountains**) **3** still stand at the former cross-roads of via Austria and via Cardines. Baroque in design, two of them are now kept in the **Regional Museum 4** which is about 1-1/2 miles from the cruise pier along the waterfront, and which houses among its works of art a collection of Renaissance paintings, including one by native-born Antonello da Messina.

The **Sanctuary of Christo Re** (King Christ) **5** enjoys a prominent position on a hill overlooking the city and harbor. Originally a Norman castle, it may have been constructed by Richard the Lionheart. Serving as a royal residence, then a prison in the 19th century, it was rebuilt after the 1908 earthquake and is now a crypt containing the Messinese who died in World War II.

An original baroque fountain can be seen down the street from the Catalans.

Taormina Attractions

A medieval town and fashionable resort of undisputed charm, Taormina stands perched above the Ionian Sea, its steep stairways and twisting paths providing views of verdant hillsides covered with palms and pines. On clear days the active volcano of Mt. Etna dominates the southwest horizon, its massive peak rising to nearly 11,000 feet. Taormina's famous **Graeco-Roman amphitheater 1**, built by the Greeks in the 3rd century BC, is beautifully situated to embrace this magnificent coastal setting of sea, sky and snowcapped mountain. Enlarged and rebuilt by the Romans in the 2nd century AD, the theatre today hosts an annual summer arts festival.

Just inside the town's north gate (Porta Messina) is the **Piazza Vittorio Emanuele 2**, site of the town's ancient Greek agora and later a Roman forum. The **Palazzo Corvala 3**, now housing a tourist information centre, was restored in 1945 and its features, spanning three historic periods of construction, include an Arab tower. The **Santa Caterina Church 4** was built in the 17th century on the site of the Roman odeum, the remains of which are visible inside the church. The town's main street of Corso Umberto I, called 'Valeria' in ancient times, leads to Piazza Aprile – a large square overlooking the sea and site of the 17th-century **Chiesa di San Giuseppe 5** and **Chiesa di Sant-Agostino 6**, built in 1448 and now the town library.

Farther along Corso Umberto I is the town's cathedral – **San Nicola** (Mother Church) **7** – which is similar in plan and from the same period as the Messina cathedral. A slight detour leads to the **Convent of San Domenico 8**, begun in 1374. Other sights

Taormina's Graeco-Roman amphitheatrer (above) and Piazza Aprile (below).

include the **Naumachie** (a Roman wall that protected a large cistern) **9**, and the ruins of **Castello Saraceno** **10**, which sits on the site of the ancient acropolis and is reached by a long stairway. A stroll through the **public gardens** **11** is also recommended. **Shops** selling local handicrafts line the Via Teatro Greco (leading to the amphitheater) and Corso Umberto I.

South of Taormina are the coastal cities of Catania and Syracuse. **Catania**, like Messina, is a port of access to Taormina. The city was heavily damaged in World War II, and in past centuries has been struck by earthquakes and volcanic eruptions, including one in 1663 when a mile-wide stream of lava flowed over the city. The 19th-century composer Vincenzo Bellini was born in Catania and his former home is now a museum. The cathedral (originally built in the 11th century) contains Bellini's remains, as well as the chapel of St. Agatha, the city's patron saint.

Syracuse (Siracusa) is best known for its Archaeological Park which contains a 5th century BC amphitheater – one of the most complete Greek theaters to survive from antiquity – as well as the ruins of a Roman amphitheater. Near the entrance to the park is Latomia del Paradiso, a garden area where a series of quarries served as prisons for the defeated Athenians who attacked Syracuse in 413 after it had become a rival city.

Sardinia

The large and mostly mountainous island of Sardinia is as much renowned for its beautiful beaches and blue-green seas as its historical landmarks. This pastoral island does not lack, however, a fascinating past. A centre of trade in prehistoric times, Sardinia was mentioned in Egyptian texts as early as the 13th century BC, and remnants of those distant days lie scattered across the island in the form of conical stone towers (called *nuraghi*). The island became a source of grain and salt for the Romans. Then, with the fall of Rome, it was invaded by various forces. From the 11th to 14th centuries, Sardinia passed back and forth between Genoa and Pisa as they fought for supremacy over the island. The House of Savoy, a dynasty of western Europe, was eventually awarded Sardinia in 1720 in exchange for Sicily (which went to the Holy Roman Emperor) and Duke Victor Amadeus II became the first king of Sardinia, its kingdom including Savoy, Piedmont and Nice.

Italy's famous revolutionary hero Giuseppe Garibaldi, born at Nice in 1807, served as a youth in the Sardinian navy. He was a man of action and when revolution swept across Europe in 1848, Garibaldi fought for Sardinia against Austria. In 1851 he bought part of the small island of **Caprera**, which lies off Sardinia's **Costa Smerald**a (Emerald Coast) of low cliffs and idyllic coves. He had, by then, abandoned the republican cause to throw his support behind Victor Emmanuel II, king of Sardinia, and in 1860 Garibaldi led the victorious conquest of Sicily before crossing to the mainland to conquer Naples. After relinquishing his conquests to Sardinia, he retired to his island property and shortly thereafter Victor Emmanuel II was proclaimed king of a united Italy.

When the Aga Khan, cruising the Mediterranean by yacht, sought shelter from a storm along the Costa Smeralda in 1965, he was smitten with the scenic beauty that had attracted the seafaring Garibaldi a century earlier. He built the upscale resort village of **Porto Cervo** and thus began the Costa Smeralda's incarnation as a chic enclave for wealthy vacationers, many of whom arrive by luxury yacht. Less-developed (and less expensive) beach resorts lie west of Porto Cervo along the island's northern tip of beach-fringed bays.

Ports of call on Sardinia include **Porto Torres** and **Alghero** – a 14th-century walled town and popular resort with sandy beaches and limestone cliffs where the Grotto of Neptune, a huge cavern, has been carved by the pounding sea. Six miles north of Alghero, on the road to Porto Torres, is a concentration of prehistoric tombs carved into the hillside, their

Shore Excursions

Sardinia Ship-organized shore excursions from **Alghero** include a walking tour of this and other walled ports, scenic drives to the dramatic headland at Cape Caccia, a stop at the prehistoric ruins at Palmavera, and a visit to Bosa, where fine lace is made. Shore excursions at **Cagliari** include a walking tour of its medieval Castello district, and a drive to the archaeological site of Nora.

chambers connected by corridors. Bronze statuettes depicting people, gods and animals have been retrieved from the tombs and nuraghi of Sardinia's earliest inhabitants. These are on display at the Archaeological Museum in **Cagliari**, the island's capital and a port of call for cruise ships. Cagliari was a Pisan stronghold during the wars with Genoa from the 11th to 14th century, and its Romanesque-Gothic cathedral, extensively rebuilt, reflects this Pisan influence, as does the massive Tower of St. Pancreas, built by Pisans in 1304. The city also has a Roman amphitheater.

As in the rest of Italy, food in Sardinia is an important matter. If **lunching** in Cagliari, try the Catalan lobster. *Ricci* (sea urchins) are also very popular.

Alghero with the cliffs of Cape Caccia in background.

CROATIA

CRUISE ROUTES

ROUTES: ------

Miles

0   60

N

ITALY

Ravenna

Ancona

Venice

Gulf of Venice

ADRIATIC SEA

Rijeka

RAB

Zadar

CROATIA

Dalmatia

Split

BRAC

VIS

KORCULA

KORCULA

LAGOSTA

BOSNIA

AND

HERZEGOVINA

Mostar

Sarajevo ★

MELITA

Dubrovnik

KOTOR

MONTENEGRO

CHAPTER SIX

CROATIA
AND MONTENEGRO

Croatia's island-dotted Dalmatian coast, famous for its scenic beauty, has been coveted by Roman emperors, Venetian doges, Turkish sultans and Hungarian kings. The mainland is dominated by the Dinaric Alps, their steep slopes forming a dramatic backdrop for the convoluted coastline's harbors and headlands. Immediately offshore lies a string of islands said to number over 1,200, where pine-scented coves and secluded beaches are lapped by the clear blue waters of the Adriatic Sea.

Dalmatia's History

When Dalmatia was swapped between Austria and France in the 19th century, Napoleon incorporated this rugged territory into the Illyrian provinces, thus reviving a name from ancient times.

Subduing the Illyrians had never been easy. The Ancient Greeks avoided the warlike Illyrian tribes, and it was only after the Roman province of Illyria was established in the 3rd century BC that Dalmatia was finally subdued and incorporated into Illyria under Augustus (35-33 BC). Two centuries later the future emperor **Diocletian** was born near the Dalmatian port of Salona (modern Split). He rose from humble beginnings to high military command in the Roman army, which proclaimed him emperor in 284 AD.

Diocletian eventually appointed three co-emperors to protect the Roman Empire from invasion. This dividing of the empire into four political sections was initially successful, but ultimately failed due to quarreling among Diocletian's successors. As for Diocletian, he abdicated in 305 and retired to his castle at Salona (Split), refusing to return and help restore stability to the empire, despite the urgings of his former co-emperor Maximiam who had

Dubrovnik's medieval walled town is a world heritage treasure.

abdicated at the same time. Gardening had become one of Diocletian's favorite pastimes and a source of happiness. Dalmatia's climate and soil are ideal for growing olives, grapes and oranges, as well as herbs such as sage and rosemary, but Diocletian was especially proud of his cabbages, and no longer interested in pursuing power.

The eventual fall of Rome brought chaos to Europe and in the 7th century the city of **Dubrovnik** was founded by Roman refugees fleeing Slav invaders, who in turn settled in Dubrovnik. The city became a link between the Latin and Slavic civilizations, and a powerful merchant republic. Over time, massive stone walls and forts were constructed to protect the medieval seaport from enemy attack.

In 1000 AD, the rising sea power of Venice sent its newly formed navy to the Dalmatian coast to defeat the pirates who hid out among the many islands, from where they staged repeated raids on Venice. When the Venetian doge Pietro Orsielo II captured the town of Korcula, his victory marked the final defeat of the Dalmatian pirates. Venice soon controlled the Adriatic, with the exception of Dubrovnik, which maintained its autonomy even while under various protectorates, including the Byzantine Empire, Venice (1205 to 1358), Hungary and Turkey. Not until 1808, when its government was abolished by Napoleon, did Dubrovnik relinquish independence.

Following World War I, Italy finally regained a foothold in Dalmatia when it received Zadar and several islands under the terms of the Treaty of Rapallo. Croatia, which had been part of the Austro-Hungarian Empire prior to World War I, was incorporated into the new Kingdom of the Serbs, Croats and Slovenes, its name changed in 1929 to Yugoslavia – a federation of six republics, namely Serbia, **Croatia**, Bosnia and Hercegovina, Macedonia, Slovenia, and **Montenegro**.

The German army invaded Yugoslavia during World War II and Dalmatia was placed under Italian control. Yugoslavia's occupation by Axis Powers was met with organized resistance by guerrilla warriors fighting from mountain strongholds. Leading this resistance was Josip Broz, who had adopted the name **Tito**.

Born in a Croatian village, the son of a blacksmith, Tito began his march to power as a soldier, then as a union organizer and political agitator. By 1945, Tito was the virtual dictator of Yugoslavia. Upon his death in 1980, ethnic tensions amongst the federation's member republics resulted in a violent breakup. Croatia was the second largest Yugoslav republic when it seceded on June 25, 1991. A six-month battle with federal troops (mostly Serbian) ensued and Croatia's independence was recognized by the European Community on January 15, 1992.

Croatia At A Glance

About 5 million people live in Croatia; the majority are Roman Catholic who use the Roman alphabet of western Europe. A minority (12%) of the population consists of Eastern Orthodox Serbs who use the Cyrillic alphabet of eastern Europe. Some Italians live in and around the city of Zadar (Ital. Zara), the historic capital of Dalmatia.

The country is nearly 22,000 square miles in size (about the size of Vermont) and encompasses Dalmatia, most of Istria, Slavonia, and Croatia proper, where the capital of Zagreb is located. A river plain lies in the east, where farming is a major industry, while the Adriatic coastline to the west is mostly mountainous, its many bays and harbors sheltered by a chain of islands. Tourism, fishing and farming thrive along the scenic Dalmatian coast, its climate similar to coastal California.

Travel Tips

Currency: The unit of currency is the Kuna (HRK), which consists of 100 lipas, but the euro is widely used. The approximate exchange is US$1 = 5 kuna. Major credit cards are accepted at most shops and restaurants. ATMs are widespread.

Telephones: Phone cards can be purchased at post offices, open Monday through Saturday from 8:00 a.m. to 8:00 p.m. Dial 901 for an international operator. Personal calling card access codes: AT&T 0800-22 0111; MCI 0800-22-0112; Sprint 0800-220-113.

Shopping: Croatian handicrafts include embroidery and fine lace, woolen and leather items, woodcarvings, ceramics and filigree jewelry. Shops remain open throughout the day, possibly closing for an hour or two over lunch.

Dining: Seafood such as calamari, cuttlefish, shrimp, lobster and oysters are featured in Dalmatian dishes, often cooked in olive oil and seasoned with garlic and local herbs. The Italian influence is enjoyed in a prevalence of pasta, pizza and risotto (rice cooked in meat sauce and seasoned with saffron).

Dubrovnik

An important seaport and tourist resort, Dubrovnik has emerged in recent years as a popular port of call for cruise travellers. Of primary interest is the city's historic section – a medieval fortress built on a promontory. Stone walls up to twenty feet thick encircle the old town, which has retained and restored much of its medieval architecture, earning it UNESCO recognition as one of the world's heritage treasures. An earthquake and fire in 1667 destroyed much of the city and in 1991-92 Dubrovnik withstood damage while under siege by the Yugoslav army.

On Your Own

The ships either anchor in the bay opposite the Old Town, or dock in Gruz Harbor, about 1.5 miles northwest of the old town. A regular shuttle bus runs between the cruise port and a stop just outside Pile Gate, one of the entrances into the walled town, which is open to pedestrian traffic only. The cruise port is a pleasant place for waterfront strolls, and the shuttle bus winds through an attractive residential area that lies between the port and the walled town. Taxis are also available at the pier. Several money exchange offices are located in or near the cruise terminal. Public phones are located at the cruise terminal and these accept personal calling cards. Phone cards can be purchased at the port building's post office. The Dubrovnik Tourist Board is located near Onofrio Fountain on Cvijete Zuzoric Street (see map).

Restaurants are found throughout the Old Town, with outdoor cafes lining the Prijeko. The main shopping streets are Stradun and Od Puca.

Dubrovnik's Old Harbour.

Local Attractions

Pile Gate ▮1▮, which dates from 1537, marks the starting point of a walking tour through the Old Town's cobbled streets and marble-paved squares. Set in a niche over the gate's Renaissance arch is a statue of Saint Blaise, the city's patron saint.

After passing through Pile Gate, visitors come upon **Onofrio Fountain** ▮2▮, one of Dubrovnik's best known landmarks and a popular gathering place for locals. Built in 1438 as a water supply system, the fountain was damaged in the 1667 earthquake but 16 of the original sculptures still adorn it.

Also in the immediate vicinity is the 14th-century **Franciscan Monastery** ▮3▮ which houses one of Europe's oldest pharmacies, founded in 1317 and still func-

Shore Excursions

Dubrovnik Dubrovnik's outlying areas can be visited by ship-organized shore excursions. These include the seaside resort of Cavtat (where Edward VIII and Wallace Simpson honeymooned) and the walled town of Ston, considered a smaller version of Dubrovnik. Some sample shore excursions:
• Walking the city walls & visiting the Maritime Museum (4 hrs, $55)
• Dalmatian Coastline & Wine Tasting (4.5 hrs, $95)
• Neretva River Boat Ride & Lunch (7.5 hrs, $100)
Consult your cruise line's website for more detail.

tioning. Medical books and laboratory equipment are on display in the monastery's museum. The monastery, its Gothic porch and

DUBROVNIK

ornamented cloister having survived the 1667 earthquake, also displays a painting that depicts the city as it looked before the great earthquake.

Placa (also called the Stradun) is the Old Town's main street and is lined with **shops** and **restaurants**. Numerous narrow lanes lead off Placa and are interesting to explore. Europe's second-oldest **synagogue** is located in the block between Boskoviceva and Zudioska.

At the eastern end of the Placa, overlooking the harbor, is the Old Town's main square, dominated by the **Clock Tower** , first built in 1444 and most recently restored in 1929, its two bronze figures regularly ringing out the hours.

Several historic buildings are located around the square, including **St. Blaise's Church** , constructed in the baroque style in the early 1700s. It occupies the site of a 14th-century church from which were recovered two stone statues and a gilded silver statue of Saint Blaise (Dubrovnik's patron saint), now displayed in the existing church's main altar.

The 15th-century **Rector's Palace** , reflecting late Gothic and early Renaissance styles, was built to house the offices and private chambers of Dubrovnik's governing rector. The building, today used for concerts during the Summer Festival, is now a museum with furnished rooms depicting how the aristocracy once lived. The 16th-century **Sponza Palace** originally served as the town's mint and customs house, and now houses the State Archives, which includes a priceless collection of manuscripts.

The **Dominican Monastery** , built between the 14th and 16th centuries, contains a collection of Renaissance paintings by local and Italian masters.

A tour of the **fortifications** encircling the Old Town, built between the 8th and 16th centuries, affords panoramic views of the city and surrounding sea. Numerous forts (shown on map)

Dubrovnik's Old Town, overlooking the harbor and Lokrum Island.

were built within and without the massive stone walls, which are still used for salt panning.

Split

The Roman emperor Diocletian put the seaport of Split on the map when he built his magnificent palace here for his retirement in 305 AD. Situated on the outskirts of Salona, an ancient city founded by the Romans, the palace was transformed into the city of Spalato (now Split) when the people of Salona fled here in the 7th century to flee invaders. Split eventually became an archiepiscopal of the Roman Catholic Church and a flourishing port of medieval Dalmatia.

Today Split (pop. approx. 200,000) is a major commercial centre, where shipbuilding and other industries thrive. Yet, its scenic location and historic monuments have made this seaside resort an important tourist

destination and an increasingly popular port of call for cruise passengers. Diocletian's palace is the most impressive of the city's Roman ruins, but other ancient structures include the cathedral and baptistery (both originally Roman temples), the town hall and parts of the walls and gates.

Shore excursions include a Split walking tour (2 hrs, $40), plus scenic drives to neighboring towns and the ruins of the Roman city of **Salonae**. A half-day trip to

The waterfront area of Split.

Korcula's inner harbor.

Krka National Park and its famous Krka River waterfalls is offered by some cruise lines, as is canoeing, cavern snorkeling, and kayaking around the medieval town of **Trogir**, which occupies an island and contains a splendid 13th-century cathedral and several Renaissance palaces.

Rab

The pastoral island of Rab (Ital. Arbe) was under Venetian rule from the 10th century until 1797. Today a popular seaside resort, the island, 40 square miles in size, has retained its ancient walls and ruins of the palace of the Venetian governors. Also of interest are the 12th-century cathedral and medieval palace where the archbishop resided.

Korcula

The beautiful island of Korcula (Ital. Curzola), lying off the Pelijesac Peninsula, is covered in pine forests, pastures and vineyards. Colonized by Greeks in the 4th century BC, Korcula became a medieval stronghold for pirates conducting raids on Venice.

According to some sources, the famous Venetian traveller Marco Polo was born on Korcula. The island's chief town, also called Korcula, has retained its medieval cathedral and fortifications.

Kotor, Montenegro

Forty miles south of Dubrovnik, along the scenic Dalmatian coast, lies the splendid Gulf of Kotor, its

---

Shore Excursions *Kotor*

In addition to a walking tour of the walled town (2 hrs), other escorted shore excursions in Kotor include a motorcoach ride to **Perast**, its baroque manors built by merchant sea captains, one of the finest being **Buovic Palace** (1693). At Perast harbor, board a motor launch for a 10-minute cruise across Boka Bay to an islet occupied by the baroque church Gospa od Skrpjela (Our Lady of the Rocks) (3.5 hrs). Another escorted excursion combines a walking tour of Kotor with a motorcoach ride up a steep, winding road to the village of **Njegusi** and to Montenegro's former capital of **Cetinje**, founded in 1482, where the National Museum is housed in the former royal palace and features the state apartments. (5.5 hrs)

St Nicholas Church

St Mary's Church

St Luca's Church

Steps to Viewpoint

0   100
N   Yards

Maritime Museum

Western Gateway

Clock Tower

Pjaca od Muzejo

Trg Oktobarske Revolucije

Kotor Fjord

St Tryphon Cathedral

Jadranski Put

KOTOR

fjord-like reaches bordered by limestone cliffs. Hidden at the head of its innermost inlet is the medieval port of Kotor, its well-preserved walls and buildings a World Heritage Site. Ruled by the Republic of Venice from 1420 to 1797, Kotor's architecture reflects the Venetian influence. Buildings of note include St. Tryphon Cathedral and the 17-century Grgurina Palace, which houses the Maritime Museum – a tribute to Kotor's seafaring past when it was one of the Adriatic's major naval powers. Kotor (pop. 14,000) is the oldest town in Montenegro. First colonized by Greeks in the 3rd century BC, then part of the Roman and Byzantine empires, Kotor passed to Austria in 1797. The republic of Montenegro, formerly part of Yugoslavia, declared its independence in 2006.

A bird's eye view of Kotor.

MONTENEGRO'S LAST MONARCH

Nicholas I was a young prince when he inherited the throne of Montenegro from his uncle Danilo II in 1860. He ruled Montenegro until 1918, when he was forced to flee invading Austrian troops. While in exile, Nicholas resisted his country's union with Serbia under a Serbian king but was deposed. His five daughters had all married into the ruling houses of Europe, including that of Serbia where an ongoing feud between two rival dynasties had existed for decades. Nicholas died in exile in 1921, at the age of 80.

CHAPTER SEVEN

MAINLAND GREECE

Greece is a mystical land of impassable mountain ridges and fertile plains filled with olive trees and orange groves. Monasteries dot pine-forested slopes and isolated valleys run down to the sea. Strabo, a Greek geographer from the 1st century BC, wrote that 'the sea presses in upon the country with a thousand arms', for no point in Greece is further than 65 miles from the coast. With limited natural resources, the Greeks have always looked to the sea for their livelihoods, through fishing, shipping and trade. Today the country's merchant marine is one of the largest per capita in the world, and an extensive ferry system connects Greece's mainland ports and widely scattered islands.

This seafaring tradition harks back to ancient times when the first stirrings of Western civilization began on the shores of mainland Greece, then spread outward, across the Mediterranean Sea, to far-flung islands and distant coastlines. Many of our modern institutions, such as democracy, are based on concepts that originated in classical Greece. Theater began with the Greek dramatists and the foundations of 20th-century architecture, law and philosophy can be traced to Greece.

The early Greeks' pursuit of both knowledge and pleasure is reflected in the myriad of words they have given the English language, such as arithmetic and aphrodisiac, platonic and erotic. The Greek gods and heroes are part of our everyday vocabulary, their names associated with everything from spacecraft to jogging shoes, as in Apollo (the god of light) and Nike (the winged goddess of victory). And when satellites beam us televised coverage of the Olympic Games, the torch-bearing runner who lights the eternal flame is reenacting yet another time-honored ritual rooted in ancient Greece.

When Athens hosted the summer games in 2004, the Olympics returned to their country of origin for the first time since the modern games began in 1896. The Men's Marathon was raced on its ancient course, retracing the route run by Pheidippides in 490 BC when bringing news of victory over the Persians. The route starts

Porch of the Caryatids.

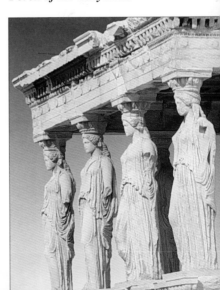

in Marathon and ends in Athens, at the Panathinaiko Stadium, its horseshoe-shaped marble-clad seating built for the 1896 Olympiad as a replica of the ancient stadium that once stood on this site. Few could witness such an event without recalling the glory that was Greece.

Greece at a Glance

The term Greek derives from *Groeci*, the Latin name for a small Hellenic tribe of ancient Greece, and the Greeks refer to their country as Hellas. About 10 million people live in Greece and the faith of the majority is Eastern Orthodox. Greek, with a variety of local dialects, is the dominant language, and the well educated speak a more classical version of the language than the masses. English is widely spoken. The Greek alphabet has fewer letters than the English, and when a Greek word or name is translated into English there are often several variations in the spelling.

The scenery of Greece is diverse, ranging from pine-forested mountain slopes to sandy beaches. Although only 25% of the land is arable, farming is a major industry. Goats and sheep are raised in the arid mountain pastures and the crops grown in the valleys below include corn, wheat, citrus fruits, olives and grapes. Greece's large urban areas are the capital of Athens (including the port of Pireaus) and Thessaloniki in Macedonia. Since 1973, Greece's form of government has been a presidential republic.

Travel Tips

Currency: The unit of currency is the euro. Most banks are open from 8 a.m. to 1 p.m., Monday through Friday. The currency exchange dispenser at the National Bank of Greece on Syntagma Square in Athens is open 24 hours a day.

A restaurant in Navplion.

Dining: The Greeks usually have lunch at 2 p.m. and dinner after 8:30 p.m., but restaurants often open earlier in tourist-oriented centers. A typical Greek meal begins with a plate of *mezedes* (hors d'oeuvres) such as salami, fish, *dolmades* (stuffed vine leaves) and *tiropites* (cheese pies). Main dishes include *kalamaraki* (squid fried in olive oil) and *moussaka* (a baked casserole of mincemeat, eggplant, onions and other ingredients). Olive oil is used extensively in Greek cooking and salads, along with fresh herbs and cheeses such as feta. For dessert, try a *baklava* – layered pastry with nuts, which is often served warm. Ouzo, a colorless liqueur and Greece's national aperitif, is served either neat or watered down, which turns it milky.

Shopping: Stores generally are open from 9:30 a.m. to 8 p.m., with some closing for several hours in mid-afternoon. Bartering is acceptable in Greece. The country's excellent handicrafts include ceramics, wood carvings, handwoven carpets and embroidered tablecloths. Wool sweaters, leather goods and gold or silver jewelry are often good buys. Fishermen's caps and natural sponges are popular souvenirs.

Telephoning: Most phone booths require a pre-paid phone card (which costs about 12 euros) for making long distance calls; these are sold at kiosks and telephone offices. Personal calling card access codes are: AT&T 00-800-1311; MCI 00-800-1211; SPRINT 00-800-1411; CANADA DIRECT 00-800-1611.

Athens

Athens, the capital and largest city of Greece, is situated on a plain dotted with low hills, the most famous of which is the **Acropolis** – 'high point of the city.' This is where the **Parthenon**, a masterpiece of classical Greek architecture, has stood for more than 2,000 years. Constructed of white marble in the 5th century BC, when Athens was at its height as a military power and a center of intellectual life, the Parthenon has survived centuries of wars, sieges, sackings and pilferings. Dedicated to the virgin goddess Athena, this ancient temple rises above the congested streets of downtown Athens as testament to the city's glorious past.

At the foot of the Acropolis lies the ancient marketplace, the **Agora**, where democracy originated and the seeds of Western culture were sown. The proud and patriotic citizens of ancient Athens supported the statesman **Pericles**, whose reforms included payment for jury duty, enabling

---

MUST SEE:

- The Acropolis, where the Parthenon and other ancient monuments are located.
- Ancient Agora, beside the Acropolis.
- Plaka neighborhood – good place to find souvenirs.
- Changing of the guards in Syntagma Square.

If you're spending more than a day in Athens, also visit Lycavittas Hill (for sweeping views of the city) and the National Archaeological Museum.

The venerable Parthenon stands atop the Acropolis.

even the poorest citizens to serve. Pericles, a patron of the arts, commissioned the city's best architects and sculptors to design and oversee the completion of the Parthenon and other great buildings, including a theater for staging the plays of Euripides and Sophocles. It was during this Golden Age of Athens that **Socrates** strolled barefoot in the streets, engaging people in dialectic conversation and rational debate.

Years later, as the 5th century BC drew to a close, Athens faced ruination at the hands of its rival city-state Sparta. After succumbing to Sparta in the Peloponnesian War, Athens attempted to regain its past glory, rebuilding both its navy and the fortified walls that protected the city and connected it to the port of **Piraeus**. But the city-state had lost its imperial status and Athens declined into a provincial city. Its great contributions to civilization endured, however, as Hellenistic culture spread Athenian achievements throughout the world.

On Your Own

Athens is a sprawling metropolis of 3.3 million people and is one of Europe's most affordable cities. Its major historic sites are situated right in the downtown core, within walking distance or a short taxi ride of one another. The heart of Athens is pedestrian-friendly, with traffic restricted inside the commercial center.

Extensive transportation improvements were made in and around Athens in preparation for the 2004 Olympics. The new international airport is located at Spata, about 18 miles east of the city center, and is connected by a six-lane highway and a rapid transit rail line, the latter providing 20-minute connections.

Taxi fares are relatively cheap compared to the rest of Europe, but not all drivers can speak English. Have the name and address of your destination written on a piece of paper and confirm the fare beforehand. If you're setting off from an Athens hotel, ask the concierge to arrange a taxi for you. Expect a luggage surcharge.

If you are making same-day connections between a flight into Athens and a cruise, you are well advised to arrange for a transfer with the cruise line.

Connections between downtown Athens and the port of **Piraeus** (a distance of six miles) can be made by taxi (6 to 9 euros, depending on traffic and amount of luggage) or on the subway system. The green subway line (No. 1) connects the port with Monastiraki Square in downtown Athens. If you plan to return to the port by taxi after a day of sightseeing in Athens, be sure to allow at least an hour in case the traffic is crawling.

One of the best ways to visit Athens for the day while your ship is docked in Piraeus, is to book your cruise line's 'On Your Own' shore excursion (if available). This excursion includes a brief city tour by motorcoach before you are dropped off at Syntagma Square. From there, you can explore Athens for about six hours, then reboard the motorcoach at the same spot for the return drive to Piraeus. (7.5 hrs; $37)

Dining in Athens. For lunch, try one of the cafes lining Theorias Street just below the Acropolis in Plaka. If you're staying a night or two in Athens, try the rooftop garden restaurant of the Titania Hotel at 52 Panepistimiou Avenue. For a truly memorable meal, Orizontes Lykavittou – atop Lykavittos Hill – is widely considered one of the finest restaurants in Athens. At the base of Lykavittos Hill is a square where families gather at modest outdoor cafes. Kolonaki Square is where you will find trendy coffee shops and restaurants.

Shopping: Some of the best streets for souvenir hunting are in the vicinity of Monastiraki Square in the Plaka neighborhood. The market on Pandrossou Street sells a selection of handicrafts, and the pedestrian mall that runs along the north side of the Agora is lined with stalls selling leather goods, silver jewelry and an array of ceramics, including Grecian urns, busts and statuettes. Fashionable stores are found on Ermou Street, while the city's most chic fashion boutiques are on Tsakalof Street off Kolonaki Square.

Athens Attractions

The main travel information bureau is located on **Syntagma (Constitution) Square 1**, a centre of activity with hotels, banks, coffee shops, bars and night clubs surrounding the square. Overlooking the Square's east side is the **House of Parliament**, originally constructed (1836-1842) as a palace for King Otto, Greece's first monarch, and Queen Amalia. The Tomb of the Unknown Soldier (1929) stands

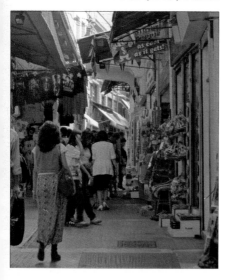

Shopping in Plaka (above). The changing of the guard in Syntagma Square (below).

in front where it is guarded day and night by two soldiers. A changing of the guard takes place every hour.

Just south of the Parliament Building is the **National Garden 2**, designed for the Royal Palace and first planted between 1838 and 1860. Further south, along Amalias, is the **Arch of Hadrian 3**, built of Pentelic marble. (Penteli is one of the mountains surrounding the basin of Athens.) On the northwest corner of the site is the **Temple of Olympian Zeus 4**, completed in 131 AD by the Roman emperor Hadrian.

To the west of Amalias lies the lovely neighborhood of **Plaka**, where narrow stone-paved streets wind past neoclassical homes and sidewalk cafes. On foot is the best way to approach the Acropolis, and a morning ascent along the quiet roads of Plaka will reward you with enchanting, ever-changing vistas. On the upper slopes is **Anafiotika 5**, a village of small white houses erected in the 1830s by master builders from the Aegean island of Anafi, who were hired by the first King of Greece to build his palace. To stave off homesickness while living in Athens, they recreated their island village along the edge of the Acropolis. One of Plaka's most famous structures is the

Shore Excursions *Athens*

The Acropolis is, not surprisingly, featured in many of the shore excursions available at Athens. These usually involve a motor-coach ride from the port to downtown Athens where a walking tour of the Acropolis is combined with shopping in the Plaka district and lunch (7.5 to 9 hrs, $114 - $130)

Some tours combine a visit to the Acropolis with a drive to ancient Corinth or to the ruins of Mycenae on the Peloponnese peninsula (9 hrs, $124). Half-day tours are available to the Acropolis (4 hrs, $50).

A private vehicle holding up to 8 passengers, with a guide and driver, costs about $600 for a half day and $1,000 for a full day.

Most cruise lines provide a motorcoach shuttle from the port into Athens (see On Your Own) (7.5 hrs, $37). For more detail, consult your cruise line's website or the excursions booklet supplied with your cruise documents.

Temple of Olympian Zeus (right).

A street in Plaka (bottom).

Monument of Lysicrates 6, a round structure built in about 334 BC. Its engaged columns are the oldest known example of exterior Corinthian capitals. Along the northern edge of the Plaka area is **Cathedral Square 7** where the city's Great Metropole Cathedral, built in the mid-1800s, overshadows the much smaller Little Metropole, built during the 12th and 13th centuries.

The **Acropolis** was regained by Greece in 1833 when the Turkish guard departed. The sacred rock, which had been used as a fortress for 1,500 years, was then declared a national monument. Archaeological work began almost immediately to excavate and restore the site, and what we see today is the result of extensive reconstruction. A mosque built inside the Parthenon during Turkish occupation was torn down, as were ramparts, walls and a Frankish tower. Restoration work is ongoing and has taken place within the Parthenon since 1983.

The cafe-lined streets of Plaka lead up to the Acropolis.

Entrance to the Acropolis is made along a processional way that passes through the colonnaded buildings of the **Propylaea 8** its interconnected stone structures including the Temple of Athena Nike. This imposing entrance prepares you for the sight of the **Parthenon 9** the great temple of Athena. Designed by the architect Ictinus and built using white, fine-grained marble, the columned Parthenon is a masterpiece of refinement and restraint. Originally it housed a colossal statue of the goddess Athena, which was created by the famous sculptor Phidias, her skin made of ivory and her draperies of beaten gold. Other temples on the Acropolis include the **Erechtheum 10**, the roof of its south porch supported by the figures of six maidens, called the

Caryatids. These famous figures are all copies of the originals, four of which are housed inside the Acropolis Museum. The fifth is being restored, and the sixth was removed by Lord Elgin in 1806; it is now on display in the British Museum.

Situated on the southern slope of the Acropolis are the **Ancient Theatre of Dionysos 11**, originally built of wood then reconstructed with marble during the 4th century BC, and the **Odeion of Herodes Atticus** (the Herodeion) **12**, which was built in 161 AD by a wealthy Athenian and is still used today for summer concerts. West of the Acropolis is the **Areopagus (Hill of Ares) 13** on which the city's supreme court of law once stood. This outcrop of slippery stone is also the spot from which St. Paul delivered his first sermon to the Athenians in 51 AD.

The road below the Areopagus connects the Acropolis with the **Agora**, the 'gathering place' of ancient Athens. Political meetings, religious festivals, dramatic

Monuments atop the Acropolis (above) include the Caryatids of the Erechtheum (right).

contests and athletic competitions took place in this civic and commercial centre, where temples and altars stood alongside law courts and libraries. Philosophers such as Socrates strolled the open squares and shady colonnades, while chariots wheeled along a broad street called the Panathenaic Way, which was the annual scene of a grand procession that ascended the Acropolis

Ancient Theatre of Dionysos (right). Odeion of Herodes Atticus (below).

during the festival of the goddess Athena. The town's craftsmen and merchants lived on the southern edge of the Agora, in modest homes with inner courtyards. On the nearby hill of Pnyx, in full view of the Acropolis, Athenians would gather to hear famous orators – such as Pericles – deliver their speeches.

The **Stoa of Attalos** 14, rebuilt in the 1950s according to its original design, is a classic example of Greek civic architecture. Originally a shopping arcade with 21 shops on each of its two floors, the Stoa now houses the **Agora Museum** and contains excavated items of everyday use in the ancient Agora, including bronze ballots from the law

Temple of Hephaistos (top). Tower of the Winds (middle left). Stoa of Attalos (bottom left).

CITY ATTRACTIONS
(1) Syntagma (Constitution) Square
(2) National Garden
(3) The Arch of Hadrian
(4) Temple of Olympian Zeus
(5) Anafiotika
(6) Monument of Lysicrates
(7) Cathedral Square
(8) Propylaea
(9) Parthenon
(10) Erechtheum
(11) Ancient Theatre of Dionysos
(12) Odeion of Herodes Atticus
(13) Areopagus (Hill of Ares)
(14) Stoa of Attalos
(15) Roman Agora
(16) Temple of Hephaistos
(17) Church of the Holy Apostles
(18) National Archaeological Museum
(19) The Academy of Athens

Academy of Athens .

courts and terracotta animals from a child's grave. Behind the Stoa of Attalos is the **Roman Agora 15**, a marketplace completed in 10 BC, its marble-paved pedestrian mall once lined with colonnades, shops and shrines built with financial assistance from Julius Caesar and the Emperor Augustus. Still standing is the **Tower of the Winds**, an octagonal structure which served as a water-clock, compass and weather-vane.

The **Temple of Hephaistos 16** was dedicated to the goddesses Hephaistos and Athena, both patron divinities of the arts and crafts. Built in 449 BC, the Temple housed statues of the two goddesses and is today one of the best preserved Greek temples of ancient times. A fountain house, its water supplied by an underground terracotta pipeline, once stood beside the site now occupied by the **Byzantine Church of the Holy Apostles 17**, built in 1000 AD and restored in the 1950s.

The **National Archaeological Museum 18** houses an impressive collection of antiquities extending from Neolithic to Roman times. The **Academy of Athens 19**, completed in 1887 and flanked by columns topped with statues of Athena and Apollo, is a fine example of neo-classical architecture. The summit of **Lycavittos Hill** can be reached by funicular, footpath or road, and provides panoramic views of the city and surrounding area – a spectacular sight when the sun is setting.

Peloponnesus

First inhabited as early as 4000 BC, the Peloponnese peninsula was gradually colonized by Greek-speaking Mycenaeans, whose advanced civilization (also referred to as Helladic) rivaled that of Crete, the center of Minoan culture. From 1600 to 1400 BC they competed for maritime control of the Mediterranean, with the Mycenaeans finally triumphing after several devastating earthquakes struck Crete.

In the 14th and 13th centuries BC, war-like northern tribes invaded the Peloponnese. As they swept southward, their Ionic tribe assimilated with the Mycenaeans and the center of Greek culture became Mycenae. This era is now called the Heroic Age, thus named for the incredible feats of Hercules and the events described in Homer's *Iliad* and *Odyssey*, including the Trojan War (c. 1200 BC).

When a new wave of invaders called Dorians arrived in about 1100 BC, their arrival marked a cultural decline. Many of the displaced Achaeans left and migrated across the Aegean Sea to Asia Minor. The conquering Dorians built huge stone buildings, and Argos, Corinth and Sparta became powerful city-states. Corinth, strategically situated on on the Isthmus of Corinth and protected by a citadel, became a wealthy maritime power and rival of Athens in the 7th century BC. Sparta was Corinth's traditional ally and, by the 6th century BC, was Greece's strongest city. Located in a mountain-walled valley, Sparta became an armed camp, its culture dominated by war. Sickly boy babies were abandoned in the mountains, while those fit for military service were taken from their mothers at the age of seven to begin training. State business was conducted in secrecy while serfs, closely monitored for fear of insurrection, farmed the land.

All of Greece's city-states participated in the Isthmian games, held at Corinth every two years in spring, and the Olympic games, held in summer every four years at Olympia. The warring city-states were as proud of a victory at the Olympic games as they were of winning a battle, and this nationalistic spirit fueled a keen competitiveness among the participants. Home-coming champions were hailed as heroes and showered with gifts and privileges. The Games began in 776 BC, possibly earlier, and running was initially the only event. Over time, new events were added, including the pentathlon, chariot racing and a foot race with armor. Greek women held their own games called Heraea.

The Olympic games were eventually discontinued in the 4th century AD by the Romans, who had conquered the Peloponnesus in 146 BC. The once-powerful Peloponnesian League of city-states allowed prolonged power struggles and wars with Athens, and each other which weakened the cities and opened the door to foreign invasions – a situation that would prevail until an 1821 rebellion in the Peloponnesus launched the Greek War of Independence.

Navplion (Nafplio)

Not only is Navplion a fascinating port of call, it provides access to the famous sites of **Mycenae, Epidaurus** and ancient **Corinth**. Ships anchor off Navplion and tender their passengers ashore, where the town's sights are within walking distance, although it's a strenuous hike up to the Palamidi fortress.

Navplion's name derives from Nauplius who, according to Greek mythology, was the son of Poseidon and father of Palamedes, a hero of the Trojan War. The old quarter, situated on a peninsula, is medieval in character. It was originally built by the Venetians when Venice was a dominant sea power in the Mediterranean.

Navplion Attractions

The **Bourtzi** , an island fortress at the harbor entrance, was built by the Venetians in 1473. Looming high above the red-roofed buildings is another Venetian fortress, the **Palamidi** . It was successfully stormed by the Ottoman Turks in 1715, when they captured the town. The view from the Palamidi is breathtaking and can be gained either by ascending the stone steps that lead to its 700-foot summit (a climb best made in the coolness of early morning) or by taking a taxi or ship-organized excursion.

At the foot of the Palamidi, beside the Cultural Center of Navplion, is the Tourist Information Office. A few blocks away is **Three Admiral Square** , named for the English, French and Russian admirals who defeated an Egyptian fleet that was bringing reinforcements to the Turks during the Greek War of Independence. Elegant neoclassical townhouses overlook this square on V. Konstantinou Street, which leads west to **Syntagma (Constitution) Square** where, on its west

Cruise ship anchors off Navplion on the Peloponnese peninsula.

side, the Archaeological Museum is situated, housing a collection of Mycenaean artifacts.

Greek insurgents took Navplion from the Turks in 1822 and the town was, from 1830 to 1834, the first capital of independent Greece, its first National Assembly convening next to the museum in a Turkish mosque on Staikopoulou Street. Both Konstantinou and Staikopoulou are picturesque pedestrian streets lined with restaurants and shops. Side streets with stone steps lead off Staikopoulou, up the hillside toward **Akronafplia** , a barren hilltop fortified over the centuries by various occupants and now the site of two hotels which can be reached by a **lift** or by a road that runs past **Arvanitia** , a fully serviced beach. The town's **promenade** is pleasant for strolling with its waterfront cafes and views across the harbor.

Ship-organized **shore excursions** from Navplion generally include a half-day coach trip through the scenic countryside to Mycenae, Epidaurus or Corinth, often with a stop at the top of Palamidi on the way back to the ship. One option for passengers interested in viewing a Mycenaean ruin is to visit nearby

Tiryns, 3 miles away (US$25 return fare by taxi). Although not as extensive as Mycenae, this ancient citadel was the mythological birthplace of Hercules. Its impressive entrance ramp evokes a sense of past power, when the palace was protected by two massive walls with an outer and inner gate designed to trap attackers between the walls.

Mycenae, 13 miles north of Navplion, is one of Greece's most famous archaeological sites. These ancient ruins, which were the center of the Mycenaean civilization, are shrouded in a dark history of murder and betrayal. Agamemnon, the great king of Mycenae, is a tragic figure of Greek mythology. He belonged to the deadliest of dysfunctional families, a curse having been brought upon it by his grandfather Pelops. Agamemnon's father didn't help matters by murdering his brother's children and serving

The Bourtzi fortress (above).

An elegant square on V. Konstantinou Street (below).

them for dinner. When Agamemnon left for the Trojan war, he sacrificed his eldest child to guarantee good winds for his sailing ships. This deed incurred the hatred of his wife Clytemnestra, who murdered Agamemnon upon his return. To avenge their father's death, Orestes and Electra murdered their mother.

Several hundred years later, the poet Homer wrote about Mycenae and his writings were used by the 19th-century archaeologist Heinrich Schliemann to provide clues as to where to dig at this ancient site. Spurred by Homer's references to gold, Schliemann's dramatic discoveries included royal tombs filled with gold treasures. The site's heavy fortifications and massive masonry

Akronafplia

0   300

Yards

STAIKOPOULOU

MARTIOU

PLAPOUTA

V. KONSTANTINOU

Sidiras Merarhias

Amalias

Alexandrou

V. Olgas

Othonos

Polizoidou

SIGROU

Tender dock / smaller cruise ships also dock here

Tender

include the **Lion Gate**, Europe's oldest monumental sculpture, which in ancient times was closed by a double wooden door sheathed in bronze and secured with a wooden bar. The largest of the beehive tombs, located outside the walls of the city, is the Treasury of Atreus (also called Agamemnon's Tomb).

Epidaurus, situated 15 miles east of Navplion (US$60 return taxi fare), is an ancient sanctuary and the site of Greece's best-pre-served amphitheater. Greek drama lives on at the 14,000-seat theatre of Epidaurus, which was considered beautiful and harmonious when built in the 4th century BC and is still acclaimed for its excellent acoustics. Since the theater's restoration in the 1950s, theatrical events have been staged here each summer, including the late Maria Callas performing the title role of Bellini's opera, *Norma*. In September 1997, to commemorate the 20th anniversary of the famous diva's death, friends from the world of opera gathered for a seaboard ceremony off Epidaurus. As a recording of her voice resounded across the water, olive wreaths were tossed into the Aegean Sea, where her ashes had been scattered two decades earlier.

Old Corinth, 40 miles from Navplion, has been occupied by Romans, Goths, Crusaders, Ottoman Turks and Venetians. Corinth was finally returned to Greece when captured by Greek insurgents in 1822, only to be destroyed by an earthquake in the

Palamidi fortress in Navplion.

1850s. A new city was founded nearby, and the ancient ruins remaining at Old Corinth include a Temple of Apollo, Roman amphitheater and hilltop fortress. A short distance away is the four-mile-long Canal of Corinth, built between 1881 and 1893, which cuts across the Isthmus of Corinth. Its sheer rock walls rise 285 feet above the water on both sides, accentuating the narrowness of the canal, which can be transited only by small ships. Until this canal was built, a narrow neck of land connected the Peloponnese peninsula with central Greece. In ancient times this isthmus served as a land bridge for tribes migrating into the area from the north but it eventually posed a barrier to trading ships traveling between the Adriatic and Aegean seas. The citizens of Corinth, with harbors on both sides of the isthmus, solved the problem and grew wealthy in the process by building a connecting road across which they hauled ships on rollers.

Katakolon

Olympia, located about 15 miles from the port of **Katakolon**, was an important center of worship and the venue for the Panhellenic Olympic Games. Situated in the beautiful valley of Alpheios, the site contains ruins of the great temple of Zeus which housed a statue by Phidias, the famous sculptor whose works adorned the Parthenon. Counted among the Seven Wonders of the World, this colossal ivory and gold statue of Zeus sitting on an ornamented

throne was later removed to Constantinople where it was destroyed by fire in 475 AD. Other sculptures from the Temple of Zeus are on display in the nearby **Archaeological Museum**, along with the outstanding statue of *Hermes with the Young Dionysos* by Praxiteles (c. 340 BC). Ruins associated with the Olympic games include the remains of the Gymnasium and the Stadium. The sacred flame of the modern Olympic games begins its journey here with a torch-lighting ceremony held in front of the Temple of Hera, the oldest Doric temple in Greece.

Shore excursions from Katakolon focus on Olympia, with motorcoach drives to the nearby site, a walking tour and, possibly, a visit to the Archaeological Museum (3 to 7 hrs; $55-$115).

A small cruise ship is pulled through the narrow Corinth Canal.

Githio

The hill-top town of **Mistra (Mystras)**, about 30 miles from the port of **Githio**, is the most representative example in existence of a Byzantine city from the 14th and 15th centuries. The medieval castle overlooking the town was built in 1249 by Frankish crusader Guillaume de Villehardouin. He and his knights were defeated 10 years later by the Byzantines, who built a palace for the emperor as well as numerous churches and monasteries decorated with beautiful frescoes. The town, its wealth generated by a lucrative silk industry, grew down the hillside, with the upper and lower sections connected by two gates. The lower town contains most of the monasteries and churches, while the upper town contains the Palace of the Despot (a rare example of civic Byzantine architecture), an adjacent church and the Frankish castle, which is reached after a 30-minute ascent. The magnificent view from the castle includes a bird's eye look at the gullies of Mt. Taygettus – where the Spartans are said to have tossed sickly babies. Nearby modern Sparta bears little resemblance to the ancient city-state that once dominated the central Peloponnese peninsula. Relying on their military power for protection, the Spartans didn't bother building walls, so only a few temple ruins remain.

Malvasia

The fortified island village of Malvasia, a unique and intact medieval town, is joined by a causeway to the Peloponnese mainland where a modern tourist resort, with fine beaches, lies in contrast to the Byzantine churches and Venetian mansions contained within the walls of Malvasia. A fortress in the Middle Ages, Malvasia was also a commercial port which exported malmsey wine.

Central / Northern Greece

Itea

On the northern shores of the Gulf of Corinth, the port of Itea accesses the ancient site of **Delphi**, where the great temple to Apollo was first built in the 6th century BC. Apollo, one of the most important Olympian gods, was associated with prophecy, and Delphi was the seat of ancient Greece's most famous and powerful oracle. Pilgrims seeking help brought gifts which lined the Sacred Way leading to the temple, where a priestess sat on a tripod inhaling divine vapors and uttering oracular messages. It has long been speculated that the 'divine vapors' Pythia inhaled were volcanic gases, and geologists now surmise that a major fault zone below the temple provided pathways for seeping gases, including ethylene and methane – known to have narcotic effects. Delphi played a unique role amid the warring city-states, for its splendid setting on the lower slopes of Mt. Parnassus was a meeting place for the important Amphictyonic League, as well as the site of the Pythian Games, held every four years.

Volos

Meteora, about 75 miles from the port of Volos, is a surrealistic sight of barren rock formations rising from a flat, fertile plain. Their geological origins still a mystery, these pinnacles of rock became a place of refuge for monks during the Middle Ages. What began as small cells evolved into great monasteries holding rich murals and religious treasures, and they form a surreal sight perched atop columns and crags of black rock. Ropes and pulleys are still used for transporting provisions, but visitors can now walk up steps cut into the precipitous slopes. These who make the strenuous climb are rewarded with sweeping views of the plain of Thessaly – ringed by mountains, including Mount Olympus, which separate Thessaly from the plains of Macedonia. An escorted **shore excursion** entails a two-hour motorcoach ride to Meteora where the road terminates at the base of the rock pinnacles. You are then taken on a guided climb up the stone steps to view the monastic buildings at the top and take in the sweeping views. (8.5 hrs, $90)

Thessaloniki (Salonika)

Macedonia's port of Thessaloniki is Greece's second-largest city and was named the 1997 Cultural Capital of Europe. Its world-renowned museum houses treasures of Philip of Macedon, father of Alexander the Great, and in 1997 it hosted a special exhibit of priceless icons, manuscripts and other objects never before seen outside the monasteries of **Mount Athos**. Consisting of 20 monasteries of the Eastern Orthodox Church, this theocratic community is perched high above the water on the southernmost tip of the Khalkidhik peninsula. Since the first monastery was founded around 953 AD, this community of monks has been allowed to govern itself by committee and its strictly enforced rules include the banning of all females and dogs. When US ambassador Thomas Niles visited Mount Athos in 1994, he chose to sleep outside one of the monasteries on a cot (as did the rest of his large retinue) rather than be separated from his beloved dog, Mr. Wheat. In 2004, a stove fire engulfed one-third of the buildings at Mount Athos but spared the most important ones.

Monastery of Saint Nicholas Anapafsas, Meteora.

CHAPTER EIGHT

THE GREEK ISLES

The only way to see the Greek isles is slowly, by boat. At least that's what Cary Grant told Doris Day in the 1962 comedy, *That Touch of Mink*, when he likened these islands to fine paintings. "You mustn't rush up to them," he said. Anyone who has stood at a ship's rail and watched the sun rise above a Greek isle will know exactly what he meant. A seaborne arrival, as the morning sun warms the terraced hillsides and whitewashed houses of a sleepy fishing port, is a travel experience of unsurpassed romance.

Greece has more than 2,000 islands, comprising about one-fifth of the country's total land area, yet only some 200 are inhabited. When the Greek government announced a plan in 1995 to resettle some of its uninhabited islands, the response – both domestic and foreign – was overwhelming. Thousands of people from all walks of life sought to move to one of the many islands left abandoned after World War II when their inhabitants emigrated in droves to the cities. Whether or not Greece's repopulation plan is successful, it's obvious the allure of the Greek isles is as strong as ever.

For general information and travel tips on Greece, please see pages 260 and 261.

THE CYCLADES

The Cyclades, comprising about 220 islands in total, spread across 1,000 square miles of the Aegean Sea. Serving as stepping stones for migrating tribes in ancient times, these scattered islands were inhabited before 4000 BC by a primitive people who gradually developed a culture called Cycladic (Greek for *circular*). **Delos** was the center of this culture, with other islands forming a rough circle around it.

Today the island group's administrative center is on Syros, but its historical heart remains on Delos – the mythical birthplace of Apollo. According to Greek legend, Zeus's lover Leto was cursed by his jealous wife. A pregnant Leto wandered the earth until the god Poseidon took pity on her and gave her a place to rest by anchoring the island of Delos with four diamond columns. There Leto

Mykonos Harbour is a popular port of call in the Greek Islands.

gave birth to Zeus's children – a girl named Artemis and a boy named Apollo, who became important Greek gods.

The Cyclades are quintessential Greek islands, with their charming fishing harbors and seaside villages. Box-shaped houses climb the hillsides and dome-roofed chapels cling to cliffsides, their dazzling whiteness appearing in stark contrast against the deep blues of the sky above and the sea below. The most popular of the Cyclades are the tourist-oriented islands of Santorini and Mykonos, which lies close to uninhabited Delos.

Mykonos (Mikonos)

This arid island, 35 square miles in size, is the most cosmopolitan of the Cyclades. Although extremely popular with tourists, Mykonos has retained a Cycladic charm with its whitewashed houses and hilltop windmills. Shops, cafes and tavernas line the town's waterfront area while serious shoppers will delight in wandering the town's winding backstreets. Originally designed to disorient marauding pirates, these

MYKONOS

twisting alleyways are now lined with boutiques frequented by the rich and famous. Jacqueline Onassis and Elizabeth Taylor are among the famous women who have shopped at Galatis on the town's **main square (Platia Manto)** ▮, also referred to as Taxi Square.

Little Venice ▮, a neighborhood south of the main harbor, is where you'll find local artwork and handicrafts. The waterfront buildings in this section are a reminder of the island's Venetian period, as is the **Roman Catholic Cathedral** ▮, its entrance hall bearing the coat of arms of the Ghisi family who took over

The whitewashed, sunbaked buildings of Mykonos.

A ship at anchor off Mykonos.

Shore Excursions *Mykonos*
Shore excursions include a beach visit (4 hrs, $35), a walking tour of the town (2.5 hrs, $60), an island tour (3 hrs, $60) and a boat ride to Delos for a tour of the ruins (3.5 hrs, $65). Several local operators also provide excursions to Delos, selling tickets at the boat dock.

Mykonos in 1207. Next door is the **Greek Orthodox Cathedral** **4** and nearby, on a promontory overlooking the sea, is the **Church of Paraportiani** **5**, its cluster of whitewashed chapels a much-photographed sight. A short distance away is the **Folklore Museum** **6**, housed in the 300-year-old house of a former sea captain. Other local museums are the **Aegean Maritime Museum** **7**, the *The ancient ruins on Delos.*

Archaeological Museum **8** and a **working windmill** **9** on the east side of town. More windmills stand on a headland south of Mykonos town.

The island's south coast boasts a string of beautiful beaches, which are a short taxi or bus ride from the town. **Psarou** **10**, one of the finest (and busiest) of these beaches, features restaurants and a variety of watersports. **Plati Yialos** **11** also has restaurants and is popular with families. The beaches lying to the east – Paranga, Paradise, Super Paradise and Elia – are designated nude beaches, and can be reached by boat from Plati Yialos or by road from Mykonos town.

Delos – The smallest of the Cyclades, this tiny island was of great importance in ancient times, when its temple of Apollo held the treasury of the Delian League – a confederation of maritime states led by Athens. Council members of this league, which was formed in 478 BC to finance a war against Persia, would meet on the politically neutral island of Delos and contribute funds, troops and ships to the league. Its treasury was moved from Delos to the Athenian Acropolis in 454

BC but the island continued to prosper, becoming the site of a thriving slave market in the 2nd century BC. Sacked by Mithridates VI of Pontus (modern Turkey) in 88 BC, Delos never recovered and was abandoned near the end of the 1st century BC. Excavation of its temples, theaters, commercial buildings and private homes began in the 1870s and today the uninhabited island is visited by day trippers arriving solely to see its ancient ruins, which include the small sanctuary of Dionysus (dating to 300 BC), a restored temple to the goddess Isis, and the famous Terrace of the Lions, carved from marble in the 7th century BC.

Naxos

The largest of the Cyclades, Naxos is ringed with beautiful beaches and traversed with fertile valleys where olive trees and grape vines thrive in the fertile soil. An island steeped in Greek mythology, Naxos was once a center of worship of Dionysus and a member of the Delian League. The town of Naxos (Hora) runs from the harbor up a hillside, its narrow winding lanes lined with stone houses and leading to a Venetian castle. White marble and granite have been quarried on Naxos since antiquity, and monuments from various periods can be found throughout the town, including fine Byzantine churches and the castle with its tower and battlements. The local archaeological museum in Naxos also contains some notable exhibits.

Santorini (Thira)

Myth and modern science meet on the island of Santorini, believed by many to be the lost kingdom of Atlantis, which was destroyed by a volcanic explosion in about 1500 BC. This popular belief endures despite claims by

Cruise ships anchor below the spectacular cliff-top town of Fira.

Greek philosopher Aristotle that his teacher Plato invented this fabled city as an allegory for his fellow Athenians, using Atlantis to illustrate a Utopian state.

The stunning setting of crescent-shaped Santorini does little to dispel the island's legendary past. Set on the exposed rim of a submerged volcano, Santorini's harbor is a flooded crater. Cruise ships anchor in this watery caldera and tender passengers ashore to the base of an idyllic clifftop town where a switchback staircase ascends the crater wall. The town of **Fira** can be reached on foot, by donkey or by cablecar. Whatever your chosen mode of ascent, the view from above is spectacular.

Across the bay from Fira lies the quiet island of Thirasia, a fragment of the caldera's rim that was once joined to the main island until an eruption in 236 BC. Dotting the bay are the smaller Burnt Islands, which rose from the caldera in subsequent eruptions. Palia Kameni emerged in 196 BC, and Nea Kameni was formed and enlarged by a series of eruptions, the first occurring in 1711, the second in 1866, and the most recent in 1925. In the past, a reliable warning of an imminent eruption occurred when the surrounding sea turned a milky color due to an increase in underwater sulphur emissions.

Before the catastrophic eruption of c. 1500 BC, Santorini was colonized by Minoans from Crete. Archaeological digs indicate these people heeded the warning earthquakes and abandoned the island before the massive explosion. The island was next settled by Phoenicians, followed by Laconians from the Peloponnese peninsula, under their leader Thira, which is the official name of the island. A new center was established on the island's east coast, its archaeological remains dating mainly from late Hellenistic and Roman times. From the Middle Ages onwards, the island was called Santorini

Fira town is perched high above the harbor on Santorini.

Shore Excursions *Santorni*

Shore Excursions in Santorini include various motorcoach tours of the island, some with a stop at the village of **Oia** and a local winery (4 hrs, $65). Also offered is a boat ride to Nea Kameni volcanic crater for a hike to the summit (2.5 hrs, $40).

after St. Irene, protector of the island. The Greek god of fertility and wine, Dionysus, is also associated with Santorini where wine grapes thrive in the volcanic soil.

Santorini is today a fashionable resort, its terraced streets of whitewashed buildings lined with chic shops and restaurants. Numerous domed churches are still prominent amid the tourist attractions. Near the **cable car ticket office** **1** are the **Archaeological Museum** **2** (containing artifacts from ancient Thira) and a private museum housed in a restored mansion near the **Roman Catholic Cathedral** **3**. More churches, including the **Greek Orthodox Cathedral** **4**, are situated a few blocks south of here. **Platia Theotokopoulou** **5** is the town's main square, where tourist services are located.

At the south end of the island, near Akrotiri, is the ancient **Minoan site**. Still under excavation, it was discovered in the late 1960s by Professor Spyros Marinatos, who was trying to prove that the Santorini blast had created a tsunami wave that wiped out the Minoan civilization on Crete. This theory has been largely discredited, but what Marinatos did discover was an extensive ancient city preserved

for 35 centuries beneath tons of volcanic ash. Streets of multi-storeyed warehouses and homes, their walls decorated with vivid wall paintings, were revealed as the ash was cleared away, but the absence of skeletons indicated there had been a mass evacuation prior to the explosion. Geological evidence indicates the island was racked beforehand by earthquakes, ample warning for the island's residents. Most of the beaches on Santorini are black, due to the fallen volcanic ash.

Crete

A mountainous island of deep gorges and farm-filled valleys, Crete's long history is one of invasion and resistance. In ancient times, one of the world's

A quiet square near Agio Titos (above). Minoan vase dating from 1700 BC in Archaeological Museum (left).

earliest civilizations thrived on the island of Crete. Called **Minoan** for the legendary King Minos, its great palaces were adorned with colorful murals and enormous clay pottery.

Minoan habitation of Crete began in about 3000 BC. The island's forests supplied wood for boat building, and the residents of Crete engaged in seagoing trade. Their island lay only 400 miles from the northern shores of Egypt, where an advanced civilization influenced the cultural development of Crete. Neolithic village life evolved into an urban society centered around great palaces, such as the one at Gournia, near the modern port of Aghios Nikolaos, and at Phaestus, on the island's south coast. The Minoans developed a system of writing but built no military fortifications or religious temples. The swirling, free-flowing motifs of Minoan art were often inspired by nature, their gambolling dolphins or leaping mountain goats portrayed with a joyful fluidity of movement.

When Dorian Greeks settled on the island several centuries after the collapse of the Minoan civilization, they established dozens of city-states, with **Knossos** emerging as one of the most powerful. A center of trade, the island became a pirate haven until conquered by the Romans in 68 BC. The Byzantines were next to rule Crete, starting in 395 AD, followed briefly by the Arabs in 824, before the island was reconquered by the Byzantines in 961. Next to rule the island, from 1204, were the Venetians, who built a wall around Iraklion (then called Candia) to defend this important trading port from pirates. When the Ottoman Turks over-ran the island in the 1648, the garrison at Iraklion fought off the invaders for 21 years before surrendering in 1669.

(Above) Iraklion's Old Harbour with 13th-century fortifications. (Below) Agios Titos Church.

The indomitable spirit of the Cretans was personified in the great statesman Eleutherios Venizelos, born in Crete and educated in Athens, who returned in 1896 to play a prominent role in the island's insurrection against Turkish rule. Turkey, at the intervention of European powers, was eventually forced to evacuate, and in 1908 Crete proclaimed its union with Greece.

Crete came under invasion once again, during World War II, when British and Greek forces on the island were overwhelmed by a German airborne invasion. The German troops occupying the island eventually surrendered to the British navy in late 1944.

Famous Cretans include the 16th-century painter El Greco, and Nikos Kazantzakis, author of *Zorba the Greek.* The singer Nana Mouskouri was born in Chania, on Crete's north coast, shortly before the Second World

War, and her childhood recollections include the excitement of the olive harvest when she dipped her mother's freshly baked bread into extra virgin olive oil, made from the first pressing and flavored with fresh herbs grown in the mountains.

Iraklion (Heraklion), capital

and major cruise port of Crete, was founded by Muslim Saracens in the 9th century, before falling under Byzantine rule in 961. The walls that still ring the city were built by the Venetians after they took possession of Crete in the 13th century. The largest of the six bastions is Martinengo Bastion, where a stone slab marks the burial place of the writer Kazantzakis, who died in 1957.

On Your Own

Knossos is the main attraction for passengers arriving at Iraklion and can be reached by taxi (about US$30 return) or by shore excursion. Other excursions include a half-day tour to the Minoan ruins at **Phaestos**. These ruins, set on a plateau, are not as extensive as those at Knossos, but the drive across the island offers an opportunity to see more of Crete's scenic landscape.

A taxi into town costs about US$5, but it's a fairly pleasant and easy walk from the cruise dock. Follow the waterfront to the **Old Harbour 1** for a look at its Venetian fortifications, then proceed up Avgoustou toward the town's central platia (square), named for the great statesman Eleftherio Venizelou. Along the way you'll pass some beautiful neoclassical buildings and the Byzantine church **Agios Tito**s **2**, named for Crete's patron saint, who converted the people of Crete to Christianity.

There are several outdoor cafes at **Platia Venizelou 3** and, standing in the center of the square, is a marble Renaissance fountain called The Lions. Across the street is the **Agios Markos** (St. Mark) **4**, built by the Venetians in the 13th century and now housing an exhibition center. The maze of back streets lying east of the square contains more outdoor cafes and a selection of shops, including the boutiques on Daedolou Street, which leads to **Platia Eleftherias 5**. Here, on the square's north side, are the **Visitor Information Office** and the **Archaeological Museum 6**. Built between 1937 and 1940, the museum stands on the site of a Catholic monastery that was destroyed by an earthquake in 1856. The museum grounds contain gardens, benches and a coffee shop. Inside the museum is an extensive collection of Minoan artifacts, including original wall paintings from the palace at Knossos.

About three miles from Iraklion is the site of the famous Minoan palace at **Knossos**. Built on a hillside, the original palace was destroyed by an earthquake around 1700 BC, then rebuilt on an even grander scale and serviced by a complex drainage and water-supply system. Although it was damaged by another earthquake around 1450 BC, excavations of the 'new' palace have revealed a labyrinth of rooms and passages, porticoes and staircases, richly decorated with lyrical wall paintings.

The palace was built around a central courtyard and boasts excellent masonry construction. The columns were originally made of wood – those we see today are reproductions. English archaeologist Sir Arthur Evans spent years uncovering the ruins (between 1898 and 1935) and reconstructing the buildings. Some archaeologists have criticized these reconstructions, but they do offer the lay person a

Minoan wall art at Knossos (above right). Ruins of the palace of Knossos (right).

good idea of what the palace looked like in Minoan times. Highlights of the site include the Queen's Megaron, approached by the Grand Staircase, which is decorated with the Dolphin Fresco. Adjacent is the Queen's Bath, containing a terracotta bathtub.

Many legends are associated with this great palace, including the myth of the Minotaur – a monster with the head of a bull and the body of a man – who was confined within a labyrinth beneath the palace, where he devoured sacrificial youth sent as tribute from Athens.

The Dodecanese

Pronounced *doh dek en ees* and meaning Twelve Islands, this island group in the eastern Aegean Sea is situated much closer to the shores of Turkey than those of Greece. Yet Greek culture has endured on these islands, despite centuries of foreign occupation, since antiquity. Initially influenced by the Minoan civilization of Crete, the Dodecanese were eventually settled by the Dorians, who had established the Greek city-states of Sparta and Corinth before migrating across the Aegean Sea. Those who landed on Rhodes discovered a fertile island blessed with a subtropical climate.

Rhodes

When the Greek cartographer Eratosthenes compiled a map of the known world in the 3rd century BC, the central point on his chart was the island of Rhodes.

Situated only 12 miles from the shores of Asia Minor (modern Turkey), the busy port of Rhodes was a trade link between East and West. Built in 408 BC as a planned 'modern' city with a grid system of streets and a water/sewage system, it was protected by a fortified wall. These were prosperous times for Rhodes and, after withstanding a siege in 305/4 BC, the city commissioned three local sculptors to create a colossal bronze statue of Helios, the sun god, which was erected at the harbor entrance but later destroyed by an earthquake. Rhodes was one of the most beautiful and organized cities of the Hellenistic world. The arts and sciences flourished, and Rhodes became a center of learning, its 800-seat theater used for teaching philosophy and oration, with Julius Caesar among those who studied there.

Rhodes eventually declined economically, descending into a period of obscurity that lasted until the Knights of St. John landed on its shores in 1306. A religious-military order founded in Jerusalem in the middle of the 11th century, the Knights of St. John had been driven from the Middle East by Arab forces and were stationed on Cyprus when their Grand Master negotiated a deal to purchase Rhodes from the Genoese, who were then administering the Dodecanese Islands.

The Knights of Rhodes, as they called themselves during their 213-year rule of the island, were supported financially by the feudal

The Colossus of Rhodes.

lords of Europe, for they were spearheads of Western expansionism and defenders of Christianity against the Arab 'infidels'. The order was a hierarchical organization of knights (noblemen), chaplains and sergeants (sons of freemen), who hailed from seven European nations – Provence, Auvernge, France, Italy, Aragon, England and Germany. Each national group was called a 'tongue', had its own 'inn' or meeting place within the fortified city, and was responsible for defending a specific section ('curtain') of the wall.

Prosperity returned to Rhodes under the Knights. Their imposing Palace of the Grand Master stood on the town's highest ground, while the winding streets below teemed with merchants, both local and foreign, as well as bankers, artists and tradesmen. Goods arrived and departed by ship, including perfumes, saffron, pepper, caviar and wax. Wheat was imported from Cyprus and Sicily, wine from Crete and Italy. Hostilities between the Knights and the Turks were set aside in favor of trade – silks and carpets from Asia Minor were exchanged for woolens and other commodities from Western Europe. Local laborers produced textiles, soap and sugar, and major building projects undertaken by the Knights kept the masons employed. The sounds of feasting and carousing spilled into the streets while the wealthy nobility strolled the town's beautiful gardens in their elegant clothes.

All of this prosperity came to an end when Turkish forces laid

(Above) Old back street of Rhodes.
(Below) Street of the Knights.

(Above) The walled fortress town of the old city. Sea Gate is one of several fortified entrances (left).

siege to mighty Rhodes in 1480. With a fleet of 170 ships carrying 100,000 soldiers, the Turks mounted attack after attack, finally taking the Tower of Italy and penetrating the city walls. Knights raced from other parts of the city to fight the invaders, who finally retreated after a bloody battle and soon sailed away. An earthquake struck Rhodes the following year, completing the devastation wreaked by the Turkish siege, but the Knights rebuilt the town and helped the struggling populace by providing tax exemptions and wheat distribution.

More than 40 years passed before the Turks attacked again, bombarding the town's landward fortifications while a huge fleet blockaded the harbour. Led by Sulayman I, thousands of Turks were killed but they relentlessly continued their attack until the townspeople, running out of food and the will to resist, convinced the Knights to surrender. On January 1st, 1523, the Knights and about 5,000 Rhodians boarded ships and set sail for Crete, leaving Rhodes to the Ottoman Turks. The Turks held the Dodecanese for the next 400 years, until they were occupied by Italian forces in 1912. Captured by the Allies during World War II, the islands were returned to Greece in 1947.

On Your Own

The cruise ships dock in the city's commercial harbor, opposite the medieval fortress of Old Rhodes.

It's a short distance to the walled town where you could easily spend an entire day wandering the cobblestone streets of this medieval fortress. Or, spend half the day exploring Old Rhodes and the other half of the day on an escorted tour to Lindos (see box).

A motorized trolley travels from the harbor to the ancient acropolis (also called Monte Smith, for a British admiral), which overlooks the walled town.

Buses run regularly between Rhodes and Lindos; the Rhodes **bus station** is located north of the Old Town's north wall. The return taxi fare to Lindos from Rhodes is about US$85.

D'Amboise Gate was named for a French Grand Master.

Rhodes Attractions

A World Heritage Site, the town of Rhodes was badly damaged by earthquakes in the mid-1800s. Many of its buildings were repaired during the Italian occupation, but further damage was caused by incendiary bombs during World War II. The Greek Archaeological Service is now in charge of its restoration and conservation.

The **Gate of the Virgin** and the much-photographed **Sea Gate** 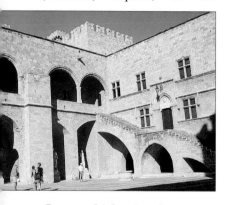 both provide access into the walled town from the harbour front. Not far from the Sea Gate is busy **Platia Ippokratous** 3, its outdoor cafes, shops and fountains overlooked by the Kastellania (Courthouse) of the Knights. Nearby, off Mousio (Museum) Square, is the

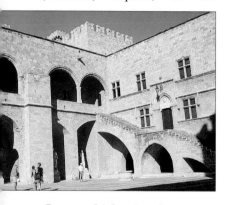

Courtyard (above) and outer gardens (below) at Grand Master's Palace in Rhodes.

Archaeological Museum 4, housed in the New Hospital of the Knights, which is one of the most handsome and best preserved buildings from the time of the Knights. Here the sick were cared for by physicians under the supervision of eight 'brothers' – one from each 'tongue' (nationality) of the Order.

The Hospital's north side runs along **Ippoton (Street of the Knights)** 5, which was the most important thoroughfare in the medieval town. It ran through the middle of the Collachium, a section of town once separated from the rest by an inner wall. The knights lived inside the Collachium, spending their days engaged in military exercises and prayer. Each 'tongue' had an 'inn' along the Street of Knights at which its members could gather to dine and discuss matters. At the top of the Street of the Knights stands the **Grand Master's Palace** 6. Built on the site of a Byzantine citadel, the Palace became the town's administrative centre and was the last refuge for its citizens during times of attack.

Left to crumble by the Turks and damaged by earthquakes, the final blow to the Palace occurred in 1856 when some gunpowder stored in the vaults of the nearby Church of St. John blew up, leaving only the palace's ground floor standing. The Italians restored and modified the palace between the two world wars, when it became a residence and headquarters for Fascist Minister C.M. de Vecchi. Interior highlights of the Palace include a grand stair-

Shore Excursions *Rhodes*
• Walking tour of Old Rhodes & motorcoach ride to Lindos; lunch included (8 hrs, $130)
• Walking tour of Old Rhodes & motorcoach ride to ancient acropolis (2.5 hrs, $50)
• Motorcoach ride to acropolis & Lindos (3.5 hrs, $50)
• Motorcoach ride to Lindos & guided walking tour (4 hrs, $55)
• Motorcoach ride to Tsambika Beach & swimming (4.5 hrs, $45)

Modern-day Rhodians favor scooters for getting around the Old Town (above). Bronze deer at the harbor entrance (below).

case, made of marble, which leads to the upper storey. There a series of vaulted halls contain carved furniture, Chinese vases and marble sculptures from the Hellenistic period, including a copy of *Laocoön* that was created in the 1st century BC by three Rhodian sculptors. The expansive floors of these chambers are covered with Hellenistic and Roman tile mosaics brought by the Italians from buildings on the island of Kos.

North of the Street of the Knights is **Platia Argirokastrou** **7** where the ancient ruins of the Temple of Venus (Aphrodite) are situated opposite the **Freedom Gate** **8**. Beyond this gate is Mandraki Harbour, the ancient port that was guarded by the Colossus of Rhodes. Today a bronze deer stands on either side of the harbor entrance. During the reign of the Knights, the **Fort of St. Nicholas** **9**, which stands at the end of the stone pier, was an important fortress protecting the harbor from Turkish assaults; the tower now houses a lighthouse. The three windmills still standing on the **Mole of St. Nicholas** **10**

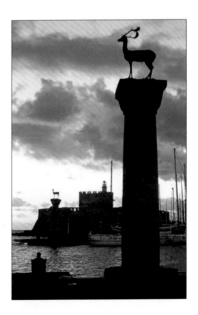

were used by the Knights for grinding wheat. West of the medieval town is the **ancient acropolis** 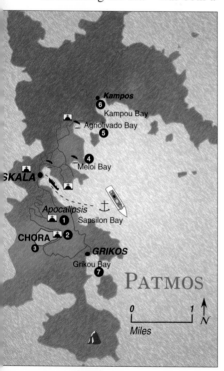 where the walled ruins include the Temple of Apollo, the Odeum and the Stadium.

Lindos – Before the town of Rhodes was established in 408 BC, Lindos was a major naval and trading center on the island's southeast coast. The town's acropolis – a promontory rock overlooking the sea – was both a fortress and sanctuary housing a temple of Athena. In the year 51 AD, the Apostle St. Paul landed by small boat in the bay and introduced Christianity to the island. The ancient acropolis was further fortified during the Byzantine period, then by the Knights.

A hike up the stairway leading to the fortress rewards visitors with a panoramic view of two crescent-shaped beaches and the hillside village of Lindos, its narrow streets and whitewashed mansions from the 17th century. The Byzantine church of the Panayia was built in the 15th century, and later decorated with wall paintings.

Patmos

The serene and scenic island of Patmos has been a place of pilgrimage ever since St. John the Evangelist landed on its shores in 95 AD. One of three apostles closest to Jesus and author of the fourth Gospel, an elderly John was banished by the Roman Emperor Domitian to the tiny island of Patmos, where he sought shelter in a cave. Now called the **Holy Grotto of the Apocalypse** 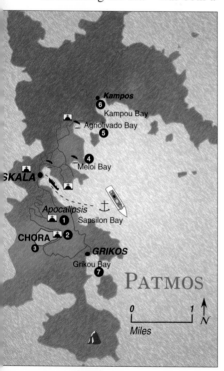, it was in this cave that God revealed to John a

A ship's tender heads ashore at the Greek island of Patmos.

Skala's waterfront (above). A shaded street in Skala (right).

magnificent yet terrifying vision, described in the Book of Revelation, which John spent the next 18 months dictating to his disciple Prochorus.

Ten centuries later, the Byzantine monk Hosios Christodoulos, who had built a monastery on the island of Kos, traveled to Constantinople to request permission to found the **Monastery of Saint John the Divine** on Patmos. His request was granted, in exchange for his holdings on Kos, and construction of the monastery commenced in 1088, its thick walls and battlements built to protect the main church, several chapels and a treasury of icons and gold-embroidered vestments. Its forecourt is decorated with frescoes illustrating the life of St. John, and its library contains priceless books and manuscripts, including one from the 6th century containing portions of St. Mark's gospel. The fortress-like monastery stands on a hill above the whitewashed village of **Chora (Hora) 3**, which is a labyrinth of interlocking lanes, houses and bell-topped chapels.

On Your Own

Patmos is an ideal island to tour independently because it is small and the roads are fairly quiet. The large cruise ships anchor outside the small port of **Skala** and tender their passengers ashore. A taxi stand with a dispatcher is located near the cruise ship quay and tender dock. Taxi drivers will transport visitors up the hill to the monastery, then return at an appointed time to bring them back down, for a fare of about US$20. Buses also run between Skala and Chora. It takes about half an hour to walk the path up

(Above) A tiny square in Chora. (Left) Fresco in Monastery of St. John the Divine. (Bottom) Natural sponges, harvested in local waters, are sold on Patmos.

to the cave, then on to the monastery. Scooters can be hired in town and cost about US$10 for two hours.

Beaches on the island can be reached by hired boat or by road. Just north of Skala and within walking distance (about 20 minutes) is the sand and gravel beach at **Melloi** 4 . Further along is the sandy beach at **Agriolivado** 5 . One of the island's best beaches is **Kambos** 6 , a ten-minute taxi ride or 20-minute boat ride north of Skala. **Grikou Bay** 7 , below Chora, has a sandy beach.

Shore excursions include a motorcoach ride to the grotto and monastery of St. John (2.5 hrs, $48), and a scenic drive to the grotto of St. John, the white-washed village of Chora and coastal Grikou (2.5 hrs).

Kos

An ancient cultural center, the island of Kos is where Hippocrates founded a school of medicine in the 5th century BC. In the following century, the Sanctuary of Asklepios became famous as a healing center, its terraced buildings encompassing the Temple of Asklepios and the Stoa, which housed the medical school. The island also prospered during Hellenistic times as a naval base for the Ptolemaic dynasty of Egypt. The Graeco-Roman town of Kos contains an odeum built in imperial times, as well as a castle built by the Knights of St. John. Its Roman-era villas were decorated with fabulous floor mosaics, many of which were removed by the Italians in the 1930s to the Grand Master's Palace in Rhodes.

Northeast Aegean Islands

Lying off the coast of Turkey, these remote and widespread islands include rugged **Limnos (Lemnos)**, volcanic in origin, its fertile soil used for growing wheat and fruit trees. Sacred to the Olympian god Hephaestus (originally an Asian fire god), Limnos was a colony of Athens in c. 500 BC and excavations at Hephaestia have revealed a theater of the Hellenistic period. With the decline of the Byzantine Empire, Limnos was eventually seized in 1479 by the Ottoman Turks. A fortress overlooks the fishing harbor at Myrina, the island's capital and primary port.

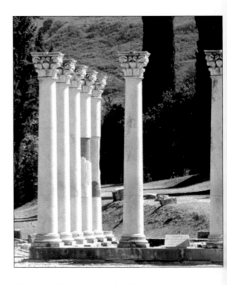

The ancient ruins on Kos.

Lesbos (Lesvos) became a cultural center of Greece in the 7th century BC. The female poet Sappho, who wrote love lyrics to other women, was born here in the early 6th century BC and the term 'lesbian' is derived from the name of her island home. Aristotle and Epicurus are among those who taught at the island's Philosophical Academy. Lesbos was captured by Ottoman Turks in 1462 and, along with Limnos, was returned in 1913 to Greece. Olive groves and citrus fruits flourish on the island's fertile hillsides. Mitilini is the chief town, its harbor overlooked by Gattelusi Castle, constructed by the Byzantine emperor Justinian. The Theatre of Mytilene, built in Hellenistic times on the slope of a hill, is where Pompey reportedly sat on a luxurious throne and watched performances lauding his military successes.

Ionian Islands

This chain of lush, mountainous islands lying off the west coast of Greece is shrouded in myth – both ancient and modern. The island of Ithaca was, according to Homer's legends, the home of **Odysseus** who, in the course of his 10-year odyssey, struggled with angry gods and insistent sea nymphs before returning home to his waiting wife and son.

A modern Greek tale unfolded on another Ionian island – the tiny isle of **Skorpios** – when its owner, the shipping tycoon **Aristotle Onassis**, married one of the world's most famous women, Jacqueline Kennedy, in October 1968. Born in Turkey, Onassis was 16 when he left his homeland in 1922 to revive the family tobacco business in Argentina. Receiving Greek citizenship in 1925, Onassis bought his first ship in the early 1930s and, upon marrying the daughter of an influential Greek ship owner in 1946, Onassis, his father-in-law and a brother-in-law formed the most powerful shipping clan in the world. Onassis, founder of Olympic Airways, was no stranger to controversy when he set his sights on the widely-admired widow of President Kennedy. Mrs. Kennedy had been placed on a pedestal following her husband's assassination and, like a fallen Greek goddess, she stunned the world with her marriage to Onassis, whose fortune at the time was estimated between $500 million and $1 billion.

Shipping has long been big business in the Ionian islands. **Corfu** (Kerkira) was settled in 730 BC by Corinthian colonists, who then competed with Corinth for the shipping trade in the Adriatic. An early naval battle was waged between these two maritime rivals in 665 BC, and this was just the beginning of numerous wars and invasions that would, over the centuries, leave their mark on each of the Ionian Islands. During the 14th and 15th centuries the maritime power of Venice seized all the islands from the Byzantine Empire, and they remained part of the Venetian Republic until it fell in 1797. The islands were then transferred by treaty to France, only to be seized two years later by a Russo-Turkish fleet. In 1807 Russia returned them to France, but they were soon occupied by the British navy and remained under Britain's protection until they were at last ceded to Greece in 1864.

The lovely Ionian Islands are known for their dramatic cliffs and sugary white beaches.

Corfu (Kerkira)

Corfu has long been considered one of Greece's loveliest islands. Homer wrote glowingly about Phaeacia – a luxurious and joyful island whose seafaring people welcomed sailors – and it's quite likely Corfu was this island, upon which Odysseus was shipwrecked. Other poets and writers since Homer have been smitten with the beauty of Corfu, including Goethe, Oscar Wilde and Lawrence Durrell. Shakespeare, in *The Tempest*, may have modeled Prospero's island on Corfu.

The Turks also coveted Corfu, but the island's inhabitants resisted Turkish invasion, including two famous sieges in 1537 and 1716. Corfu is a fertile island, and its major industries are farming, fishing and tourism.

On Your Own

Corfu town, one of Greece's largest medieval towns, is beautifully preserved, its cobblestone alleyways winding past churches, fountains and statues. The ships dock west of the town, and most cruise lines provide a motorcoach shuttle into the town center where your escort remains at a central meeting point while you independently explore Corfu town (3.5 hrs, $30).

If you would like to see the sights south of the town center, buses travel regularly between the Esplanade and Kanoni. Buses also run regularly between Corfu town and Palaeokastritsa on the island's west coast.

Corfu Town's mostly pedestrian streets are filled with shops

The large medieval town of Corfu is beautifully preserved.

and tavernas, as well as important medieval buildings. On the west side of town stands the Venetian-built **New Fortress 1**, originally constructed in 1577, its maze of tunnels and moats later modified by the French and British, whose citadel stands at its heart. On the

Shore Excursions *Corfu*

Shore excursions in Corfu include a walking tour of the Old Town and a motorcoach ride to various island attractions.

Full day tours include lunch and cost about $100. Half-day tours (4 hrs) cost about $40 and combine a walking tour of Corfu with one or two island attractions.

opposite side of town, on a promontory once guarded by a moat and bridge, are the remains of the **Old Fortress** built by the Venetians in 1546.

The town's main square – the **Esplanade** – contains a cricket pitch and Victorian bandstand, and is bordered on its west side by Georgian and Venetian townhouses, their overhanging balconies decorated with wrought-iron railings. The Liston – an arcaded sidewalk of cafes and restaurants – was built by the French under Napoleon. This beguiling blend of architecture is repeated throughout the historic quarter – the 16th-century red-

domed **Church of St. Spyridon** , the 17th-century Venetian lodge now housing the **Town Hall** , and the 19th-century colonnaded **Palace of St. Michael and St. George** , built as a residence for the British Lord High Commissioner. Another beautiful building houses the **Corfu Literary Society** , the oldest in Greece.

It's a pleasant walk along Garitsa Bay to the **Archaeological Museum** , with its fine collection of excavated artifacts. At the south end of the bay is the **Church of Saints Jason and Sosipater** , a 12th-century Byzantine church decorated with beautiful icons. Just south of the bay, near the public beach, is the **Palace of Mon Repos** 🔟. Set amid gardens, this mansion was built in 1831 as a summer residence for Britain's Lord High Commissioners. It became a royal residence and was the birthplace of Prince Philip, Duke of Edinburgh, who is a grandson of George I, the Danish prince who reigned as Greece's king from 1863-1913. Greece abolished its monarchy in 1973, when the country became a presidential republic, and in 1990 the Palace was expropriated by the Greek government.

About a mile past the Palace of Mon Repos is **Kanoni** 🔟, with its captivating view across a mountain-bounded inlet dotted with two idyllic islets: one joined to shore by a narrow causeway and containing the monastery of Vlacherna; the other covered with green foliage which all but hides its 13th-century chapel. South of Kanoni is the gaudily grand **Achilleion Palace** 🔟, which was used as a springtime retreat by Germany's Kaiser Wilhelm II in the early 1900s but is perhaps better known as the casino set used in the James Bond movie *For Your Eyes Only*.

The cliff-edged coves of **Palaeokastritsa (Old Castle)** 🔟, on the island's west coast, are also exceptionally beautiful. Palaeokastritsa, its beautiful beaches and turquoise waters considered by some archaeologists to be the ancient site of Homer's city of the Phaeacians. The sea caves here can be explored by peddle boat. For panoramic views of the coves,

follow the road west of Lacone to the **Byzantine monastery** 🔟, perched atop a cliff, or carry on further to **Bella Vista** 🔟 – a natural terrace overlooking the sea, which is situated near the ruins of Angelokastro, a 13th-century fortress.

(Above) The monastery on Kanoni island.

(Below) Grand staircase of the Achilleion Palace.

CRUISE ROUTES

ROUTES: - - - - - -

N

Miles

0   75

BULGARIA

GREECE

BLACK SEA

Edirne

Istanbul

MARMARA SEA

Gelibolu (Gallipoli)

Çanakkale

Troy

Dardanelles

LESBOS

CHIOS

AEGEAN SEA

İzmir

Selçuk
Ephesus

Kuşadası

Bodrum

KOS

Marmaris

RHODES

SEA OF CRETE

Iraklion

CRETE

TURKEY

Bursa

Ankara

CENTRAL ANATOLIA

Boğazkale

Nevşehir

Göreme

Cappadocia

Konya

Çatalhöyük

Perge
Aspendos
Side

Antalya

Kemer

Kaş

Adana

Antakya (Antioch)

SYRIA

CYPRUS

Lefkoşa

Nicosia

Famagusta

Limassol

CHAPTER NINE

TURKEY,
THE BLACK SEA AND CYPRUS

Part Europe, part Asia, Turkey is a unique Mediterranean destination – exotic, mysterious and steeped in history. Arching gold beaches and lush stands of palm and cypress trees are juxtaposed with ruins dating back to before the Bronze Age.

If ever there was a Garden of Eden, it may well have been situated in a narrow valley of south-eastern Turkey where researchers have found DNA traces of the founder crop of einkorn wheat. This region, on the edge of the ancient Fertile Crescent of Iraq, is where agriculture and the origins of collective society began 10,000 years ago.

Yet, despite its ancient past, Turkey is very much a modern nation. A democratic republic, Turkey has embraced westernization while retaining its exotic eastern culture.

Turkey at a Glance

Turkey's population, about 63 million, is almost exclusively Sunni Muslim. The official language is Turkish – not Arabic – and English, French and German are widely understood. Turkey covers an area over 300,000 square miles, with more than 5,000 miles of coastline. European Turkey is largely rolling agricultural land while the Asian side of the country is bordered by the Black Sea Mountains to the north and the Taurus Mountains to the south. This part of Turkey is dominated by the vast semi-arid plateau of Anatolia, although parts of the lower interior are lush and fertile, with numerous rivers and lakes.

Travel Tips

Currency: The unit of currency is the New Turkish lira (YTL) introduced in early 2005. This eliminated six zeros from existing Turkish Lira with bank notes now starting at 1 YTL (1 YTL is worth about $.70 US). US currency is accepted everywhere and ATM machines issuing Turkish lira at competitive exchange rates are located at most ports.

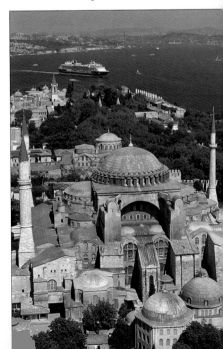

A Celebrity ship departs Istanbul.
Haghia Sophia in foreground,
with Topaki palace behind.

The excellent Metro transit system can be boarded near the Eminönü docks with stops throughout "Old Stamboul."

Visa: Passengers visiting by ship for a day do not normally need a visa. However, if Istanbul is a home port where a stay for a few days is planned, citizens of the United States and Canada will require a visa obtained either beforehand or upon entering the country. If arriving by airplane, a visa can be obtained at a kiosk within the airport. The cost for US citizens is about $20 but for Canadians the cost is $60.

Health Concerns: Inoculations for cruise passengers planning to stay a few days in Istanbul or along the Aegean coast are not necessary. However, if you intend to travel further inland before or after your cruise, you should consult your physician.

Getting Around: The taxi fare from Ataturk International Airport to downtown Istanbul is about US$25. However, it is a good idea to agree beforehand on a price with the driver by showing him the written name of your hotel. More economical are the government-owned, HAVAS buses which carry luggage and charge about US$3 per person. These green-and-yellow buses are stationed outside the exit area of the arrivals level and have three drop-off stops: Aksarray in the old part of Istanbul; Sishane just over the Ataturk Bridge; and Taksim, in the Beyoglu area.

Taxis are a good way to get about in Turkey and are reasonably priced. For example, the fare from Taksim to the Sultanahmet mosque is about US$15. Another efficient way to get around is by the ubiquitous dolmus (meaning 'stuffed' – which they often are at rush hour). These small buses are usually tan coloured, with their destinations displayed on the windscreen. Payment, in local currency, is made as you get off. Istanbul's Metro, a sort of art-deco street car, is also good – and cheap.

Dining: Turkish cuisine is renowned for its excellence and variety. Popular dishes include *kebap* which is grilled or roasted meat, and fish. Restaurant dinner hour normally begins at about 7:00 p.m. A popular alcoholic beverage is *raki* – the grandfather of absinthe-type drinks – which goes well with hors d'oeuvres and is traditionally enjoyed prior to the main meal of the day. Turkey

Turkey is a fascinating study of contrasts between its history of Muslim traditions and its adaptation to the modern world.

produces some good wines from the Thrace, Anatolia and Aegean regions. *Buzbag*, a popular red from Anatolia, is often touted as Turkey's most original wine.

Although Turkish coffee is very good, tea is more popular with the Turks. The favorite tea (cay) is deep red and known as 'rabbit's blood'. Served piping hot with sugar in small, tulip-shaped glasses, it is often offered as a traditional expression of hospitality.

Opening Hours: Most stores open by 10:00 a.m. and many business hum along well after 6:00 p.m. The covered bazaar in Istanbul is open from 8:00 a.m. to 7:00 p.m. but it is closed on Sunday. Bank hours seem to vary but generally the doors open at 8:30 a.m., closing at noon for lunch and re-opening from 1:30 until 5:00 p.m. Museums are open between 10:00 a.m. and 4:00 p.m. every day except Mondays. An exception is Topkapi Palace, which closes on Tuesdays.

Shopping: Turkey is renowned for its carpets and kilims (fine carpets for walls), tiles and porcelain, and silks. Turkey is also an excellent place to buy jewelry,

View from the Bosphorus of Istanbul with Blue Mosque at left, Hagia Sophia in the middle, and Topkapi Palace to the right.

Meerschaum pipes, brass work and leather products. Handmade ceramic tiles, bowls, plates and other pottery are also widely available, their colorful designs often replicated from 17th and 18th century works.

Turkish merchants are well known to enjoy pre-sale banter and haggling is part of the process. It is very common for a merchant to offer you tea and ask you to sit down while he tells you about his wares. If you are seriously looking to buy something, this is an aspect of Turkish culture to be enjoyed. The art of bargaining starts with a figure about half the asking price and settles at between 60 and 80 per cent of the merchant's initial price.

Turkey's History

The world's first settlement is thought to date back over 8,000 years to a Neolithic centre at Çatalhöyük, about 120 miles northeast of the coastal resort city of Antalya. The entire Anatolian plateau harbored numerous tribes, but it wasn't until the Hittites moved west into the Capadocian area around 1800 BC that Turkey's history began. With their capital at Bogazkoy (70 miles east of Ankara), the Hittites were the chief power and cultural force in western Asia from 1400

to 1200 BC, successfully smelting iron and posing a threat to Babylonia, Syria and Egypt.

By 1000 BC, the Hittite empire had been subdued by invaders and it was also around this time that Ionians, fleeing Dorian invaders on mainland Greece, began settling along the coastline of Aegean Turkey. The region's fertile land and excellent harbors provided prosperity for these Greek pioneers and various cities thrived, particularly **Ephesus**.

Well before the Romans arrived in Turkey, one of the world's greatest cities was being settled by the Greeks on a small promontory on the Sea of Marmara. Legend has it that a Greek soldier named Byzas received direction by the Delphic oracle, who advised him to settle "opposite the land of the blind". When Byzas stood at the first hill of **Istanbul** (where Topkapi Palace now stands), he saw opposite the Greek town of Chalcedon (now Uskudar) and concluded the oracle meant the Chalcedonians were blind not to have settled where he stood. If legends have any truth, he was right. Standing at Topkapi's Mecidiye Kösk, viewing the Bosphorus and Golden Horn flowing together into the Sea of Marmara, is a scene of great beauty. Byzas established his colony on the acropolis of the city in 667 BC, making Istanbul now over 2,600 years old.

Politically, the city's position held great importance. Ancient Byzantium was ideally situated to control shipping to and from the

Black Sea and, straddling Europe and Asia, it was a critical trade portal between the Orient and Europe. Surrounded on three sides by water and with substantial land walls, it was virtually impregnable to attack.

For almost 1,000 years, Byzantium was little different from other Greek cities of Asia Minor, with first the Persians, then the Spartans and the Athenians gaining control of the city. Eventually, Byzantium, like most other cities of the Mediterranean, fell under Rome's rule, becoming an important port and garrison for the Empire. So things remained until the 4th century, when an event unparalleled in the history of the Roman Empire occurred: the voluntary retirement of Emperor Diocletian. This caused an eruption in the Empire as armies aligned with three competing Caesars, one of whom – the victor– is known as **Constantine the Great**.

Some historians point to Constantine as the single most influential ruler in western civilization and perhaps no one more

deserved the title of 'Great' than did Byzantine's first emperor. Constantine moved the Roman capital to Byzantium and on the 11th of May in 330 he formally dedicated the city, now called Constantinople, to the God of the Christians. Today, the most visible remains of Constantine's building effort is his column near the entrance to the Covered Bazaar.

The Byzantine Empire reached its apex during the reign of Justinian I, from 527 to 565 AD, when its borders stretched from Spain to Iraq. Many edifices and magnificent churches were built across the Empire during this time, the most magnificent being the Hagia Sophia, built near the acropolis of the city.

Though the Byzantine Empire remained relatively intact for another 500 years, the ebb was apparent by the 11th century with the permanent loss of Asia Minor to the Turks which greatly diminished Constantinople's ability to defend its European possessions.

Mosiac of Justinian I in Basilica S. Vitale, Ravenna, Italy.

Imperial Byzantine emblem.

The Byzantine Empire's fortunes darkened irrevocably during a chaotic period following a power struggle for the throne early in the 13th century. In 1204 the Venetians, enlisted by the usurper Alexius IV, attacked the city under the guise of the Fourth Crusade and for the first time in almost a thousand years, the city fell. Pillaging of the city stripped it of most of its splendor and wealth and many of these treasures were taken to Venice. This sacking of the Greek Orthodox capital of Constantinople by Latin Roman Catholics made permanent the schism between the two great Christian religions.

The Latins were finally pushed out of Constantinople in 1261 by the Byzantine emperor Michael Palaeologus. His son Andronicus enjoyed a long reign of over 40 years, during which time the Empire declined. However, through his patronage of the arts, Byzantium flowered culturally. But the end for the great Byzantine Empire was quickly approaching. The Ottoman Turks, successors to the Seljuk dominance of Asia Minor, conquered Bursa in 1326 and Nicaea in 1331. With the sudden death of Andronicus III in 1341, the Empire convulsed in a bitter civil war, followed by the Black Plague. Militarily and financially spent, Byzantium had few allies and was forced into an appeasement policy with the ever-encroaching Ottoman Turks.

Finally, in 1453 the Turks succeeded in surrounding the Queen of Cities and on May 29th, using a specially made cannon (the largest the world had known), they blasted a hole in the Theodosian Walls and took the city. Their leader, Mehmet II, was 21 when he made his triumphal entry into the city. Mehmet, called Fatih (the Conqueror), made Constantinople his capital and restored the city's greatness with a massive rebuilding program and by bringing in populations from other towns.

The Ottoman Empire enjoyed another 100 years of expansion which culminated with **Süleyman the Magnificent's** capture of

Belgrade, Budapest and very nearly Vienna. However, the reign of his son Selim II, known as The Sot, marked the slow decline of Ottoman influence. Corrupted from within by palace intrigues and by the violent resistance of the Janissaries – an elite corp of the Ottoman army – to any reforms, the Empire's steady decline followed. While Europe embraced new battle tactics and technology, Ottoman Turkey continued using methods from the 15th century.

In the early 19th century the sultan Mahmut II ushered in an era of reform but suffered political and military setbacks, such as the loss of Greece in 1830. Mahmut eliminated the Janissary Corps, created a new, more modern army and supported the improvement of education, thus laying the foundation for secularization throughout Ottoman society. He also banned turbans, which were replaced with the Moroccan fez.

Throughout the 19th century, succeeding sultans continued to spend extravagantly, building huge palaces along the Bosphorus such as the **Dolmabahçe Palace**. Serious conflicts, such as the Crimean War, drained the Empire's

(Top) Gentile Bellini's portrait of Fatih (the Conqueror). (Below) Dolmabahçe Palace, Bosphorus.

finances, and by 1881 the Empire was on the brink of bankruptcy. The government was forced into taking loans at high interest rates and making political and trade concessions with European powers.

The unravelling Ottoman Empire collapsed when Turkey blundered into the First World War on the side of Germany. Despite winning the tactical battle of Gallipoli, Turkey's fate was tied to that of Germany. With Germany's surrender in 1918, it was over for the Ottoman dynasty. Plans were made to alter Turkey's borders, with Greece the main benefactor. However, the European allies, which helped land Greek troops at Izmir in May of 1919, underestimated the determination of the Turkish people to hold onto their country. The Turks rallied around the hero of the Battle of Gallipoli, Mustafa Kemal (known later as Ataturk – "father of Turkey"), who hastily organized an army and routed the Greek invaders in a counterattack that began in late August 1922. Within a few weeks, the Turkish mainland was completely liberated, an armistice signed and the Ottoman dynasty abolished.

In July 1923, the Turkish government signed the Lausanne Treaty with European powers. Ankara became the capital of the new Turkish State and the Republic was proclaimed, with Mustafa Kemal elected president. The new Turkey's ideology was, and remains, Atatürkism. Its basic principles stress the republican

Fishermen gather near the cruise ship dock at Karaköy.

form of government, representing the power of the electorate. A secular administration, it supports nationalism, modernization and a mixed economy with state participation in many of the vital sectors. Although the country's democracy is underpinned by a military determined to keep Turkey secular, the process of participatory democracy continues to work for the country.

Istanbul

The Queen of Cities, as Istanbul has been called over the centuries, is one of the most fascinating ports in the world. If Istanbul is the home port for your cruise, you should try to add at least two days for touring the city. Although no longer the capital of Turkey (which moved to Ankara in 1923), an aura of power remains in Istanbul, for it is still the country's financial and business center, and home to most of its head offices. Called Constantinople for over 1,500 years, its name was formally changed to Istanbul (meaning 'to the city' in Turkish) in 1930.

On Your Own

Istanbul is a safe city to stroll and its main attractions are also quite accessible by foot from the cruise dock. The best place to start touring this magnificent city is the **Galata Bridge**, near the cruise port at **Karaköy**. The view is expansive and beautiful, taking in the Bosphorus, the Golden Horn, the Sea of Marmara and the old city. A thousand years of architecture, from the Theodosian walls (completed in 447 AD) to the Topkapi Palace (built in 1465), can be seen in a glance, while below, on the river, ferries jockey for position at the docks.

Galata Bridge joins Karaköy with the Eminönü dock area. Near the bridge is one of the city's important mosques, the **Yeni Cami** **1**, meaning the New Mosque, for it was the last of the great classical Ottoman mosques built (in 1663).

About halfway along the **Eminönü** dock area will be your first opportunity to hitch a ride on Istanbul's excellent **Metro**, which

View from Galata Bridge to Kadiköy where cruise ships dock.

MUST SEE:

Like Rome, Istanbul has many must-see sites and first time visitors cannot go wrong focusing on the old city of Istanbul.
Hagia Sophia, touted by art lovers and architects around the world as the greatest monument of the bygone Byzantine Empire.
Topkapi Palace – a rare glimpse into the mystery and splendor of the Ottoman era.
Blue Mosque one of the most beautiful mosques in the world, renowned for its tiles.
Kapali Çarsi, also known as the Grand Bazaar; whether or not you are in the market for a carpet, you have to visit this fascinating labyrinth of shops.

winds through the city. You can also catch the Metro just outside of the **Sirkeci Train Station** a few hundred paces further along. However, there is still much to see on foot, as you walk up old Constantinople's first hill, beginning with the Sirkeci Train Station – termination of the famous **Orient Express** which made its first run to Istanbul in 1888. Further along, are the palace walls and **Alay Köskü** (sultan's gazebo) **2** where the sultan observed the comings and goings of his Grand Vizier across the street. The entrance to the Vizier's palace and offices was known as the **Sublime Porte**, the diplomatic reference to Turkey for hundreds of years. Nearby is the first entrance to the grounds of **Topkapi Sarayi**, the Great Palace of the Ottomans.

Topkapi Palace **3** – Built by Mehmet the Conqueror in 1467, Topkapi Palace was, for 400 years, the residence of sultans and the center of imperial administration. The palace is the most extensive structure of Ottoman architecture, covering an area almost half the size of Monaco. It took its name from the Cannon Gate of the Byzantine sea-walls, which translated into Topkapi in Turkish. It was not until the reign of Süleyman the Magnificent (1520-1566), at the urgings of his Russian wife Roxelana, that accommodations for wives and concubines were included at the palace.

Now a museum complex, the Topkapi Palace contains unrivalled collections of porcelains, armor, jewels and other objects of

CITY ATTRACTIONS
(1) Yeni Camii (new mosque)
(2) Sultan's Gazebo - Sublime Porte
(3) Topkapi Palace
(4) Archaeological Museum
(5) Hagia Sophia (Aya Sophia)
(6) Sultanahmet (Blue Mosque)
(7) Hippodrome
(8) Yerebatan Cistern
(9) Constantine's column
(10) Covered (Grand) Bazaar
(11) Istanbul University
(12) Beyazit Tower
(13) Kariye Camii -
     St. Saviour in Chora
(14) Tekfur Saray (Byzantine Palace)
(15) Fatih Camii
(16) Süleymaniye Camii

art formerly belonging to the sultans. Visitors can wander freely throughout the grounds' public areas. There are two entrances into the first court, with the northern one (near the Alay köskü) taking you to the **Archaeological Museum 4**, the Museum of the Ancient Orient and the famous Tiled Pavilion. The southern gate, known as the Bab-i Hümayun or Imperial Gate, is the main entrance. This gate also takes you by the old Byzantine church of **Hagia Eirene**, built during Justinian's reign at about the same time as Hagia Sophia.

The **Archaeological Museum** was the first systematic attempt by the Ottoman Empire to preserve the nation's antiquities and it contains the superb Alexander Sarcophagus, discovered at Sidon (modern Sayda in Lebanon) in 1887. (This sarcophagus derives its name from carved sculptures depicting Alexander the Great hunting.) The **Museum of the**

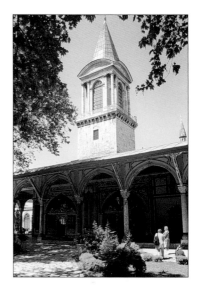

Topkapi Palace.

Ancient Orient's collection isn't large but is of great importance with its pre-Islamic Arab artifacts, as well as Babylonian and Assyrian exhibits.

Leaving the grounds of the first court, you pass through the

Shore Excursions *Istanbul*

With ships docking very close to a city crammed with attractions, the cruise lines have numerous excellent tours available.

• **Istanbul Sampler** tour gets you to the old city with a walk to three or four famous sites (7 hrs, $60).

• **Bosphorus Cruise** – affords a rare view of the grand Ottoman palaces along this famous strait. This tour usually takes in some shopping and sites in the old city (7 hrs, about $100).

• **Ciragan Palace** tour (9 hrs, about $200). Tour historic sites, visit the Grand Bazaar and lunch at the luxurious Ottoman palace.

• **Architectural Wonders Of Istanbul** – Some cruise lines offer tours showcasing the architectural works of Sinan, who designed the Suleymaniye Mosque. Includes two or three mosques and a visit to the Grand Bazaar ($40).

• **Topkapi Palace** tour (5 hrs, about $60). This tour focuses on the famous palace used by Ottoman sultans for 400 years. Visit includes treasury and harem.

Recommended: Many cruise lines offer a Best of Istanbul tour (9 hrs, about $100) which is a history walk and scenic drive, focusing on the major sites in the old city. Usually includes shopping in the Grand Bazaar. Good value.

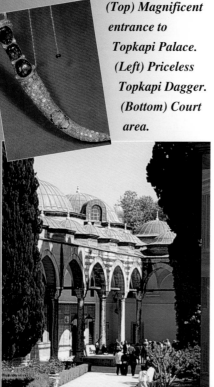

(Top) Magnificent entrance to Topkapi Palace. (Left) Priceless Topkapi Dagger. (Bottom) Court area.

impressive Bab-üs Selam (Gate of Salutation). Built into the wall to the right of the gate is the **Executioner's Fountain**, where he would wash his hands and sword after performing a decapitation outside the gate. The inner palace grounds contain many important exhibits and attractions. For Muslims, the most significant is the **Pavilion of the Holy Mantle**, displaying the sacred relics of the Prophet Muhammad, including his sword and robe (the Holy Mantle).

The **Treasury of the Topkapi Palace** is considered one of the richest in the world. Among its priceless artifacts, which were made for the sultans, is the famous **Topkapi Dagger**. The centrepiece of the 1960s film *Topkapi*, the dagger's sheath is pierced with diamonds and its gold hand is set with huge emeralds.

Hagia Sophia (Church of the Divine Wisdom) 5 – On first entering this venerable building, one senses the volume of history it has withstood. First a church, then a mosque, and now a museum, Hagia Sophia has been in existence for nearly 1,500 years. Considered one of the most beautiful buildings ever constructed, it was the largest church in Christendom until the construction of St. Peter's Basilica in Rome.

Standing just outside the Imperial Gate of the Topkapi Palace, the Hagia Sophia is the third edifice of the same name to rest on the site. The first church, dedicated in 360 AD, was destroyed by fire during a mob riot, as was the second church during the Nika Revolt in early 532,

THE SULTAN'S HAREM

For the sultans, home was the harem. These private apartments housed, in addition to the sultan's four main wives (the maximum number under Islamic law), his concubines and numerous relatives (including confined princes), eunuchs, guards and servants. At the height of its use, the Topkapi Palace population numbered over 3,000. Numerous staircases, corridors and courtyards are linked by narrow passageways, exuding the claustrophobic world of palace intrigue where, for generations, the women behind the sultan – often his mother – controlled the reins of power.

On half a dozen levels, hundreds of attractive girls and women lived their existence almost exclusively within the walls of the harem. They usually came from non-Muslim parts of the empire (Islamic law forbidding enslavement of Muslim women) and were almost always captured in war or bought on the slave market. Because life for these women was so privileged, some parents would voluntarily send their daughters to Istanbul, even after slave trading was banned in the 19th century.

Girls came to the harem as young as five years of age. After training for domestic duties, they became a *cariye* (a concubine of the lowest rank). They could then begin to assume greater importance, for each was the potential mother of a sultan. The sultan normally had about a dozen favorite concubines, and if one became pregnant she was called *kadin efendi*. If she successfully brought a child into the world, she acquired the title *haseki sultan* and given her own apartment.

If the child was male and the mother a favorite of the sultan, she could become one of his four official wives. Depending on the woman's power and skill, she would do her utmost to maneuver her son as heir to the throne. Roxelana, a wife of Süleyman, went so far as to convince the sultan to kill his first son so that her alcoholic son, Selim II, would assume the throne.

(Above) The gardens overlooked by Hagia Sophia. (Below) 19th-century view of Hagia Sophia .

during the early years of Emperor Justinian's reign. Successfully putting down the riot with the help of his general Basilierus and the considerable backbone of his wife Theodora, Justinian resolved to build the grandest church ever, regardless of expense.

The architects, given carte blanche and 10,000 workers, began the project just five weeks after the riots. Provincial governors were ordered to send to the capital any surviving classical remains that might be incorporated into the new edifice. In response, eight porphyry columns of the pagan Sun Temple of Rome were sent, as were eight green marble columns from Ephesus.

The church was completed in 537 and according to Procopius, the historian of the day, it greatly impressed the Christian world. With a huge dome over 100 feet in diameter, 160 feet high and pierced with 40 windows, it appeared "suspended from heaven by a golden chain." To most observers, the church seemed nothing less than a miracle. When Justinian first walked into the church, he stood silent for a long time before uttering, "Solomon, I have surpassed thee."

What makes Hagia Sophia such an architectural marvel is not the height nor breadth of the dome, but the two semi-domes at either end. In addition to lengthening the nave, the semi-domes give the observer, on first entering the church, an unobstructed view to the top of the church. Decorative aspects of note include the beautiful marble casings throughout the interior, such as the butterfly marble over the main entrance. The unique capitals of the columns, with their surface decoration of acanthus (symbolizing heaven) and deeply undercut palm foliage, produce an effect of lightness and strength. Monograms on the capitals are those of Justinian and Theodora.

The mosaics of Hagia Sophia are one of the most fascinating aspects of this church. Although various figures adorned the church in the 6th through 8th centuries, these were removed during the iconoclastic years which ended in 846 with a burst of new work. Important mosiacs include those at the east end of the south gallery, next to the apse, depicting the Empress Zoe and her third husband, Constantine IX, on either side of Christ. Just to the right of this mosaic is an imperial portrait showing John II Comnenus and Empress Eirene with the Mother of Jesus holding an infant Christ. A side panel shows the heir, Prince Alexius, who ascended to the throne at 17 but died shortly thereafter.

The most significant of the Byzantine mosaics in Hagia Sophia is the sad and beautiful

(Top) South aisle of Hagia Sophia. (Above) Empress Zoe and Constantine IX with Christ. (Below) The Deesis.

Deesis, located in the east wall of the buttress in the south gallery. Likely produced in the early 14th century, this work is an example of Constantinople's cultural renaissance after the restoration of the city from the dark years of Latin control. Although most of the mosaic is lost, the facial features of its three subjects remain intact and show Christ, with an expression of grief, flanked by the young Virgin on one side and a pleading St. John the Baptist on the other.

Sultan Ahmet Camii (The Blue Mosque) 6 – Built by the young Sultan Ahmet I between 1609 to 1616, the Blue Mosque is widely considered the city's most splendid. The domes and semi-domes cascade gracefully from the summit within a stand of six slender minarets which represented that Ahmet was the sixth Sultan. Ahmet was an enthusiast about his mosque and often pitched in to speed up construction. He didn't have long to enjoy it for he died of typhus, at the age

View across Hippodrome and Blue Mosque to Marmara Sea.

of 28, within a year of its completion. His tomb is at the northwest side of the mosque.

When walking the short distance from Hagia Sophia to the Blue Mosque, visitors enter a square that was the heart of ancient Byzantium. Law courts, a large public library and a book market all stood where gardens now flourish. The main entrance to the Blue Mosque is at the eastern side of the courtyard and, as with all mosques (*camii* in Turkish) you must remove your shoes before entering.

The Blue Mosque's reputation as a must-see attraction is deserved, for the interior is stunning. Four fluted piers, pushing towards the center, resemble trunks of huge trees as they disappear into the arching canopy of the dome and four semi-domes. Sunlight, filtered and diffused by coloured glass, pours in from 260 windows. Along the lower part of the walls, especially in the galleries, is a profusion of beautiful blue and green Iznik tiles, for which the edifice is named.

Just to the west of the Blue

Mosque is the ancient **Hippodrome** **7** where chariot races and other events entertained the citizens of Constantinople. An immense structure, it could seat 100,000 spectators. The central line of the race course is still visible today and was marked by obelisks and columns, three of which remain.

The **Egyptian Obelisk**, from the 15th century BC (erected in the 4th century) is about 65 feet in height and is actually the top third of the original obelisk. The sculpted reliefs around the base depict Emperor Theodosius sitting in his box at the Hippodrome, holding a head wreath to honor a winner.

The middle column, called the **Serpent Column**, is the oldest Greek monument in the city. Erected in 479 BC in the Temple of Apollo at Delphi, it was brought to the city by Constantine the Great. The **third column**, erected by Emperor Constantine VII Porphyrogenitus in 940, is over 100 feet high and was once plated in bronze gilt, which was

(Above) Interior of Blue Mosque.
(Below) Egyptian Obelisk.

removed during the Latin conquest. A favourite pastime in early Ottoman years was to climb this column as a daring feat.

It's about a 25-minute walk from Sultanahmet to the Covered Bazaar and you may want to take this opportunity to board the Metro at the station just west of the Hippodrome on the Divan Yolu. Just a few steps from this station is the fabled **under-**

ground cistern [8] known as the **Yerebatan Saratu** (underground palace). This giant reservoir, built in the 6th century, was supplied with water from the Belgrade Forest 12 miles west. Supported by 336 columns, the cistern was the main water source for the city and was specifically built to survive periods of siege.

The **Divan Yolu** has been the main road of this city for over 2000 years. The Milion (first mile) started at an archway just beyond Haghia Sophia and from this point all distances in the Byzantine Empire were measured. The first Metro stop along Diva Yolu is called Çemberlitas which refers to the nearby **Column of Constantine** [9], sometimes referred to as the Burnt or Hooped Column. This column was erected in 330 to mark the city's dedication and a number of relics, including bits of the True Cross, are reportedly sealed beneath its foundation.

Turning north from the Hooped Column, you soon encounter the walls of the Nuruosmaniye Mosque and the entrance, through a shaded courtyard, to the Bazaar.

Beggars and peddlers often line the walkways leading to the Bazaar and occasionally a musician can be heard.

Kapali Çarsi (Covered Bazaar) [10] – Also known as the Grand Bazaar, this is a huge labyrinth of shops, banks, cafes, restaurants, mosques and a post office crammed into a grid of narrow streets and protected from the elements by a multitude of domed and vaulted roofs. Come prepared to spend. It is the world's largest covered bazaar and, with 4,000 shops, the place to buy Turkish souvenirs. Whether you are interested or not in a carpet, you'll be approached by numerous young men wanting to show you their selection. If you are interested in a carpet or kilim, this is a good place to shop – the selection is excellent and the competition for business is intense.

Located northwest of the Grand Bazaar is the **Istanbul University** [11] and the **Beyazit Tower** [12] – built as a fire lookout in 1828. The University dates from just after the Conquest in 1453.

West of the Bazaar along Millet Caddesi, are the beautiful **Theodosian Walls**, first built in the fifth century by Theodosias and fortified many times right up to last Byzantine emperor, Constantine XI. The Topkapi Gate is where the Turks first blasted through on May 29th, 1453. These walls inspired Lord Byron to write they were the most impressive of all ancient ruins he had seen. Although crumbling, the walls testify to the survival of this great

Interior of Grand Bazaar.

city for over 1,000 years. Extending more than four miles from the Sea of Marmara to the Golden Horn, the walls were actually a system of three defences with an outer moat (where the highway now is), an outer wall and the main inner wall studded with 96 towers. Although the first phase of the walls was completed in 413 under Theodosius II, a violent earthquake in 447 destroyed much of what had been built. Reconstruction began immediately and within two months the walls were rebuilt and were far stronger – successfully repelling Attila the Hun shortly after.

From the Edirnekapi gate, it's a short walk to the beautiful **Church of St. Saviour in Chora (Kariye Camii) 13** and the haunting ruins of **Tekfur Saray 14**, an annex to the nearby Byzantine Palace of Blachernae. The palace facade is decorated with geometrical designs in red brick and white marble, typifying latter Byzantine architecture of the 13th and 14th century.

For many visitors to Istanbul, seeing the Chora church is a priority. The phrase 'in Chora' means

THE LOWDOWN ON CARPETS

The creation and use of carpets in Turkey dates back to at least 2500 BC, with depictions on rock tombs showing men with implements used for rug weaving. The cool, mountainous region stretching from Turkey to Persia, where sheep fleece and camel and goat hair grow long and fine, is where the art of carpet-weaving reached its peak in the 16th century. Lying east and southeast of Ankarra, this famous region of carpet production is among the few places in the world where carpets are still hand-made. Marco Polo claimed the best and most beautiful carpets in the world came from Konya in this area of Turkey.

The most common material used in Turkish carpets and kilims is sheep's wool, and weavers still use the time-honored double knot, or Gordes knot. A well-made woollen carpet can take one or two weavers up to a month to make, and prices range from US$80 for small throw rugs to several hundred dollars for larger carpets. Silk carpets can be priced in the thousands of dollars.

The quality of a carpet depends on the quality and type of wool, and the number of knots per square inch of surface which can vary from 40 to 1,000 knots. Traditional woollen Turkish carpets are more vibrant and brighter than Persian carpets and often contain patterns dating back many centuries. Kilims, flat woven rugs without any pile, are very popular because of traditional Turkish design and deep colors.

Patterns found in Turkish carpets not only indicate the vintage of the design, but also the region where the carpet was most likely produced. Motifs from nature include birds, camels and flowers. Other patterns utilize symbols, such as arrows for courage, and colors, such as blue to represent the infinite. Prayer mats are distinguished by the pointed shape of their central panel.

The ruins of the last Byzantine palace – Tekfur Saray.

'in the country' and the original church (of which nothing now remains) stood outside the walls built by Constantine. The present building dates from the late 11th century, with elaborate remodelling carried out in the 12th and 14th centuries. The mosaics and frescoes of this church are regarded as the most important series of Byzantine artwork in the world, exquisite in detail and anticipating the great Renaissance which soon took hold in Europe.

A visit to the mosques of **Fatih** **15** and **Süleymaniye** **16** as well as **Valens Aqueduct**, which spans the valley between the two mosques, is well worth the effort. The Fatih Mosque, largest mosque in Istanbul, named after **Mehmet the Conqueror**, is more sombre in appearance than the Blue Mosque, but is nonetheless impressive, if only for its sheer size. It is said that when Mehmet the Conqueror found his mosque was not quite as high as Hagia Sophia he ordered the architect's hands cut off. Both the architect and Mehmet are buried behind the mosque, and visitors can view the tomb of the great conqueror.

The **Süleymaniye Mosque**, the second largest in the city, is one of Turkey's finest imperial Ottoman mosques and is representative of the 'Golden Age' of the Empire. Designed by the great architect Sinan, the Mosque was completed in 1557 and stands just below Istanbul's third hill, on a slope down to the Golden Horn. A structural masterpiece, it assured Sinan's place as a genius of architecture. At the entrance is a grand porticoed courtyard with columns of rich marble and granite. At the corners of the courtyard rise four minarets, representing Süleyman as being the fourth sultan to reign in Istanbul. Cleverly disguising buttresses and eschewing aisles and numerous columns, Sinan created a vast interior enlivened by light filtered through beautiful stained glass windows. Süleyman's majestic tomb is located behind the mosque and his catafalque is capped by the huge white turban he once wore.

The **Valens Aqueduct** was built about 375 AD to bring water from the Belgrade Forest into the centre of the city. Although damaged by earthquakes, it was kept in good repair by the Byzantine emperors and the Ottoman sultans, and was used until the late 19th century when it was replaced by a modern water distribution system.

Dolmabahçe Palace – Many Turks in the late 19th century saw in this palace all that was wrong with the Ottoman Empire. Excessive, expensive and out of

touch with the rest of the country, the Dolmabahçe Palace's construction helped bring the empire to the point of bankruptcy. An inlet was filled in to form the palace site (Dolmabahçe means 'filled-in garden') and a royal park was created with a series of kiosks and pavilions built close to the Bosphorus. The sultan Abdul Mecit decided to build a much larger and more luxurious palace, designed in a neo-baroque style and completed in 1854. The opulent furnishings of the palace included the largest chandelier in the world, weighing four-and-a-half tons and hanging in the State Room.

The palace was home to the last sultan, Mehmet VI, whose ignominious departure entailed being smuggled aboard a British frigate. The palace was also the principal residence of Mustafa Ataturk, who died here in November 1938.

Karaköy and Beyoglu

The districts of Karaköy and Beyoglu, on the north side of the Golden Horn, are almost as old as the main city and were for centuries home to 'foreign' merchants and dignitaries. Karaköy is the Turkish name for the old **Galata** area, which was once the Genoese stronghold. A walled mini-city, Galata had a reputation for debauchery.

Beyoglu is the Turkish name for the old **Pera** district, and was actually an upper-middle class suburb of Galata. During the 18th and 19th centuries, along a road

which became known as the Grand Rue de Pera, palatial mansions and embassies were built. You can take the 19th-century tram part way along Grand Rue de Pera – now called **Istiklâl Caddesi** – or explore on foot. Just off Galatasaray Square, halfway along Istiklâl Caddesi, is an avenue which leads to **Tepebasi** and the site of some renowned grand hotels. The best known of these is Pera Palas, which was built in 1876 as the terminal hotel for the Orient Express.

(Top) Fascinating old Pera District. (Right) Galata Tower affords good views of old city.

At the south end of Istiklâl Caddesi, where the avenue forks to the right, is the entrance to the underground funicular railway known as the Tünel, built in 1875 and dubbed 'The Mouse's Hole' by locals. It takes just over a minute to descend to the bottom of the hill near the Galata Bridge. Another route is to turn left down the steep street of Galip Dede Caddesi to see the famous **Galata Tower**. Built in 1348 as the apex of Genoese fortifications, it has been restored and houses a restaurant on its upper levels with magnificent views.

The Turkish Coast

The **Dardanelles**, known in ancient times as the Hellespont, is a famous strait and the site of many legendary events. Leander swam across this strait nightly, from Asia to Europe, to meet his beloved Hero, a Greek priestess. This romantic gesture was repeated by the poet Lord Byron, to prove it could be done. Armies have crossed this strait, including that of Alexander the Great.

One the most tragic battles of the first world war, resulting in the death or injury of over 500,000 soldiers, also took place

at the Dardanelles, and is known as the **Battle of Gallipoli** after the nearby town. The plan was set in motion by a young Winston Churchill, then First Lord of the Admiralty, who saw a chance to seize Constantinople and secure a route to Russia, England's ally. However, Churchill prematurely sent a British fleet into easy gun range of the hills overlooking the strait and, after a number of ships went down, the navy retreated to wait for land troops. By the time the Allied army was ready, two months later, the Turks had fortified their position. The landing of allied forces at Suvla on the west coast of the peninsula resulted in severe casualties of British, Australian and New Zealand troops, as well as for the Turks. The man most directly responsible for the Turkish victory was the future president of Turkey, **Mustafa Kemal Ataturk.** Ataturk remains greatly venerated and his picture is often seen in stores throughout Turkey.

About 20 miles (32 km) south of Çanakkale lies the ancient Hellenic city of **Troy**, site of the legendary Trojan war described by the Greek poet Homer in his work the *Iliad*. Long dismissed as fiction, the city was only discovered in the latter part of the 19th century by the German archaeologist Heinrich Schliemann. Uncovering the ruins in a series of mounds, Schliemann proved, by Homer's description, that there was indeed a great city just west of the Dardanelles.

Mustafa Kemal Ataturk (1881-1938), first president of Turkey.

Although the ruins of Troy are not impressive, the fortifications are well preserved and certainly convey the scene to those familiar with the famous story of Paris, Helen, Achilles and Odysseus. At the entrance to the archaeological site stands a replica of the famous wooden horse.

Shore excursions from **Çanakkale** include visits to both Troy and its nearby museum (about $65) or to the Battlefield of Gallipoli ($65, about 6 hours) which includes crossing the Dardanelles by ferry. Although there is a fair bit of hiking involved, this is a highly recommended tour for war buffs.

Kusadasi

This popular port of access to Ephesus has become a frenetic resort town serving the ruins-bound travellers. Although there are some decent beaches to the south of the town, they are usually busy. However a walk across an extended causeway links the town to pretty **Pigeon Island**, with a 13th-century Byzantine castle surrounded by gardens and restaurants. The town bazaar is a good place to shop.

Ephesus

This is one of the most important archaeological sites in the Mediterranean. not only for the fine examples of classical architecture but for a rare view into the life and architecture of classical Rome. Of great importance for over a thousand years, Ephesus at one time rivalled Rome for opulence and beauty. The ruins are extensive

> ## Shore Excursions
> *Kusadasi* Kusadasi, drop port for visits to Ephesus and area, offers travelers various tour combinations, many of which focus on the ruins. A basic tour of Ephesus, about $50, takes three or four hours and is good value.
> • Ephesus, St. John's Basilica & Virgin Mary Shrine. Great way to see the three most important Ephesus sites in day. About $70.
> • Turkish village visit (Sirince) and tour of Ephesus Museum with its impressive collection of Hellenistic and Roman artifacts ($50, about 4 hours).

and parts are well preserved. One can easily visualize this bustling port city that was once home to over 300,000 citizens.

Located near the mouth of the river Cayster (now Kuçuk Menderes), Ephesus (Efes in Turkish) was first settled by Ionian Greeks around 1100 BC. The site was a place of worship for a native nature goddess associated with the Greek goddess Artemis, and around 550 BC a large temple was built in her honor. Over the next few centuries the city changed hands many times and continued to thrive as a Greek seaport until

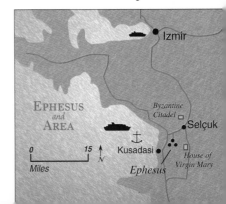

133 BC, when it was taken by the Romans and used as the leading city of their Asian province. Its great Temple of Artemis, renamed the Temple of Diana by the Romans, was considered one of the Seven Wonders of the Ancient World, although little remains today.

As the terminus of the famous Silk Route and the world capital of the slave trade, Ephesus was wealthy and secure for over 500 years, even surviving a sacking by Goths in 262 AD. In the 5th and 6th century, it remained the second-most important city, after Constantinople, in the Byzantine Empire.

Soon, however, Ephesus began to decline with the sacking of the city by Arabs in 716 AD. The Byzantine government also could not afford the annual expense of dredging and soon the harbor completely filled with silt. The city lost its value as a port and by the end of the 8th century Ephesus was reduced to little more than a village. With the advent of the Ottoman Empire, it was completely abandoned. The site was re-discovered by a British archaeologist in 1869, after six years of searching. Most of the ruins visible today date from the Roman period of the 1st century BC to the 2nd century AD.

EPHESUS

1) Market Gate (Gate of Macaeus & Mithridates)
2) Byzantine Fountain
3) Octagon
4) Brothel
5) Temple of Hadrian
6) Baths of Scholastica
7) Fountain of Trajan
8) Gate of Hercules
9) Hydreion
10) Monument of Memnius
11) Square of Domitian
12) Museum of Inscriptions
13) Fountain of Pollio
14) Toilets / public
15) Basilica / town hall

Exploring Ephesus

Ephesus actually begins near the parking lot where the orginal harborfront existed a few hundred yards to the west. Also near the car park is where the **Church of Virgin Mary** (also know as Double Church), is located. This church got its name after the Church of Councils was held in 431 when it was decided that Mary would be known as the "bearer of God". Pope Paul VI led prayers at this spot when he visited Ephesus in 1967.

From the site entrance at the souvenir market you can walk east along the wide **Arcadian Way**. This avenue was first built in the Hellenistic period but was restored in the fifth century and, as it links the city with the sea, it is also referred to as Harbor Street. Arcadian Way leads east for over five hundred yards to the Great Theatre.

Built during the reign of Claudius in about 60 AD, the **Great Theatre** could seat over 25,000 spectators and was the scene for gladiator fights in the 4th and 5th centuries. If you

(Top) Library of Celsus, (below) Ruins of Prytaneion, (bottom) the Apostle Paul spent two years in Ephesus, mainly in jail.

House of the Virgin Mary was declared a shrine by the Vatican.

climb up to just the first tier of rows, you can enjoy an excellent view over the city's old colonnaded main street, once lined with statues and lit by oil lamps at night. The walk along Marble Way takes you past the Lower Agora (marketplace).

One of the most beautiful pieces of architecture remaining in Ephesus is the **Library of Celsus**, built in the early 2nd century by a Roman consul as a memorial to his father. The library once contained over 10,000 scrolls and books. Statues of the four virtues adorn the niches between the columns.

Along **Curates Street** are many interesting ruins including the Temple of Hadrian and ruins of various houses and public buildings. Under the marble-paved street runs the largest sewer system of the city. At the east end of the ruins is the **State or Upper Agora** where large transactions of government took place. The **Odeon**, a building with a capacity of 1400, was built in the 2nd century AD for concerts and drama.

The **Apostle Paul's** connection with Ephesus (described in Acts 17-19) occurred during his second and third missionary journeys into Anatolia between 53 and 57 AD. For three years, with Ephesus as his base, Paul wrote letters and preached to the locals, urging them to put aside their idols of Artemis. "Gods made by human hands are not gods at all," he wrote. This outraged the local silversmiths, who enjoyed a lively trade making Artemis statues, and they provoked a riot that resulted in Paul's incarceration. Forced to leave Ephesus upon his release, Paul journeyed to Jerusalem where he was arrested, sent to Rome and executed during the persecutions of Emperor Nero.

House of the Virgin Mary: According to legend (which began with a German nun in the 19th century) St. John the Apostle brought Mary to Ephesus around 38 AD. She retired to a cottage at Meryemana near Selcuk and there died a few years later. The stone cottage was declared a shrine by the Vatican in 1896 and several popes have visited the site, including Pope Benedict XVI in 2006.

Selçuk

When the port of Ephesus began to fill in with silt, residents moved a few miles to the northeast and settled near the ancient **Temple of Artemis**. The town was below the prominent Ayasuluk Hill upon which the **Byzantine Citadel** was built in the 7th and 8th century. When the Turks overran Ephesus in the 12th century, the fortress (known as Ayasuluk Castle) was rebuilt and much of what remains is from the Ottoman era. The town of Selçuk (pop. 30,000), the modern name for Ephesus, benefits greatly from tourism.

St. John's Basilica: Built in the 6th century by the industrious emperor Justinian, the church is regarded as the most magnificent of the buildings from the Byzantine Period. It is located at the southern foot of Ayasuluk Castle and is said to be built over the grave of John. While in Ephesus he wrote the *Book of John* as well as his three letters.

(Top) The Byzantine Citadel with ruins of Temple of Artemis in foreground. (Middle) The important naval port of Izmir also has one of the best bazaars in Turkey. (Below) The Clock Tower and the miniature Hisar Mosque are two landmarks of Izmir.

Izmir

Turkey's third largest city and second largest port, **Izmir** is also an important military base and a NATO command center of southeast Europe. Of the original Hellenistic city-states situated along the Turkish Aegean coast, only Izmir (known until this century as Smryna) survived. It was possibly the birthplace of Homer, and was the largest and most prosperous city of Asia Minor. Unfortunately, it bears little evidence of its ancient past, yet it's an interesting city to stroll with several sites situated close to the

Hadrian's Gate in Antalya.

Antalya

This beautiful city is situated far enough south to receive good weather during the shoulder seasons and is often referred to as Turkey's Riviera with miles of golden sand stretching north to Kemer. The old port is situated on a small cove surrounded by ancient fortifications. The steep hillside was first settled in the 2nd century BC and fell under Roman control soon thereafter. The Emperor Hadrian visited the city in 130 AD, an event commemorated by a triumphal gate which is still in excellent condition. During the Middle Ages, Antalya was a Byzantine stronghold and an important staging point for shipping troops and supplies to the Holy Land during the Crusades. Captured by Seljuk Turks in the 12th century, it became the most important port on the Mediterranean coast and fell under Ottoman rule in the 15th century.

Mermerli Beach is situated about one and a half miles from the Kaleiçi District. In between, Ataturk Park provides cool shade

downtown. These include the **Roman Agora**, just a few blocks from the main centre of town, the **main bazaar**, the **Clock Tower** and the 16th-century **Hisar Mosque**.

South of Izmir and Kusadasi is the resort town of **Bodrum** which occupies the site of ancient Halicarnassus. Bodrum offers many attractions, including a fascinating Museum of Underwater Archaeology which features Byzantine ships housed in the magnificent crusader castle overlooking the harbor. The Castle of St. Peter was built in the 15th century by the Knights of St. John using stone quarried from the ruins of the Mausoleum of Halicarnassus (one of the Seven Wonders of the Ancient World). In the castle's English Tower, the banquet hall has been restored and visitors can enjoy a glass of wine while reading graffiti that was carved into window niches by homesick knights. A dolmus can be taken to the pretty fishing villages of Turgutreis and Gümüslük.

and good views of the Mediterranean Sea and Taurus Mountains.

Perge (10 miles 16 km from Antayla), was settled by the Hittites as early as 1500 BC. St. Paul stopped here on one of his journeys, when Perge was an important city of the area.

The Black Sea

When the Latin poet Ovid, famous throughout the Roman Empire during the time of Augustus, was inexplicably exiled to a Black Sea outpost in 8 AD, he poured his despair into a five-volume work called *Tristia* (sorrows). By the late 19th century, the Black Sea region was no longer regarded as a place of exile but rather as a fashionable retreat for members of the Russian nobility. Count Leo Tolstoy spent his last summers at a cottage overlooking the Black Sea, and Anton Chekhov wrote *The Three Sisters* while staying at a Crimean resort. The 1917 Bolshevik Revolution replaced the privileged classes of czarist Russia

with Communist party leaders and Kremlin military brass, yet they too followed the aristocratic tradition of retreating to a Black Sea dacha (country cottage) each summer. Former Soviet president Mikhail Gorbachev was vacationing at his villa in the Crimea in August 1991 when he was placed under house arrest during an unsuccessful coup d'état in Moscow.

The lands bordering the Black Sea have changed hands many times over the centuries. Navigated since prehistoric times, the Black Sea contains mud that is rich in hydrogen sulphide, which causes the water to look black. Sheltered from the north by mountains, the Black Sea's waters remain warm year-round and its coastline was colonized as long ago as the 8th century BC by the ancient Greeks. Eventually the Greek colonies fell under Roman rule, and the founding of Constantinople increased the strategic importance of the Black Sea. Its southern shores remained mostly under Byzantine control following the decline of the Roman Empire, but its northern shoreline was invaded by Tartars and the area became part of the Mongol empire. In the 13th century, the Genoese ventured into the Black Sea where they established prosperous coastal commercial settlements. The Turks followed in the 15th century, and their expanding Ottoman Empire soon controlled all of the Black Sea coast.

In the 18th century, Russia, under Catherine the Great, began to flex its military muscle by annexing the Crimea. This region had become independent of the Ottoman Empire and was blocking Russia's access to the Black Sea. Russia, in addition to its ongoing disputes with the Ottoman Emprie over control of the Bosperous and Dardanelles, was eager to expand into the Balkans in pursuit of warm-water ports accessible to the Mediterranean. These imperial

ambitions were thwarted by the Crimean War of 1853 to 1856, in which the allied powers of Turkey, England, France and Sardinia defeated Russia when, after a long and bloody siege, its naval base of Sevastopol in the Crimea fell.

Military alliances had changed dramatically by the time a World War II meeting took place at nearby Yalta in 1945, attended by British Prime Minister Churchill, American President F.D. Roosevelt and Soviet Premier Stalin. Cloaked in secrecy, the agreements reached by the 'Big Three' included territorial concessions to the Soviet Union, with Roosevelt later accused of delivering Eastern Europe to Communist domination. The Soviet Union has since collapsed, and the Crimea, once called the 'Soviet Riviera' because of its subtropical climate and numerous resorts, has returned to quieter times.

Ports of Call

Yalta is the largest resort in the Ukraine-administered Crimean peninsula. Many of its hotels, sanatariums and guest houses were built as villas by the Russian nobility, and the nearby town of Livadiya became a summer residence of the Russian czars in 1861. The Livadiya palace, built in 1910, was the meeting place of the Yalta Conference in 1945 and is now a sanatarium.

The Ukrainian port of **Odessa** was the leading Soviet Black Sea

(Top) Yalta Conference in 1945 took place at Livadiya Palace.

port before the dissolution of the Soviet Union, and its cosmopolitan population consists of Ukrainians, Russians, Jews and Greeks. Originally an ancient Greek colony called Odessos, the port became a Tatar fortress and trade center in the 14th century. Odessa's cultural attractions date mainly from the 19th century and include a university, a historical museum, an astronomical observatory, a ballet theater, an opera house and a picture gallery.

The French statesman Armand Emmanuel du Plessis duc de Richelieu served Russia as governor of both Odessa in 1803 and the Crimea in 1805, and a monument to Richelieu stands at the top of a magnificent flight of granite steps leading to the harbour. These steps were the scene of a famous workers' riot in 1905 when the mutinous crew of the *Potemkin*, a Russian battleship of the Black Sea Fleet, arrived in port.

Constanta, Romania's main seaport and a popular seaside resort, began as a Greek colony called Tomi, and became Ovid's place of exile in the 1st century AD. Ovid, whose erotic and mythological poems later became a primary source of inspiration for the artists of the Renaissance, wrote his final works at Tomi. In the 4th century, Constantine the Great changed the city's name to Constantiana. Captured by the Turks in 1413, the port city became part of Romania in 1878. Local sights include an Orthodox cathedral, several museums and extensive Roman and Byzantine remains.

An excursion into **Bucharest**, Romania's largest city, takes visitors into the heart of Walachia. The 'bread basket' of Romania, the principality of Walachia was founded in the late 13th century when the Mongol wave receded and local inhabitants descended from their mountain refuges. Vlad IV, who ruled Walachia in the mid-15th century, maintained order by sentencing 20,000 people to death in the space of six years. His practise of impaling Turkish prisoners earned him the name Prince Vlad the Impaler and, as the son of Prince Vlad Dracul (Vlad the Devil), he also became known as Dracula or son of the Devil. Bucharest was the residence of the Walachian princes and became the capital of Romania in 1861. Much of the Old City was demolished by President Nicolae Ceaucescu during the 1980s to make room for a model socialist-planned city. Historic landmarks include several churches from the 17th and 18th centuries; the Museum of Romanian History was built during Ceaucescu's dictatorship.

Like many Black Sea ports,

Varna began as a Greek colony, then passed to the Roman Empire in the 1st century AD. Under subsequent Byzantine rule, the city's 5th-century basilica and 6th-century fortress were built. Then, in 679, the Byzantine emperor Constantine IV was defeated by the Bulgarians, a Turkic-speaking people called Bulgars, who had merged with earlier Slavic settlers and adopted their language. The first Bulgarian empire was established in 681 but was eventually subjugated by the Byzantines in 1018. The second Bulgarian empire rose in 1186 but was absorbed by the Ottoman Empire. Varna was captured by the Turks in 1391 and the 1444 Battle of Varna was the last major attempt by Europe's Christian Crusader forces to stem the Ottoman tide. Not until 1878 was Varna and the rest of Bulgaria liberated from Turkish rule.

Sofia, the capital of Bulgaria, has undergone several name changes. The city flourished under the Roman emperor Trajan as Sardica. Following its destruction by the Huns in 447, the city was rebuilt by the Byzantine emperor Justinian I and renamed Triaditsa. The Bulgars renamed the city Sofia or Sophya in 1376. Soon after, Sofia passed to the Ottomans and became the residence of Turkish governors overseeing the Ottoman Empire's Balkan possessions. Situated on a high plain surrounded by the Balkan Mountains, Sofia is filled with historic churches, mosques and synagogues. City landmarks include the parliament building, the state opera house, the former royal palace, the 4th-century Church of St. George and the 6th-century Church of St. Sofia.

Cyprus

In pagan times, the mountainous island of Cyprus was a centre of the cult worshipping Aphrodite, the Greek goddess of love and beauty who sprang from the foam of the sea. Ruled by a succession of ancient empires, including the Phoenicians, Egyptians, Persians and Romans, the island at one point was given to Cleopatra by Marc Anthony. Saint Paul brought Christianity to the beach-lined shores of Cyprus in the 1st century AD, and in 395 AD the island became part of the Byzantine Empire, its monks retreating into the Troodos Mountains to build secluded monasteries filled with icons and manuscripts.

In 1191 AD, Richard Lion Heart rescued and married his betrothed after her ship, en route to Jerusalem, was caught in a storm and forced ashore at Limassol. Today the island republic of Cyprus, with its liberal marriage laws, attracts Israeli couples who wish to be legally wed without undergoing the stringent rituals of Orthodox Judaism. Wedding packages often include the beach town of **Larnaca**, which is the mythical birthplace of Aphrodite.

Dubbed the Island of Love, Cyprus has also been an island of war. Taken by the Turks in 1571 following seven centuries of Byzantine rule, this bastion of Greek Orthodox Christianity became part of the Ottoman Empire, with colonists arriving in large numbers from Turkey. When Britain gained administrative control of the island in 1878, the animosity between the Greek Cypriot population and the Turkish Cypriots was firmly entrenched. Granted independence in 1960, the new country of Cyprus was soon embroiled in ethnic violence, forcing the UN to intervene and eventually partition the island into Greek and Turkish territories, which are separated by a UN-occupied buffer zone. The northern third of the island is recognized only by Turkey as the Turkish Republic of Northern Cyprus, while the southern two-thirds of the island is internationally recognized as the Greek-occupied Republic of Cyprus. Nicosia is the capital, and Limassol, on the south coast, is the chief cruise port and commercial centre of Cyprus.

Limassol's attractions include sandy beaches, an historic town centre and the Limassol Castle, where Richard Lion Heart married Berengaria of Navarre and crowned her Queen of England.

About nine miles (14 km) west of Limassol is Kolossi Castle, and another three miles (five km) further along is the ancient site of **Curium** (Kourion), where a Graeco-Roman theater overlooks the blue sea. Further to the west is **Paphos**, with its historic harbor. Attractions there include the Paphos Mosaics, which are well-preserved mosaic floors from 3rd-century Roman villas.

Shore Excursions

Limassol From Limassol, there are several shore tours of interest.

• A 4X4 scenic drive through the Phassouri Citrus Groves en route to the Crusader Kolossi Castle; includes a visit to wine-producing region. (7 hrs, $100)

• Kourion Beach – 20-minute drive to beach (2.5 hrs $36)

• Kourion, Temple of Apollo and Omodos Village (4 hrs, $30)

• Nicosia and Lefkara Village includes visit to 17th-century St. John's Cathedral (8 hrs, $100)

• Trekking in forested Troodos mountain range (4 hrs, $40)

• Paphos & Kourion Ancient Theatre, with shopping in Old Harbor area (7 hrs, $100)

CYPRUS

N

0   30

Miles

Kyrenia Range

Nicosia ★

Famagusta

Cease-fire Line

Troodos Mountains

Omodos •

Larnaca •

Paphos •

Curium (Kourion) •

Limassol

MEDITERRANEAN SEA

MEDITERRANEAN SEA

CYPRUS

Beirut ★

0   100
Miles
N

Lebanon

Tyre
Akko
Haifa
Nazareth
Tel Aviv
Ashdod
Jerusalem ★
Gaza
Bethlehem
Masada

Sy.

Sea of
Galilee

Jordan
River

West
Bank

Dead
Sea

ISRAEL

Jorda.

Alexandria

Zagazig

Port Said

El 'Alamein

Lower Egypt

Suez Canal

Suez

Sinai Desert

Giza   Cairo
Memphis

EGYPT

Eastern
Desert

Mt. Sinai

Gulf of
Aqaba

Nile River

Western
Desert

Hurghada

RED SEA

Upper Egypt

Great Sphinx

Dendera

Valley of the Kings

Luxor
(Thebes)

Esna

Edfu   Kom Ombo

Aswan
Philae   High Dam

Lake
Nasser

Abu Simbel

Chapter Ten

EGYPT
AND THE HOLY LAND

Egypt is a country of epic proportions, both historical and geographical. Its ancient civilization is measured not in centuries but in millennia, and its vast desert, covering 95% of the country's nearly 400,000 square miles, is bisected by the longest river on earth – the Nile.

The story of Egypt is the story of the Nile. Indeed, Egypt owes its existence to this river which flows its length. The river's fertile valley and fan-shaped delta cover only 4% of the country's total area but provide almost all of its arable and habitable land. The Nile has been the country's lifeblood for some 7,000 years, beginning with hunters who roamed the river valley in predynastic times. Eventually they learned to control the river's annual inundation by digging irrigation canals, and farming of the fertile floodplain began.

Supported by an agricultural society, a long line of pharaohs became almighty rulers of Egypt. They were divine kings, descended from the gods, and they oversaw the construction of colossal stone structures along the banks of the Nile. Built to preserve life beyond death, these awe-inspiring temples and tombs still stand, their imperious facades exerting a sense of power and mystery on mere mortals gazing up at them. Huge temple gates, massive columns, giant statues and of course pyramids – all were built to last for eternity and many of them have, preserved for thousands of years by an arid climate and a dry soil of sand and silt.

Egypt at a Glance

The Arab Republic of Egypt, with a population exceeding 60 mil-

The famous pyramids of Giza.

lion, is governed by a 1971 constitution. The president, elected every six years, holds executive power and the government must approve the formation of any political parties. Islamic groups are illegal, although the Muslim Brotherhood (created in 1929) is tolerated. Most Egyptians are of complex racial origin, being descended from ancient Egyptians, Berbers, black Africans, Arabs, Greeks and Turks. More than 90% of the people are Sunni Muslims, while a sizeable minority are Coptic Christians. Arabic is the official language; English and French are also spoken by the well educated. Nearly one third of Egypt's workers are engaged in agriculture and the principal crop is cotton, which is one of the country's principal exports along with petroleum and metals. The Suez Canal and tourism are important sources of foreign exchange.

Travel Tips

Currency: The approximate exchange is US $1 = 6 Egyptian pounds (LE). American currency is widely accepted.

Documentation: In addition to a valid passport, visitors to Egypt need a visa, which must be purchased ahead of time if you are arriving by ship.

Shopping: Always barter – it's expected – except in department stores. Gold cartouches are unique and popular Egyptian souvenirs, but be careful when buying gold jewelry. If you're interested in a piece, ask to see its stamp indicating the number of karats. Egyptian cotton is among the finest in the world and attractive cotton clothes, including the traditional *galibeya*, are widely sold. Handcrafted items in brass, copper and Egyptian alabaster are also popular.

Egypt's History

Ancient Egypt – its fields, towns, temples and tombs lining both banks of the Nile – was buffered from invasion by the river's natural borders. Desert plains lay to the east and west, the Mediterranean Sea to the north, and a series of cataracts south of Aswan in Upper Egypt. The shepherds then living in the Nile valley were descendants of the Hamitic branch of the Caucasian race, and their villages evolved over time into towns which became the centers of principali-

Shore Excursions

Visitors arriving by cruise ship at Alexandria or Port Said are strongly advised to take a ship-organized excursion into Cairo due to the distances involved and the heavy traffic in Cairo. The drive each way is about three hours and lunch is provided at a hotel in Cairo. Ships docking in Alexandria also offer half-day tours of Alexandria. Some cruise lines offer a special two-day tour that covers all the sights in and around Cairo and includes overnight accommodation at a leading hotel ($460). The following are a sampling of excursions:
• Pyramids of Giza & Egyptian Museum (11.5 hrs, $180)
• Pyramids of Giza & Step Pyramid (11.5 hrs, $160)
• Pyramids of Giza & Nile lunch cruise (11 hrs, $170)

ties that collectively became the kingdoms of Lower and Upper Egypt. In about 3100 BC, these two kingdoms were unified by Menes, who was believed by ancient Egyptians to be a descendant of the sun god Ra (see page 52). During his long reign, the city of **Memphis** was founded in Lower Egypt on the Nile delta, 14 miles south of modern Cairo.

Egypt's famous Old Kingdom (2682-2181 BC) emerged during the rule of Djoser (Zoser). Memphis had become the seat of the royal government and, under Djoser's reign, Egypt's territory expanded into the Sinai Peninsula. Amid a flourishing era of arts and sciences, the pharaoh's vizier Imhotep designed the **Step Pyramid** – the first great stone structure ever built. Located at the necropolis of **Saqqara**, it consisted of six massive tiers climbing to a height of 200 feet, its pyramid shape clearly visible from Memphis.

Stone construction continued to evolve and, during the reign of Sneferu, the first smooth-sided pyramid was constructed at Saqqara. This is known as the 'bent pyramid' for its sudden change of angle part-way up. Sneferu ordered another one built nearby, which was an architectural success called the 'red pyramid' because of the iron oxide in its stone. However, it was during the reign of Khufu, Sneferu's son, that the largest surviving pyramid was built at **Giza**, a plateau situated on the southwestern outskirts of modern **Cairo**.

Rising 481 feet above the ground, the **Great Pyramid of**

Visitors emerge from the Great Pyramid's burial chamber.

Khufu (Cheops) was built using an estimated 3.2 million blocks of limestone, each weighing an average of 2.5 tons. Khufu's son Khafra built a somewhat smaller pyramid at Giza, although it appears larger than Khufu's because it stands on a slight rise. The **Great Sphinx**, a representation of Khafra carved from a knoll of rock, is located next to the causeway leading from the pharaoh's granite-lined temple to his pyramid. A third pyramid, covering less than a quarter of the area of the Great Pyramid, was built by Menkaura, a son of Khafra. It took approximately 20 years to build the Great Pyramid and hundreds of thousands of workers were employed each flood season to labor on this project. After the building site was carefully leveled, the cardinal points were determined through astronomical observations, providing for a precise alignment of the pyramid's sides. The entrance is north-facing, allowing the pharaoh's mummified body to face the north star from within the burial chamber, which is located deep within the pyramid's core and reached by cramped passages. Two air shafts, straight narrow tunnels, lead from the chamber to the outside and are aligned with various stars. The apex was crowned with gold sheet, symbolizing the pyramid's association with the sun god Ra.

Much of the building stone was quarried nearby, and granite, for lining the burial chambers, was transported from Aswan. Work was carried out during the Nile's inundation, when floodwaters would have allowed boats carrying massive granite columns and heavy blocks of limestone to navigate close to the pyramids. The inundation season, when farmers were idle, was an ideal time for the pharaoh to employ them as laborers, helping to raise the

blocks – each weighing about 2 1/2 tons – into place. The method used is still open to speculation. They likely used cranes, levers and rockers, along with ramps built along the terraced sides of the pyramid. It is believed that as the outer casing of limestone was applied from top to bottom, the ramps were removed.

Egypt's second great era was the Middle Kingdom (2055-1650 BC). This period lasted nearly 400 years, during which the centre of political power shifted from Memphis in Lower Egypt to Thebes (modern Luxor) in Upper Egypt. Then, in 1550 BC, the Theban ruler Ahmose I ushered in a new era of greatness for the pharaohs of ancient Egypt. Called the New Kingdom (1550-1069 BC), these were glory days for the ancient city of Thebes, where columned temples and avenues of sphinxes were built on a massive scale. Across the river from Thebes, where the sun sets on the west bank of the Nile, lies the traditional burial ground of the New Kingdom pharaohs and their families. Cut into barren cliffsides, the tunnel entrances of these treasure-filled tombs were concealed with rocks and sand in an attempt to foil grave robbers. The Valley of the Kings would eventually contain more than 60 royal tombs, including that of the boy-king **Tutankhamun**, which was discovered intact by Howard Carter in 1922. Priceless treasures found in Tutankhamun's tomb, including the solid gold sarcophagus that held his mummified remains, are on display in the **Egyptian Museum** in Cairo.

Cairo is the capital and chief city of Egypt, with a population exceeding 13 million people. Although a modern city with wide, traffic-clogged streets, its older sections contain famed mosques, palaces and city gates built between the 7th and 15th centuries. The **Citadel of Salah El Din** was built by Saladin in 1179 to protect Cairo from attacks by Crusaders. Cairo's famous bazaar, **Khan el-Khalili**, is across the street from the mosque of Al Azhar, built in 970.

Cairo's famous suburb of **Giza**, on the city's southwestern outskirts, is where the **Great Pyramids** and the mysterious **Sphinx** loom above the desert horizon. The ancient city of **Memphis** once stood a short distance south of modern Giza and its surviving necropolis (the nucleus of which was **Saqqara**) contains the **Step Pyramid**, the first pyramid ever built.

Alexandria

Situated on a narrow peninsula, Egypt's leading port of more than three million people is built over the ruins of an ancient city once famous as a center of learning and culture. The names associated with Alexandria are legendary, starting with Alexander the Great, who founded the city in 332 BC. The city then was considered more Greek than Egyptian, with its gridded street plan and large population of Hellenistic Greeks. Its famous library and museum, no longer standing, attracted scholars such as the mathematician Euclid and the anatomist

Tutankhamun's gold mask (opposite) is displayed in Cairo's Egyptian Museum (above).

Herophilus, who founded the university's medical school.

But it is **Cleopatra**, co-regent of Ptolemaic Egypt from 51 to 30 BC, who is most often associated with ancient Alexandria. Famous for her intelligence and political astuteness (her beauty was more myth than reality), Cleopatra conducted her famous love affair with Marc Antony in a palace overlooking the East Harbour. Later submerged when earthquakes altered the city's coastline, the ruins of Cleopatra's ancient court remained hidden beneath the sea until they were discovered in 1996 by a team of French marine archaeologists.

Another famous landmark was the **lighthouse** on the island of **Pharos**, joined to the mainland by a causeway. This celebrated lighthouse, one of the Seven Wonders of the World, was built during the city's Roman occupation in about 280 BC. It was destroyed by an earthquake in the 14th century and the fortress of Qait Bey now stands on its site. The greatest of Rome's provincial capitals, Alexandria received antiquities from all over Egypt to decorate its new temples. Under Augustus, Cleopatra's Needle (now standing on the Thames embankment in London) and New York's Central Park obelisk, were brought as a pair to Alexandria from a temple at Heliopolis near modern Cairo.

Although much of ancient Alexandria lies underwater or is covered by modern buildings, there are some accessible monuments, such as **Pompey's Pillar** (a granite column erected in c. 297 AD near the temple of Serapeum) and the **Konel-Shugafa catacombs** – a labyrinth of rock-cut tombs constructed in the first two centuries AD. Excavations near the Mosque of Nebi Daniel have uncovered remains of the central city during its **Roman** period, including an **amphitheate**r, baths and a gymnasium complex.

Port Said

Located at the entrance to the **Suez Canal**, this port was founded in 1859 by the canal's builders and is named for Said Pasha, then leader of Egypt. Port Said is a fueling point for ships using the canal and is also a cruise ship port, providing access by modern highway to Cairo. The canal connects the Mediterranean Sea with the Red Sea, and is level throughout with no locks.

The Holy Land

The Holy Land is a place of pilgrimage for the world's three great monotheistic religions – Judaism, Christianity and Islam. Jews believe it was promised to them by God, Christians believe it was the scene of Jesus's life, and Muslims believe it was the site of Muhammad's ascent to heaven. Lying roughly between the Mediterranean Sea and the Jordan River, this region has long been called Palestine, a name derived from a word meaning 'land of the Philistines.' The Philistines came to the region from the Aegean in the 12th century BC and were rivals of the Hebrew people of Israel, whose name for Palestine is Eretz Israel, meaning 'Land of Israel.'

The Jews, who had left Palestine to settle in Egypt, returned around 1290. They were led by **Moses**, who delivered to them the Ten Commandments while crossing the Sinai desert. When the shepherd boy **David** killed the Philistine giant Goliath using a slingshot, his divine election was revealed. Crowned king of ancient Israel, David conquered Jerusalem, walled the city and made it his capital. His son **Solomon** built the first Temple in Jerusalem. Following his reign, the kingdom eventually fell under foreign domination, with the Jews exiled and their temple destroyed.

In 63 BC, Palestine became a Roman province ruled by puppet kings of the Herod dynasty. In about 8 BC, when word of the birth of **Jesus** reached Herod the Great, he ordered the massacre of all male babies, prompting the Holy Family to flee into Egypt.

Following a Jewish revolt in the 2nd century AD, Hadrian rebuilt Jerusalem as a pagan shrine. However, when the Roman emperor **Constantine** converted to Christianity in 312 AD, the city became a center of Christian pilgrimage, especially after Constantine's mother, Saint Helena, found what was believed to be a relic of the True Cross in Jerusalem and the location of the Holy Sepulcher (Christ's Tomb).

The rise of **Islam** and its belief that the Prophet Muhammad had ascended to heaven from Jerusalem, prompted the Muslims to build, in 691, the Dome of the Rock on the site where the Temple of Solomon once stood. When Muslims destroyed the Church of the Holy Sepulcher in 1001, this triggered a call to arms for the Christians of western Europe, and the first of several **crusades** was launched. For the next two centuries, the Christian cause in the Holy Land was carried out by armies of Latin princes and by the great military orders of the Knights Hospitalers and the Knights Templars. The First Crusade was a success, but the Second Crusade ended in dismal failure. The Third Crusade, led by England's King Richard I (Richard Lion Heart) and Philip II of France, failed to recapture Jerusalem. The last Christian stronghold of Akko fell in 1291 to the Egyptian Mamluks, who in turn were defeated by the Ottoman Turks in 1516.

In 1831, following three centuries of Ottoman rule, Palestine

Tenth Station of the Cross, Church of the Holy Sepulcher.

began opening up to European influence and Jewish settlement. With approval from the League of Nations, the British began to establish a Jewish homeland within Palestine in 1920. This caused clashes between the Arabs and the steadily growing population of Jews. In November 1947, the United Nations divided Palestine into Jewish and Arab states, with Jerusalem and its environs, including Bethlehem, to be an internationally administered enclave. Six months later the British withdrew and on May 14, 1948, the state of Israel was proclaimed. However, Israel's neighboring Arab states rejected both the partition of Palestine and the existence of a Jewish state, and fighting broke out in Jerusalem before the partition even went into effect. To this day, ongoing peace negotiations have failed to resolve the situation.

Travel Tips

Getting Around: Israel's two main cruise ports are Haifa and Ashdod. Taxis are available at the port gate in Haifa. A train station is located near the Haifa pier, and it's a half-hour ride from Haifa to Akko, costing about 10 shekels per person. From the Akko train station it's a 20-minute walk to the Crusader fortress. Nearby is a taxi dispatch office where, for about 30 shekels per person, you can arrange for a taxi ride back to Haifa.

Taxis are available on the pier in Ashdod. Tel Aviv is a 30-minute drive from Ashdod, and Jerusalem is an hour drive. Drivers will often accept US currency, but it's best to use Israeli shekels and negotiate a price.

Currency: Israel's currency is the shekel (NIS). Approx exchange rate US$1 = 4 NIS.

Language: Hebrew is the official language, although English and Yiddish are spoken.

Shopping: Handcrafted items include leather articles and embroidered, hand-woven clothing. Best buys include olive-wood figurines, gold and silver jewelry and brass candelabras. Be wary of street hawkers in Jerusalem – while one distracts you by unfurling a poster for your perusal, another could be picking your pocket.

Haifa

Haifa, the chief city of northern Israel, is situated at the foot of Mount Carmel. High on the slopes overlooking the port is the **Bahai Temple**, surrounded by Persian gardens. The domed shrine contains the tomb of Baha Allah, the 19th-century Persian founder of the Bahai faith.

Situated at the top of the Bay of Haifa is the ancient port of **Akko (Acre)**, birthplace of the Virgin Mary and the site of a medieval citadel, walled fortifications and several churches dating from the Crusades. Numerous battles have taken place along its walls, outside of which is the al-Jazzar mosque, built in 1781. Next door, housed in the mosque's former Turkish bath, is Akko's museum.

A popular shore excursion from Haifa is a day-long journey to **Galilee**, in northern Israel, where Jesus grew up and spent the first years of his ministry. Places of pilgrimage include **Nazareth**, home of Jesus and site of the Basilica of the Annunciation, Mary's Well and the Mosque of Peace. Jesus per-

---

Shore Excursions *Israel*

Shore excursions from Haifa include a day-long motorcoach tour of Nazareth and Galilee. Excursions from Ashdod include a motorcoach ride to Jerusalem for a guided walking tour of the Old City, lunch in a Jerusalem hotel and a visit to Bethlehem's Church of the Nativity. Other Ashdod excursions include a full-day trip to Masada and the Dead Sea, and a half-day tour to Tel Aviv and Jaffa.

Some cruise lines (on certain voyages) offer a two-day overland tour (between Haifa and Ashdod) to Nazareth, Galilee and Jerusalem. Meals and hotel accommodations are included; advance booking required.

formed his first miracle of turning water into wine at nearby **Cana**, and he began his first ministry at **Capernaum**, home to several of his disciples and the site of a 3rd-century-AD synagogue which has been excavated and partially restored.

Along the shores of the **Sea of Galilee**, also called Lake Tiberias, stand several pilgrim sites, including the famous Place of Baptism at Yardenit, associated with the baptism of Jesus, where the **River Jordan** flows from the lake. The resort town of **Tiberias**, one of the four holy cities of Judaism, was founded by Herod Antipas in 20 AD. Ruins of the Roman baths remain, as do some Crusader fortifications. At nearby **Tabgha**, the Church of the Multiplication commemorates the act of Jesus feeding the multitude with fish and bread, and the **Mount of Beatitudes** is where Jesus delivered the Sermon on the Mount.

Ashdod

Ashdod, a Hebrew name for 'stronghold,' is the modern port for Tel Aviv. Settled as early as the Bronze Age, Ashdod's first modern Israeli settlement was made in 1955 and its deepwater port was completed ten years later, bringing about the closure of Jaffa's ancient seaport. **Jaffa**, situated in a quiet section of Tel Aviv, was founded by the Phoenicians and named a provincial capital of ancient Egypt in the 15th century BC. Conquered numerous times throughout the ages – by Alexander the Great,

Saladin, Richard I and Napoleon, among others – Jaffa today is known for its narrow streets and a thriving artists' quarter.

Tel Aviv, the commercial and cultural center of Israel, was founded in 1909 by Jews from Jaffa. Its population grew rapidly in the years preceding and following World War II. In 1950, Tel Aviv was merged with Jaffa, and was briefly named the capital of the new state of Israel, before the capital was moved to Jerusalem.

The **Holy City of Jerusalem** is the highlight of a visit to the Holy Land. Within the stone walls of Old Jerusalem, amid the maze of narrow alleys and crowded bazaars, stand the holiest sites of Judaism and Christianity, and the third holiest site of Islam.

Standing atop Mount Moriah (Temple Mount), is the **Dome of the Rock** – a magnificent mosque built on the site of the First and Second Temples. It is centered upon the rock from which Muhammad, according to tradition, ascended to heaven on his winged steed. This same rock is where the Jews believe Abraham was poised to sacrifice his son Isaac to prove his faith in God. Dome of the Rock mosque is encased in marble slabs and Persian tiles inscribed with passages from the Koran. The nearby Mosque of El-Aksa was used for a time by the Crusaders as a residence for the knights in charge of the Temple area, who became known as the Knights Templars.

The **Western Wall** of the **Temple Mount** is what remains from the Second Temple. Also called the Wailing Wall, this is

STATIONS OF THE CROSS 1-14

Damascus Gate

Herod's Gate

Rockefeller Museum

New Gate

CHRISTIAN QUARTER

MUSLIM QUARTER

Church of the Holy Sepulchre

Antonia

Lion's Gate

Mary's Tomb

Church of All Nations

St. Stephen's Church

Jaffa Gate

JERUSALEM OLD CITY

Dome of The Rock

Golden Gate

Citadel

ARMENIAN QUARTER

JEWISH QUARTER

Temple Mount

Mosque of El-Aksa

N

0   200

Yards

Zion Gate

Dung Gate

Wailing Wall

Judaism's most holy site and it is here that Jews come to pray and bewail the destruction of their Temple.

Christendom's most sacred site is the **Church of the Holy Sepulcher**, which contains the Tomb of Christ. Situated in the Christian quarter of the city, the Church of the Holy Sepulcher houses the last five of the **Fourteen Stations of Cross**. Each station marks an event of sacred memory along the traditional route taken by Jesus, bearing his cross, to his crucifixion. Called the **Via Dolorosa**, this **Way of Sorrow** is Christendom's most hallowed road and it begins at the Antonia Tower, which marks the site of the Roman fortress where Jesus was condemned to death.

The next eight stations are marked by chapels, convents and monasteries built along the Via Dolorosa as it twists and turns its way to the Church of the Holy Sepulcher. The original basilica was built in 325 by order of Emperor Constantine, after the location of Christ's tomb was revealed in a dream to his mother Saint Helena while she was visiting Jerusalem. The first church was destroyed by the Persians in 614, then rebuilt and destroyed once more. The existing structure was built by the Crusaders in 1149 AD. Inside is a Latin shrine marking the place where Jesus was nailed to the Cross (the Eleventh Station), a Greek altar standing over the **Rock of Calvary** where the cross of Jesus was erected (the Twelfth Station), and the Stone of the Anointment where the dead body of Jesus was placed when taken down from the cross (the Thirteenth Station). The Fourteenth Station is the **Chapel of the Angel** – the site of Christ's burial and resurrection.

Opposite the Old City's eastern walls, overlooking the Dome of the Rock, is the **Mount of Olives**.

At its base stands the **Church of All Nations**, also called the Basilica of the Agony. The adjacent **Garden of Gethsemene** is where Jesus and his disciples spent the last hours before his arrest. The present church was built in the Byzantine style in the early 1920s with contributions from 12 nations. It stands on the ruins of Byzantine and Crusader churches, and houses **the Rock of Agony** upon which Jesus prayed the night before his arrest. On Palm Sunday, Jesus entered Jerusalem with his disciples through the Eastern Gate – which is where the **Golden Gate** (a 7th-century Byzantine structure) now stands and has been walled up since the 9th century.

The **Jaffa Gate** adjoins the **Citadel**, which was originally built by Herod to guard his palace. This famous landmark now houses the Museum of the City of Jerusalem. South of the Old City, in a park-like setting, is the **Keneset** (Israel's seat of government), the Israel Museum and the Shrine of the Book, which houses the Dead Sea Scrolls.

The town of **Bethlehem** – birthplace of Jesus – is about six miles south of Jerusalem, in the West Bank. The first **Church of the Nativity** on Manger Square was completed in 333 by Constantine, then rebuilt and enlarged by Justinian I in the 6th century. The low entrance door, through which visitors must stoop, was built to prevent Muslims on horseback from entering the church. Now shared by monks of Greek, Latin and Armenian orders, the Church of the Nativity is built over a grotto which is believed to be the manger where Jesus was born.

Israel's private and collective farms (*kibbutzim*) have transformed dry desert into arid farmland, irrigated by the **Jordan River**. Deep and turbulent during the winter's rainy season, it becomes a sluggish stream during the summer drought. The **Dead Sea**, fed by the Jordan River, is shrinking due to a combination of the river's reduced inflow and natural evaporation, which is caused by the lake's extremely dry and hot location. One of the saltiest water bodies in the world, the Dead Sea contains no marine life but its waters are extremely buoyant and are a source of mineral salt. The ancient cities of Sodom and Gomorrah once stood on the southwestern shore, and today beaches, spas and tourist hotels line the Dead Sea coast. **Masada**, a nearby mountaintop fortress once occupied by Herod the Great, was seized by Jewish Zealots in 66 AD, who later committed mass suicide when faced with capture by Roman soldiers. Masada was excavated in the 1960s, and today a cable car transports visitors up to the site.

In 1947, the **Dead Sea Scrolls** were found by Bedouin shepherds at Qumran. These ancient leather and papyrus scrolls contain the oldest known books of the Old Testament, and were written or copied between the 1st century BC and the 1st century AD by members of a Jewish sect whose library was secreted in cliffside caves overlooking the Dead Sea.

CHAPTER ELEVEN

MALTA,

TUNISIA & MOROCCO

Malta has no rivers or lakes, no natural resources and few trees, but its strategic location in the center of the Mediterranean has made it the jewel in many a crown. Sir Winston Churchill called this former British colony a "tiny rock of history and romance." For centuries its natural harbor – one of the finest in the world and situated at the crossroads of Mediterranean shipping – brought war and conquest to its doorstep. Following a siege by the Turks in 1565, the Knights Hospitalers fortified the port of Valletta so extensively it became one of the greatest strongholds in the Mediterranean.

Malta At A Glance

Malta (pop. 400,000) has been a republic since 1974, when the first Maltese president took office. The country's three inhabited islands are Malta (the largest), Gozo and Comino. The two official languages are English and Maltese (similar to Arabic but with an alphabet and grammatical structure derived from Latin). Italian is also widely spoken, with Malta lying just 58 miles south of Sicily. British colonial influences include driving on the left and an enthusiasm for marching brass bands, which are an integral part of the local festivals. Malta remains a bastion of Roman Catholicism

and has retained strong economic ties to Europe.

Shopping: Malta is famous for its handmade lace, silk cloth and filigree ornaments in gold and silver. Other items to look for include pottery and blown glass. The main shopping area in Valletta is Republic Street. Other shopping venues are the harborfront promenade in Sliema, and the Ta' Qali Crafts Village near Mdina. Shops are generally open from 9 a.m. to 1 p.m., and from 4 p.m. to 7 p.m. (or later) except on Sundays and holidays.

Currency: On January 1, 2008, the Maltese lira will be replaced with the euro as the country's unit of currency. Banks are open Monday to Saturday, closing in the early afternoon (mid-day on Saturday). ATMs are plentiful, and most larger shops and restaurants accept major credit cards as well as foreign currency, although their exchange rates may not be as competitive as those available at banks.

On Your Own

The cruise ships dock at Pinto Wharves, within walking distance of Valletta's fortifications. A Tourist Information Office is located in Freedom Square, just inside City Gate.

Island attractions can be reached by taking the local transit buses, painted orange and yellow, which can be boarded at the main terminus just outside the Valletta

Valletta's natural harbor is one of the finest in the world.

Shore Excursions *Malta*

Shore Excursions in **Valletta** include a harbor cruise (2 hr, $60) and city walking tour (4 hrs, $50) as well as scenic drives around the island to **Mdina** (4 hrs, $30), prehistoric sites (3.5 hrs, $50) and the **Blue Grotto** for a boat tour (4 hrs, $55). Malta can also be explored on half-day and full-day 4x4 adventures ($82 - $110), as can the neighboring island of **Gozo**, which is reached by boat (7.5 hrs, $85). Full-day tours combine a city walking tour with a drive to Mdina and includes lunch (7.5 hrs, $90).

city gates. Buses 38 and 138 go to Hagar Qim and Mnajdra; Bus 65 goes to Mdina and Rabat. Check with your ship's shore excursion office or the tourism information office in Valletta (see map) for more detail regarding bus schedules and fares.

Malta's History

Malta contains some of 'the world's oldest stone monuments, pre-dating those at Stonehenge in England. The island had already been inhabited for some four thousand years when the Phoenicians arrived in about 1000 BC. The Greeks followed, occupying the island in 736 BC and naming their colony Melita – the island of honey – for the golden-colored limestone found here. Malta later passed to the Carthagians, then to the Romans. Saint Paul brought Christianity to Malta when he was shipwrecked on the north coast in 60 AD.

When the Roman Empire was divided in 395 AD, Malta and its smaller neighboring islands of Gozo and Comino became part of the Eastern Roman (Byzantine) Empire. An Arab conquest in 870 was followed by a Norman invasion in 1090. Malta was a feudal fief of the kingdom of Sicily when Emperor Charles V of the Holy Roman Empire granted the island in 1530 to the Knights of

St. John of Jerusalem, who had been driven out of Rhodes by the Ottoman Turks.

The Knights ruled Malta until 1798, when Napoleon invaded and occupied the islands during his Egyptian campaign. The Maltese appealed to Great Britain and in 1799 Lord Horatio Nelson besieged Valletta, compelling the French to withdraw. For the next century and a half, Valletta was the headquarters of the British Mediterranean Fleet, its harbor further fortified and an extensive naval dockyard built in Grand Harbour. During World War II, Malta withstood almost daily German and Italian air raids, and in 1942 King George VI awarded the British colony the George Cross for heroism. Malta became independent in 1964 and a few years later Britain handed over the naval dockyards. A haven for NATO warships until 1979, Malta's former naval base has since been devoted to shipbuilding and dry dock repairs.

Upon joining the European Union in 2004, Malta became the smallest member nation and, as such, negotiated certain concessions regarding the potential influx of laborers (which could quickly swamp such a small country) and speculation in property ownership by non-residents. The Maltese have always been a pragmatic and resourceful people, and their small but diversified economy, which includes financial services, electronics, manufacturing and tourism, qualified the country for EU membership. Other industries include tourism and, despite the poor soil, agriculture. Nearly everything in Malta is built of golden limestone, and fresh water is produced at its seawater reverse osmosis plant, one of the world's largest, with the rest provided by wells.

Valletta

Built on a rocky promontory between two deep harbors, Valletta is named for the French Grandmaster Jean de La Vallette, who oversaw construction of the town's fortifications. Described by Sir Walter Scott as "the most superb place I have ever visited", Valletta is today the capital of Malta, its parliament housed in the Palace of the Grandmasters in the very core of the fortified town. Lining the cobbled streets, which are laid in a grid-work pattern, are the churches and inns (auberges) built by each nationality (langue) of the Knights.

Republic Street, now a pedestrian **shopping mall**, leads from Freedom Square to three adjoin-

Malta's golden limestone prompted the ancient Greeks to name the island Melita – 'the island of honey.'

ing squares in the town's center where several landmark buildings are located. **St. John's Co-Cathedral** 1 ('co' because there's another cathedral in Mdina, the former capital) was built by the Knights between 1573 and 1577, and contains the crypt of Jean de La Vallette. The magnificent interior of gold and marble contains a succession of chapels, each representing one of the Order's nationalities.

Overlooking Republic Square is the **National Library** 2, and in adjacent Palace Square stands the **Palace of the Grandmasters** 3, a masterpiece of military architecture completed in 1574. Its marble halls are graced with priceless paintings and its ground floor armory features weapons and armor from different periods.

The **National War Museum** 4 in Fort St. Elmo commemorates Malta's heroic role in WWII when the island refused to capitu-

late to relentless bombing by the Italians and Germans.

Mediterranean Conference Centre 5 is housed in the original hospital (Sacra Infermeria) of the Order of St. John, built in 1574. Restored and converted to a conference center in 1976, the hospital's Great Ward became the Exhibition Hall, one of the longest in Europe. Hospital artifacts, including silver plates upon which patients were served their food, are on display in the Fine Arts Museum, along with paintings by Tintoretto and other Renaissance artists. Regular performances are held in the **Manoel Theatre** 6, built in 1731 and featuring an opulent interior.

The **National Museum of Archaeology** 7 is housed in the Auberge de Provence. On display are pottery, sculptures and other objects found at various prehistoric sites on the islands. These megalithic stone structures – built between 3800 and 2000 BC, and dedicated to a fertility goddess – are among the world's earliest freestanding structures.

Lovely views of Grand Harbour can be enjoyed from **Upper Barracca Gardens** **8**, originally the private gardens of the Italian Knights. Nearby is **Auberge de Castille** **9**, one of the Knights' grandest inns.

Across Grand Harbour, south of Valletta, lie the three historic towns of **Vittoriosa, Cospicua** and **Senglea** – referred to as Cottonera (**The Three Cities**). Local attractions include the Folklore Museum (housed in the Inquisitor's Palace) and Maritime Museum, housed in the former bakery of the Royal Navy.

Sites of interest outside Valletta include the ancient stone temples at **Hagar Qim** and Mnajdra, and the nearby **Blue Grotto**, a stunning sea cave. Also worth visiting is the medieval walled town of **Mdina**, its labyrinth of narrow winding streets containing palaces and churches, including the cathedral dedicated to Saint Peter and Saint Paul. Close by, in the town of **Rabat**, are early Christian catacombs (underground cemeteries) and the Museum of Roman Antiquities with fine mosaics on display.

Tunisia & Morocco

The coastal lands of North Africa were once called the **Barbary States**. Initially inhabited by Berber tribes who farmed the coastal plains and lived in mountain villages, the region was colonized by Phoenicians in the 9th century BC. They founded **Carthage**, on the Bay of Tunis, which became a powerful city-state. As the Carthaginian empire grew, its expansion ultimately led to a series of wars with the rising Roman Empire. Called the Punic Wars, these conflicts were fought in three distinct stages between 264 and 146 BC.

The Second Punic War is sometimes called the Hannibalic War, for the famous Carthaginian general. **Hannibal** is considered one of the greatest military geniuses of all time for his march from Spain into Italy, crossing the Pyrenees and then the Alps with elephants and a full baggage train. A brilliant leader, Hannibal defeated the main Roman army but could not assail Rome's strong walls. By the end of the Third Punic War, the Berber States were under Roman rule, and Carthage became an important center of Roman administration under Augustus. Invasions by various barbarian peoples followed the decline of the Roman Empire, and the Barbary States were conquered by Arab Muslims in the 7th century. Although Berber-Arab conflicts were common, the Berbers were converted to Islam and formed the backbone of the Arab armies that conquered Spain in the 8th century.

In the 13th century, the Christians of Spain and Portugal began driving the Moors from the Iberian Peninsula, back across the Strait of Gibraltar into North Africa. By the early 15th century, the Portuguese and Spanish were attacking the Moroccan coast but were eventually repelled.

Meanwhile, the Ottoman Turks were sweeping westward across North Africa, led by the corsair Barbarossa, who prevented the region from falling to Spain. Tunisia became an autonomous province of the Ottoman Empire, and for the next three centuries the Barbary States were a base for Muslim pirates who staged attacks on Mediterranean shipping and raids on coastal towns. European naval powers often bombarded and blockaded the pirate strongholds, but not until 1830 was piracy eradicated.

Seeking repayment of heavy debts, the European powers of France, Great Britain and Italy intervened in Tunisia's finances in 1869. Tunisian attacks on Algeria, a French possession, prompted France to invade Tunisia and make it a French protectorate in 1881.

Major battles of World War II were fought on Tunisian soil after British General Montgomery defeated German forces in Egypt and forced them to retreat to Tunisia, where they became trapped by American and British troops occupying territories to the west, including **Casablanca**, which was the scene of a major Allied landing in November 1942.

A year later, American president Franklin D. Roosevelt and British prime minister Winston Churchill met in Casablanca, where they issued a joint declaration pledging the war would end only with the unconditional surrender of the Axis powers.

Following the war, nationalist movements intensified in Morocco and Tunisia, with both nations gaining independence from France in 1956. The Moroccan sultan became King Muhammad V, and he was succeeded by his son Hassan II in 1961, who ruled for 38 years until his death at age 70 in 1999. King Hassan was a staunch supporter of the West who worked secretly for Middle East peace.

Today, Tunisia and Morocco are moderate Arab states, although suicide bombings in Casablanca in May 2003 killed 45 people. Islam is the state religion and Arabic is the official language, with French widely spoken. Mineral production and agriculture are major industries, with citrus fruits, olives and other crops grown on the coastal plains. In Morocco, water for irrigation is drawn from artesian wells, while Tunisia is more dependent on rainfall. Desert oases, found in

NORTH AFRICA'S MOVIE ROLES

Numerous films have been shot in the mountains, deserts and walled towns (medinas) of North Africa. Scenes from *Raiders of the Lost Ark* and *The English Patient* were shot in Tunisia, as was footage for the original *Star Wars* movie and *The Phantom Menace*, in which scenes set on the planet of Tatooine were shot near the southern city of Tatouine. Morocco has served as a movie backdrop for decades. Alfred Hitchcock filmed scenes for his 1956 thriller *The Man Who Knew Too Much* at the Hotel La Mamounia in Marrakesh, and David Lean shot *Lawrence of Arabia* at locales in and around Ouarzazate, in the heart of the Atlas Mountains. A permanent film studio was founded at Ouarzazate in 1984, when *The Jewel of the Nile* was shot there. Ridley Scott shot *Black Hawk Down* and parts of *Gladiator* in Morocco, and Oliver Stone's epic about Alexander the Great utilized the Moroccan army as extras, who slept on the battlefields and provided security for the film crews.

both countries, form in places where the water table reaches the surface, often as springs. They range in size, from a pond surrounded by date palms to cities surrounded by cultivated fields. In Morocco's oasis city of Marrakesh, an 11th century sultan built a network of underground canals, still in use today, for irrigating the imperial city's extensive gardens.

Travel Tips:

Currencies: Tunisia's unit of currency is the dinar (TD) which is divided into 1000 millimes. Morocco's unit of currency is the dirham (DH), which is divided into 100 centimes.

Shopping: Shops in the medinas (old walled towns with narrow winding lanes) are generally open for business from 8 a.m. to 9 p.m. daily, with a Friday break for prayers. Bartering is done at the souks (markets) where rows of stalls sell a variety of hand-

crafted items in copper, brass and wrought-iron. Silk caftans, painted ceramics, inlaid wooden boxes and Berber carpets are all popular items, as of course are the country's leather goods. They are made of a special goatskin leather, called 'morocco,' that is dyed on the grain side and boarded or embossed to show the characteristic grain. Often crushed and glazed, morocco is hard but pliable, and valued for bookbindings and purses.

Tunisia

Tunis, located on a lake connected by canal to the sea, is the capital of Tunisia, its metropolitan area approaching two million in population. The cruise ships dock at **La Goulette**, a port suburb lying east of the city center. The winding streets of the **medina** (the historic heart of the city) contain colorful souks, the **Great Mosque** and a Turkish palace housing the **Dar Ben Abdallah**

Museum. West of the *medina* is Ville Nouvelle, built by the French during the city's colonial era and traversed by the grand Avenue Bourguiba. The Hotel Majestic, on Avenue de Paris, is an impressive example of French colonial architecture. The famous **Bardo** museum, housing one of world's finest collections of Roman mosaics, is about four miles northwest of the city center.

The site of the ancient Phoenician city of **Carthage** lies 10 miles east of the city core. Its seaside ruins are mostly of Roman origin and include baths, villas and a museum. About two miles past Carthage, along the coast, is the whitewashed, cliff-top village of **Sidi Bou Said**, which is popular with tourists who enjoy strolling the cobble

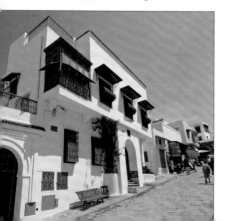

streets of this quiet residential area. Further afield, about 100 miles south of Tunis, past the port of Sousse, is the ancient Roman amphitheater at **El Djem**. This is the world's second-largest amphitheater after the Colosseum in Rome, and its thick walls are of staggering proportions.

Shore excursions in Tunis include a walking tour of the medina and the Bardo Museum combined with a drive to Carthage and Sidi Bou Said, with a stop for lunch (8 hrs, $90). Shorter half-day tours can be taken to the medina and Bardo museum (4 hrs, $45), and to Carthage and Sidi Bou Said (4 hrs, $45).

Morocco

Casablanca is called Dar-al-Baida in Arabic, but the city's Spanish name is embedded in the minds of many as the exotic setting for the 1940s film classic starring Humphrey Bogart and Ingrid Bergman. The real city bears little resemblance to the movie, which was filmed in a Hollywood back lot, but it does have a Rick's Cafe – thanks to the efforts of former U.S. diplomat Kathy Kriger, who formed a company called The Usual Suspects and raised enough capital to open a Casablanca restaurant that is reminiscent of Rick's Cafe, complete with arabesque arches and a pianist playing tunes from the 1940s. Rick's Cafe, which opened in March 2004, is located in a converted townhouse at 248 Boulevard Sour Jdide, opposite the city's bustling port.

The village of Sidi Bou Said.

Casablanca, with a population approaching three million, is Morocco's largest city and principal port. Dominating the modern city's skyline is the **Hassan II Mosque**, the world's third largest. Completed in 1993 and located near the cruise port, the mosque features marble pillars, ceramic mosaics and carved Moroccan cedar. Its minaret is the world's tallest at 660 feet and the roof over the main prayer hall is retractable.

The former imperial city of **Marrakesh**, founded in 1062, is stunningly situated at the base of the snowcapped Atlas Mountains. The city's ruling sultans and grand viziers built rambling palaces and walled gardens, where reflecting pools and palm trees stand amid a fragrant profusion of jasmine and bougainvillaea. Rising high above the winding streets of the medina is the **Koutoubia minaret**, built by the Almohad dynasty of Berber rulers in the late 12th century. It is the oldest of their three famous minarets – the other two being the Tour Hassan in Rabat and the Giralda in Seville, Spain. Other historical sites include the ornately refurbished Ali ben Youssef Medersa, a religious school founded in the 14th century.

The focal point of Marrakesh's medina is the **Djemaa el-Fna**, a huge square of non-stop activity where snake charmers and fortune tellers jostle for space with acrobats and magicians. Leading off the square is a maze of alleys filled with souks selling spices and slippers, kaftans and carpets. In contrast to

Shore Excursions

Casablanca Shore excursions in Casablanca include a city walking tour (3.5 hrs, $45) which includes shopping and refreshments, and a driving tour of Casablanca (3 hrs, $40). Out-of-town excursions are offered to Rabat (Morocco's capital) for a city walking tour (5.5 hrs, $50) and to Marrakesh (12 hrs, $130), which is a four-hour drive from Casablanca.

the cacophony of customers bartering for wares in the crowded souks, is the nearby tranquillity of the luxurious **Hotel La Mamounia**, set in an enclosed park which was originally a sultan's wedding gift to his son. This legendary hotel, with its pillared lobby and red-carpeted corridors, opened in 1922. Former guests include the Aga Khan, Richard Nixon, Orson Welles, General de Gaulle and Jimi Hendrix. Winston Churchill was a frequent guest in the 1940s and '50s, and the Churchill Suite is decorated with photos of the former British prime minister and his last unfinished painting of the gardens.

Casablanca's Hassan II Mosque.

Azamara Journey (2007)
866 passengers, 30,000 tons

Constellation (2002)
1,950 passengers, 90,000 tons

Costa Mediterranea (2003)
2,114 passengers, 86,000 tons

Crystal Serenity (2003)
1,080 passengers, 68,000 tons

AZAMARA CLUB CRUISES: This cruise line is Celebrity Cruises' deluxe brand. Azamara features 4- to 12-night Med cruises from Barcelona, Nice, Rome, Venice and Athens on finely appointed, mid-sized ships that are ideal for seasoned cruisers seeking out-of-the-ordinary destinations. Several overnight port stops and customized shore excursions are featured. Pre-cruise land tours in Italy and Greece are offered. *(azamaracruises.com)*

CELEBRITY CRUISES: Founded in 1990 by the Greek cruise line Chandris Inc., Celebrity Cruises is now owned by Royal Caribbean Cruises Ltd. and is a premium brand offering sophisticated service on contemporary ships appointed with modern art. Celebrity features a range of 7- to 13-night roundtrip itineraries from the base ports of Barcelona and Rome. Celebrity cruisetours include 5-night land tours of Venice, Florence and Rome. Officers are Greek; service staff are international. *(celebritycruises.com)*

COSTA CRUISES: Founded by a Genoa shipping family, Costa introduced its first passenger ship in 1948 and is today Europe's most popular cruise line. Costa offers an international ambiance and authentic Italian cuisine. North Americans comprise 10 to 25% of passengers on Med sailings. Costa's main base ports are Savona, Rome, Venice and Barcelona, with round-trip itineraries ranging from 7 to 13 nights. Officers and service staff are international. *(costacruises.com)*

CRYSTAL CRUISES: This luxury cruise line offers a variety of 7- to 12-night one-way itineraries between Istanbul, Athens, Venice, Rome or Barcelona. Crystal ships are spacious with all outside staterooms, most with a balcony. Crystal is known for interesting itineraries with many ports that are off the beaten track. Officers are Scandinavian; service staff is international. *(crystalcruises.com)*

CUNARD: This prestigious British line began operations in 1840 when Sir Samuel Cunard formed a fleet of ships to deliver mail between Liverpool, Halifax and Boston. Cunard, now owned by Carnival Corporation, currently operates *Queen Mary 2, Queen Victoria* and *Queen Elizabeth*, featuring traditional elegance and a British ambiance. Cunard offers a selection of one-way Med itineraries between the base ports of Venice, Barcelona and Rome, and roundtrip cruises from Southampton. Officers are British and Norwegian; service staff are international. *(cunard.com)*

Queen Mary 2 (2004)
2,620 passengers, 150,000 tons

DISNEY CRUISE LINE: This family-oriented cruise line, which debuted in the Med in 2007, offers 10- and 11-night roundtrip western Med itineraries from Barcelona that include Malta and Tunisia. Officers are European. *(disneycruise.com)*

Disney Magic (1998)
1,750 passengers, 83,500 tons

HOLLAND AMERICA LINE: This Seattle-based premium cruise line commands a loyal following, its classic blue-hulled ships featuring wrap-around teak decks and spacious staterooms. HAL's Med itineraries are diverse, covering both the major and minor ports. Itineraries include a wide variety of 10- to 22- day roundtrip and one-way cruises between various base ports, including Barcelona, Rome, Venice and Athens, with frequent overnight stays in Venice, Barcelona and Istanbul. Pre-cruise land tours are also available. In business since 1873, HAL operated transatlantic service between Rotterdam and New York before turning to cruises in the late 1960s. Officers are Dutch; service staff are Indonesian and Filipino. *(hollandamerica.com)*

Westerdam (2006)
1,848 passengers, 85,000 tons

MSC Musica (2006)
2,550 passengers, 89,000 tons

MSC ITALIAN CRUISES: This Italian line is owned by Mediterranean Shipping Company (one of the world's largest freight container companies) and offers 5- to 12-night cruises out of Genoa and Venice. The company's mid-sized ships, which include the *Lirica* (christened by Sophia Loren in 2003), appeal to experienced travellers who prefer traditional cruise liners. The mix of passengers is international. Officers and service staff are Italian. *(msccruises.com)*

Norwegian Jewel (2005)
2,400 passengers, 92,000 tons

NORWEGIAN CRUISE LINE: One of the first lines to invent modern cruising in the mid-1960s, NCL remains innovative with its unstructured dining, casual atmosphere and excellent youth facilities. NCL offers 7-day roundtrip cruises from Barcelona, and 11- to 14-day itineraries featuring Venice, Rome and Barcelona as base ports. Officers are Norwegian; service staff is international. *(ncl.com)*

Regatta (1998)
684 passengers, 30,000 tons

OCEANIA CRUISES, INC:
This deluxe line's mid-sized ships offer gourmet cuisine and attentive service in a country-club casual atmosphere. The *Insignia*, *Nautica* and *Regatta* (former Renaissance ships) offer 10- to 14-day itineraries that begin or end in Barcelona, Rome, Venice, Athens and Istanbul. Officers and service staff are international. *(oceaniacruises.com)*

Ventura (2008)
3,090 passengers, 113,000 tons

P&O CRUISES: Britain's favourite cruise line, P&O is geared to the British holidaymaker and has been operating passenger ships since the early 1800s. Formerly a division of the Peninsular & Oriental Steam Navigation Company, P&O is now operated by Carnival UK. Based in Southampton, P&O's fleet offers a variety of itineraries including 20- to 26-night Eastern Med cruises and 14- to 16-night Western Med cruises, all roundtrip from Southampton. *(pocruises.com)*

PRINCESS CRUISES: This popular cruise line, based in Los Angeles, offers a variety of 12-night itineraries in the Med. One-way cruises are between the base ports of Barcelona, Rome, Venice and Athens, and 7-day roundtrip cruises from Rome to the Western Med are also offered, as are land-tours of Italy. Princess also offers 14-night roundtrip cruises of the Western Med from Southampton, England. Princess ships appeal to a broad range of passengers with their tasteful decor, excellent entertainment, extensive children's facilities and flexible dining options. Princess ships feature an abundance of outside staterooms with private balcony. Officers are British and Italian and service staff are international. *(princess.com)*

Star Princess (2002)
2,600 passengers, 109,000 tons

REGENT SEVEN SEAS: This luxury line (formerly Radisson Seven Seas) offers a variety of 7- to 12-day itineraries between such base ports as Barcelona, Monte Carlo, Rome, Venice, Athens and Istanbul. Offering small-ship intimacy, Regent's ships feature all outside suites. Officers are Scandinavian; service staff are European. *(rssc.com)*

Seven Seas Navigator (1999)
490 passengers, 30,000 tons

ROYAL CARIBBEAN INT'L: Miami-based RCI offers a variety of 5- to 12-night roundtrip cruises out of Barcelona, 7- to 13-night roundtrip cruises from Rome, and 7-night roundtrip cruises from Mallorca. RCI also offers 14- and 18-night roundtrip Med cruises from Southampton. Pre-cruise land tours of Italy, Spain and Paris/London are available. RCI's megaships are known for their stunning atriums, sports facilities and excellent youth programs. Each ship's funnel features a rock-climbing wall – the company's trademark. Officers are Scandinavian; service staff are international. *(royalcaribbean.com)*

Brilliance of the Seas (2002)
2,112 passengers, 90,000 tons

Seabourn Spirit (1989)
208 passengers, 10,000 tons

SeaDream II (1985)
110 passengers, 4,250 tons

Silver Whisper (2001)
382 passengers, 28,250 tons

Wind Spirit (1988)
140 passengers, 6,000 tons

SEABOURN CRUISE LINE: This luxury line offers gourmet cuisine and spacious accommodations on its 200- and 450-passenger mega-yachts. Base ports are Monte Carlo, Rome and Barcelona. Itineraries feature less-visited ports and customized shore excursions. Officers are Norwegian and service staff are international. *(seabourn.com)*

SEA DREAM YACHT CLUB: Founded in 2001 by Norwegian industrialist Atle Brynestad (founder of Seabourn) this innovative company's twin yachts each carry 55 couples in relaxed and casual elegance, providing the private-yacht experience on 7- to 14-night voyages. Ports include Nice, Monte Carlo, Capri and Positano. Officers and service staff are international. *(seadreamyachtclub.com)*

SILVERSEA: Consistently rated the Number One Small Ship Cruise Line by Conde Nast Traveler, this luxury line offers interesting Med itineraries ranging from 7 to 12 days. Base ports include Lisbon, Barcelona, Monte Carlo, Rome, Venice, Athens and Istanbul. Officers are Italian; service staff is European. *(silversea.com)*

WINDSTAR: This is a premium line of high-tech sailing ships, each accommodating 150 passengers (except *Wind Surf* which carries 312 passengers). Windstar ships appeal to clients seeking both luxury and the romance of sail. The line offers 7-night Med itineraries that include some of the smaller ports along the French Riviera and Greek Isles. Base ports are Lisbon, Barcelona, Nice, Rome, Venice, Athens and Istanbul. Officers are British and service staff are international. *(windstarcruises.com)*

**PHOTO AND ILLUSTRA-
TION CREDITS:**